To Ana —
With warm
regards —
Ann F. Caron

Strong Mothers, Strong Sons

ALSO BY ANN CARON

"Don't Stop Loving Me":
A Reassuring Guide for Mothers of Adolescent Girls

Strong Mothers, Strong Sons

Raising Adolescent Boys in the '90s

▲

ANN F. CARON, ED.D.

Henry Holt and Company
New York

Henry Holt and Company, Inc.
Publishers since 1866
115 West 18th Street
New York, New York 10011

Henry Holt ® is a registered
trademark of Henry Holt and Company, Inc.

Library of Congress Cataloging-in-Publication Data
Caron, Ann F.
Strong mothers, strong sons : raising adolescent boys in the '90s
/ Ann F. Caron. — 1st ed.
p.   cm.
Includes bibliographical references and index.
1. Mothers and sons.   2. Teenage boys.   I. Title.
HQ775.C37   1994   93-25487
306.874'3—dc20   CIP

ISBN 0-8050-2499-9

Henry Holt books are available for special promotions and
premiums. For details contact: Director, Special Markets.

First Edition—1994

Designed by Paula R. Szafranski

Printed in the United States of America
All first editions are printed on acid-free paper.∞

1   3   5   7   9   10   8   6   4   2

To my sons
John, Peter, Paul, Mark

Contents

Acknowledgments   xi

Introduction   1

1. **"Welcome to the Club"**   7
   It's a Boy

2. **"Crazed with Madness"**   21
   Puberty

3. **Struggling for Identity**   39
   Searching for Who He Is

4. **"Should I Tell Him I Love Him?"**   61
   A New Relationship

5. **"My Mother Would Kill Me"**   87
   Strong Mothers

6. **Mother-Talk, Son-Talk**   111
   Communicating with a Son

7. **"Why Do They Fight So Much?"**   135
   Boys and Violence

8. **Living Up to His Potential**   159
   School and the Adolescent Boy

9. **"Get Them into Something"**   183
   After-School Activities

10. **"I Only Have Sex with Virgins"**   207
    Sex and the Adolescent Boy

11. **"Kids Do What They Want"**   231
    Alcohol and Drugs

12. **"Is My Son Gay?"**   255
    A Mother's Fears

13. **"Soon You'll Be Wanting Us to Wear Bras"**   281
    The Dilemma of Being Sensitive and Strong

Notes   289

Index   311

Acknowledgments

When the mothers in my workshops first urged me to write about boys, I hesitated because my interests had focused primarily on promoting understanding between a mother and her adolescent daughter. But after my initial research and many discussions, I became convinced that the adolescent male experience needed to be heard and understood by mothers. I, therefore, am grateful to the mothers who asked me to write about mothers and sons.

I am immeasurably indebted to the many adolescent boys I interviewed for this book. Their stories helped me appreciate what propels, motivates, inspires, aggravates, and stresses boys. I thank them for confiding in me and for trusting me to accurately report their thoughts, feelings, and advice.

A special thanks to the school principals and leaders of community centers who allowed me to interview students, and to the teachers and counselors who motivated their students to show up for the interviews.

When I talked with mothers, I marveled at their openness as they discussed their love and fears for their sons. Their voices reflect the concerns of all mothers who know the risks faced by adolescent boys in the '90s. I thank them for their confidence and willingness to share their experiences, frustrations, and pride.

The support I received from friends propelled me through the snowy days of winter, but I especially appreciated the counsel of Robin Loughman, free-lance editor and mother of two young adolescents. As my "first reader," she became a reliable and trusted sounding board. Thank you, Robin.

Also, thanks to Molly Friedrich, my literary agent, who shares my conviction about the importance of adolescent issues. She cuts through the web of contracts and publishing jargon, and I am grateful for her guidance.

My editor at Henry Holt, Cynthia Vartan, also urged me to pursue the mother-son relationship, and I am thankful for her encouragement and faith in me.

My mother, Mildred; my brother Cushing Fitzgerald; and my sisters Moira Collins and Sara Penn; their spouses and their children always bolster my confidence whenever I need reassurance that I am on the right track. I thank them.

Without my husband John's love and friendship, I may not have followed my educational dreams and writing ambitions. Thank you, John, for your unwavering and unconditional love and support.

My daughters, Elizabeth and Cathleen, lived through the publication of my book on adolescent daughters with good humor. I love them and thank them for their wisdom and affection. I especially appreciate Cathleen's editing skills and comments on both manuscripts.

When I decided to write about boys, I talked with each of my sons about his adolescence. They willingly responded to my (sometimes frantic) phone queries and embraced my enthusiasm about exploring the mother-and-son relationship. Each son contributed in his own way to this book.

John and his wife, Dede, were always ready to offer support and friendship. John helped particularly when he shared his thoughts about male development and gave me permission to use parts of a letter he wrote to us.

Peter and his wife, Jane, good naturedly answered my questions as Peter recalled some of his adolescent experiences. I was moved when Peter told me how much he appreciated my passing down advice to the "next generation," which now includes their daughter, Madeline.

Paul and his wife, Andrea, read the manuscript with the eyes of parents of two young sons, Joey and Frank. I welcomed their sharing of parental concerns and Paul's championing of sports for adolescent boys.

Our son, Mark, and his wife, Lisa, willingly responded to my requests for clarification about adolescent issues, and Mark offered excellent insights—especially when I was writing about adolescent risk-taking.

To these wonderful young men, our sons, this book is dedicated with love and gratitude.

Introduction

A father came to a discussion I was leading at his son's school and asked why I would choose to highlight mothers and adolescent sons in the era of the men's movement and its focus on male bonding. "Why aren't you writing about fathers and sons?" he queried. This father shared the men's movement's belief that mothers create problems by staying close to their sons. Take the key from under your mother's pillow, Robert Bly tells his followers through the myth of Iron John, and find your true self in the company of men. Strong mothers, warns Bly, produce weak sons.

In contrast to Bly, I champion a mother's influence on her son. Although the critical role a father plays in his son's development is undeniable, I am convinced that an adolescent son needs his mother. His early disengagement from her will inhibit, not foster, his adolescent search for a sense of self. Whereas Bly and others may advocate separation from mother and independence for himself, I propose that *interdependence* is the key that validates maleness in the nineties.

A boy who understands that he needs others just as others need him (interdependence) attains his masculinity—and his humanity. He does not find the secret by following a mythical character into the woods, by beating on a drum, or by dissolving his ties to strong women. A boy-turning-man discovers himself when he realizes that he does not exist on his own, that the qualities of both men and women must be cherished, nurtured, acknowledged—and utilized. He acquires this insight when he learns how to live and relate to others in a family and among friends. And his mother sets the tone for that experience.

Boys revealed their dependence on others (which is usually camouflaged) when I interviewed them for this book. I asked about their mothers and fathers, about life in their schools and neighborhoods. Some boys spoke with assuredness and confidence about achievement and goals. Others struggled to talk about survival and street life. Some swaggered, full of themselves. Still others voiced resentment of their fathers' absence, while a few could barely articulate any thoughts, so affected were they already by alcohol or drugs.

Although each boy spoke of unique experiences and hopes, I found a common theme. An adolescent boy wants his mother to believe in him, to be committed to him and to provide the support he needs to successfully maneuver through adolescence. As he matures, he communicates differently and his interests change, but he still desires his mother's guidance and her confirmation of his individual worth. He does not crave independence, but an acknowledgment of his individuality.

When I wrote *"Don't Stop Loving Me": A Reassuring Guide for Mothers of Adolescent Daughters*, I was bewildered by my adolescent daughters and needed to explore what lay behind our feelings toward one another. Although my sons are no longer adolescents, interviewing and writing about boys has brought me a deeper understanding of their teenage years. Talking with boys has made me more aware of the inner turmoil that dominates young male lives, and was undoubtedly present in my own sons. I always took my sons at their word and did not look for their hidden adolescent fears, deep anguish, or restless uncertainty. Now I see that their reluctance to express inner fears or self-doubt is a hallmark of adolescent boys and presents a challenge to mothers who want their sons to mature safely. When mothers don't know what their sons are feeling, guiding them becomes an even greater challenge, a challenge some mothers willingly accept and others ignore or reject outrightly.

Turning my attention to adolescent sons caused me a few anxious moments when some women accused me of abandoning the interests of girls and women. But I feel that the well-being and advancement of women is closely tied to attitudes fostered in the home. When a mother calls her son's attention to his mistreatment, disregard, or insensitivity toward girls, she is teaching respect for herself and other women. So, to the contrary, I am not ignoring women, but bringing their concerns about the male of the species to the forefront.

Mothers know that raising sons is not like raising daughters. In spite of noble efforts to eradicate male/female distinctions, the relationship between a mother and son still reflects their sexual differences. A mother in one of my workshops commented that she had been misled about the similarity of parenting boys and girls. Now that her son is a young adolescent, she feels deceived by well-meaning efforts to underplay her son's and daughter's basic differences. She, an only child, is mystified and frustrated by her son.

A woman may feel comfortable with a daughter because she has lived through female adolescence herself. She may not want to raise her daughter the same way she was raised, but at least she understands the process of becoming a woman. She can look back at her own adolescence and accept or reject her mother's ideas. In spite of her questions about some new mores that attract her daughter and her excitement about others that offer new opportunities for women, a mother always wants to strengthen her bond with her daughter.

But when mothers encounter adolescent boys, filled with

testosterone, energy, and lethargy—all at the same time—they wonder what has happened. A mother may panic when she reads news stories about shootings, drug overdoses, sex for points, and the apparent disregard many adolescent boys show for the safety and well-being of themselves and others. She suspects that growing up male means not growing up. And she has been told that mothers must back away from their sons during adolescence.

Mothers who do not give up on their sons want to know how to bridge the gap of silence and understand the process of becoming a man. A mother longs to raise a son who will not only reach adulthood, but will survive with his good qualities intact. Can sons remain safe, strong, and masculine and at the same time learn to express emotions and respect for girls and women? How does a mother encourage these traits in her son without emasculating him? In some women's circles, the words "strong and masculine" have become equated with male dominance and female compliance. I believe, however, that these words can describe a caring young man who values his male gender and his physical and mental strengths, yet visualizes himself and his future spouse as equal partners and competent, loving caretakers of children.

These young men will emerge from families who are committed to their safe passage, who cherish them and clearly speak their minds about what is important. Many families face economic and social problems that seem insurmountable, but commitment to a child, in this case a son, can override the conditions under which he lives. And mothers can make this happen.

I hope that the voices of boys, mothers, and experts I have blended in this book will help a mother understand her adolescent son and give her confidence as a parent. Frightening stories may confront her whenever she picks up a newspaper, turns on the television, looks out the window, or overhears her son's conversations. But a woman's confidence in her ability to guide her son will help him emerge successfully from adolescence.

And her confidence must not be undermined by a false assumption that teenage boys do not need their mothers.

They do need mothers, strong mothers.

1

"Welcome to the Club"

It's a Boy

We React • Communicating
Toys • Friends • Boyhood
Into Adolescence • Memos for Moms

A woman laughed as she recalled her son's birth to a group of mothers gathered to talk about their adolescent sons. "Congratulations," her mother had phoned. "You're a member of the club." "The club?" the new mother asked. "Yes," her mother chortled, "the Mothers of Sons Club."

"All my life," this woman continued, "my mother would sigh, 'Ah, mothers of sons.' She knew they had a special relationship. My father's mother adored him, worshipped the ground he walked on. My mother always commented on that." The woman telling this story has a sister, no brothers, and never quite understood her mother's apparent feeling of exclusion from "the Club."

But now as she looks at this young man who is her son, she thinks about her mother's comment. What were her own feelings when he was born? Are they influencing her effectiveness in parenting him now during his adolescence?

Each mother responds uniquely to her newborn, and emotions vary with each woman and each birth. Some women do not experience a "special" response at the birth of a son and may favor a daughter who will remain close to her the "rest of her life." She may be more comfortable with women and puzzled by how she should act with a male child. Or she may want a son, to replace a beloved father, to please her husband, or to balance the family.

Some cultures still favor sons over daughters for reasons of tradition. A news story recently reminded us that baby daughters "disappear" in China. A woman from India told me, "To have a firstborn son is definitely the done thing. I figured he would be a boy, but I wanted a girl desperately, everything was pink. My parents were very happy, rejoicing that it was a boy."

A pregnant woman may hear many theories about the advantages of one sex over the other, with some people declaring that boys are easier to raise than girls and others claiming the reverse. Hopefully, a new mother will ignore her relatives' and friends' predictions and trust her own experiences and instincts.

The mothers I interviewed who preferred one sex over the other usually cited personal reasons. "I have worked so hard to get where I am, I want to show my daughter how much I have worked and what I have attained," responded one woman hoping for a daughter.

Stating the opposite view, another woman said, "I didn't want to have a daughter because I had such a lousy relationship with my mother." She smiled, adding, "Besides, I always loved boys."

A desire to please her husband may also motivate a mother. "So many women who come into the office want to give their husbands a son," commented a nurse in an obstetrician's office. "They're disappointed when it's a girl."

Still others just want to experience the opposite sex. "I would have been disappointed if I didn't have sons," one mother reflected. "I had only one sister and she wanted to do her hair and worried about her clothes. I desperately wanted a brother to go out and climb trees with and do all the things that boys do that I thought were fun and I didn't have any access to. That was part of my life I missed."

Speaking to the desires of most mothers, one woman said gratefully, "I had hoped to have children of both sexes and fortunately we did."

We React

For the majority of mothers, the thrill of holding a healthy baby is all that matters. The anxiety and fear about labor are over and the baby can be loved as a real person. But as much as a baby is enjoyed as a baby, mothers and fathers take care of their sons and daughters in distinct ways and, according to psychoanalyst Christiane Olivier, the gender of the child is never a matter of indifference to a family.

A baby daughter, Olivier contends, is desired not because she is a girl, but for the qualities she will bring to the family—her sweetness, her lovableness, her goodness. She will be her mother's companion. A boy, however, is desired for his own sake. He is a boy, a completion of his mother, her pride and joy.

"For it is in her son," Olivier writes, "that the mother has her only chance of seeing herself in male form. This child that has come out of her belongs to the other sex, and so the woman gets the chance of believing in that ancient dream that all humans have: bisexuality. . . . Just watch how proudly she carries this son who has come along to complete her in a way that no one else can."[1]

Mothers may disagree with Olivier's assessment of the importance of gender or her belief that humans desire qualities of both sexes, but her observation that mothers and fathers "gaze" at sons and daughters differently is reflected by many mothers whom I interviewed.

One woman felt a sense of accomplishment when after two daughters, a son was born. "We did it," she exclaimed to her husband. Another who had twin sons announced with pride and a touch of superiority to an acquaintance, the mother of two daughters, "*I* hit the jackpot."

In many a mother's eyes, no one will be as wonderful as her son. She radiates as she talks about him, expecting that he will fulfill her dreams of the perfect man. A mother told me, "You look at your husband and think, Well, he isn't exactly what I want him to be. So you look at your son and think, Maybe I can make him into what I really want a man to be." Then she laughed and said, "Then all of a sudden you have these teenage sons and they aren't what you expected and everyone has to adjust."

Because mothers have never experienced what it is like to be a boy, the birth of a son presents a challenge as well as a fulfillment of a dream. With a daughter, a woman can look back at her own upbringing and emulate or reject her mother's parenting. Many mothers take my parenting workshops so they will not "mother" their adolescent daughters the way they were mothered.

But with a son a mother may feel an overwhelming responsibility. She wants him to be strong, a real man, yet able to communicate. Strong and sensitive is her ideal, but how does she arrive at that? Should she minimize the differences between boys and girls? Should she give him "girl" toys? Should she surround him with unisex playthings? How can she get her son to express his feelings and become emotionally in tune with himself? How can she raise the perfect son?

Communicating

Parents exert tremendous influence over their children and children themselves influence parents. "It is by no means evident who educates whom, the children, the parents or reverse," writes psychotherapist Kasper Kiepenheuer. "In addition to the conscious influence that is exerted mutually, children live in deep unconscious unity with their parents."[2] A child can sense a mother's feelings and moods, sometimes before she recognizes them herself. This unconscious unity connects them in the most ancient and strongest of all bonds, parent and child.

A child's personality also molds and shapes his relationship with his parents. One child may be more tranquil than his siblings, enabling his mother to respond calmly and quietly to his needs. Another may demand attention from the moment he is born, exhausting his frantic mother as she wonders what happened to her former unruffled self.

In addition to individual personalities, boys and girls develop their own gender-typical characteristics and parents can unwittingly foster these behaviors. For instance, when a toddler son aggressively demands attention—verbally, nonverbally, or physically—he usually gets noticed (how could you ignore him?). But if a toddler daughter makes similar demands, she often is corrected and doesn't receive the desired attention until she expresses her needs through words. Many parents are conforming to these age-old expectations, encouraging boys to be aggressive and girls to communicate.[3]

Mothers and fathers naturally display their own personalities and gender traits when they play with their sons. A boy quickly discovers that his father plays in a more boisterous, animated way than his mother. He excitedly awaits the appearance of his father because he knows it will be fun. His father rolls with him on the ground, throws him in the air, chases him around the room. He adores his father's hugs and knowing pats. Life with Father is stimulating; life with Mother is more comforting.

When I talk about children receiving gender messages, I am not referring to messages about talent, intellectual ability, or career choice, which are gender-neutral. I am concentrating on the messages that affect psychological and social development of boys and girls.

Studies suggest, for example, that mothers talk more about the feelings of other children with their daughters than with their sons.[4] When a girl toddler bites a playmate, hits or kicks someone, or doesn't share, her mother usually reprimands her and talks about the other child's feelings. A mother of a boy toddler, however, might respond to a similar scene by taking control of the situation and demanding that her son stop the behavior. Perhaps mothers observe a more threatening situation between boys and sense the urgency of moving in to stop the fighting. I certainly intervened quickly when my sons fought with one another, afraid that one would injure the other. I was too busy restoring order to examine why each felt compelled to respond to the other with anger.

Since three-year-old boys engage in nearly twice as many transgressions as three-year-old girls, this method of just telling them to stop is ineffective. Teaching a boy as well as a girl to respect another child may be a better way to change his behavior. Forcing him to stop hitting may work temporarily, but most mothers, like myself, would like to see a more permanent solution and longer-lasting ways of resolving conflict. Studies show that mothers who frequently remind their sons that their wrongdoing is hurting another child are more likely to have children who empathize and help another child in distress.[5] Teaching a boy to think before he strikes may discourage the fighting common among boys. As he grows, he hopefully will find more agreeable ways of getting what he wants.

A son can receive messages about empathy and care from his father as well as his mother. A father who takes care of a young son, changes his diapers, gives him a bath, and plays with him teaches him that being male does not exclude the ability to love and care for another. Fathers who actively participate in the caretaking of their children give their sons the best example of manhood. A mother and father who encourage their son to respect another's belongings, talk about other children's feelings, and show him how to ask rather than grab or demand teach their son valuable lessons in human relations.

Toys

Each generation establishes its own child-care agenda and decides what should or should not be in a son's playroom. When our sons were young and before our daughters were born, we only bought "masculine" toys: blocks, trucks, cars, puzzles, Legos. When they wanted comfort, they cuddled stuffed animals or old blankets. They satisfied their creative outlet through messy paints and clay. Instead of doll houses, they had garages. Their imaginative games included playacting, working with puppets, hiding and springing on one another. We read books and boycotted guns or weapons that encouraged aggression (I thought the boys were aggressive enough, so even G.I. Joe was banned).

When our daughters were born, baby dolls, dress dolls, and cuddly dolls finally joined the array of trucks, cars, and garages. Nowadays more parents are comfortable allowing all kinds of toys in the playroom—a more realistic approach. Many toy companies also manufacture "neutral" games and toys that are played with equal fervor by boys and girls.

In most homes, mothers find that their sons still gravitate to cars, trucks, and wooden blocks. Mothers know instinctively, and through experience, that boys and girls not only prefer different toys but often play with the same toys differently—and now research is confirming this innate maternal knowledge. A boy who breaks apart his sister's doll to see how it works is mystified by his sibling's dismay. He thinks the point of playing is to take things apart and put them back together.

Both male and female one-year-olds may play with the same toys and some continue doing so into the second year. But studies show that by the beginning of their third year, boys are playing more with "guns, blocks and trucks and girls with stuffed animals, dolls, puzzles, pegboards. And by the end of the third year, sex differences in toy play are firmly established."[6]

Nursery school and day-care teachers often are fascinated with boys who seem to ignore any kind of "girl" activities in their classroom. Although boys and girls have been choosing separate toys for as long as parents can remember (regardless of parental desires), researchers still passionately discuss why a child chooses one toy over another.

Some theorize that when toddlers are learning new skills,

parents are more conscious of gender differences and revert to stereotypes. For instance, parents in an Oregon study made more positive comments to 12- to 24-month-old boys when they played with male-typical toys than when they played with female-type toys.[7] When a boy knows he pleases his parents by playing with "boy" toys, he usually will choose those toys.

Others say that no matter what parents say or what toys they offer a child, little boys will crawl toward anything with wheels. Adults naturally think of children according to their sex and give them what they consider gender-appropriate gifts, letting children know what is expected of them. This gender knowledge gives children a sense of security—of knowing they are boys or girls. Hopefully, children also will receive messages of human behavior that extend beyond gender.

I think a son receives many cues about what it means to be a boy. Playthings are only a small part of his overall indoctrination into the world of sex differences.

Friends

Besides preferring different toys and expressing themselves in unique ways, preschool children seek out friends of the same sex. Eleanor Maccoby, a noted researcher in sex differences, observed that children look for same-sex friends and play differently with them than they do with the opposite sex. When paired with boys, girls (33 months old) frequently stood on the sidelines and let the boys monopolize the toys. But when girls played with other girls, they actively joined in the fun. Maccoby suggests that girls avoid playing with boys because of the rough-and-tumble characteristic of their play and because girls "find it difficult to influence boys"— even between the ages of three and five. The boys didn't pay any attention to the girls' requests to let them play; they listened to other boys instead. Both boys and girls played more actively and enjoyed one another more when their playmates were of the same sex.[8]

This pattern of boys' preferring boy playmates may exacerbate the sex-typed play that often is misunderstood by women who did not have brothers. When I ask groups of mothers whether they notice any differences in the way their sons and daughters interact with friends, they immediately mention the boys' rough play, their need to take up lots of space, and their activity level. Mothers who understand boys feel free to appreciate and enjoy their exuberant fun. Others can't believe the high noise level and the constant movement.

Maccoby's description of boys playing with boys sounds a little like the videos we see of British parliamentary sessions. Little boys in all-boy groups, she says, were more likely to "interrupt one another; use commands, threats, or boasts of authority; refuse to comply with another child's demands or give information; heckle a speaker; tell jokes or suspenseful stories; top someone else's story; or call another child names."[9]

No wonder a mother sometimes is astonished by her son's play. She may remember playing quietly as a child, listening to her friends and sharing. Now she is confronted with this creature who wants to dominate a group, take away a toy, have his way. She will be relieved to know that studies confirm that not only her son, but boys in general, confront one another while girls get their way by "toning down coercion and dominance, trying to bring about agreement."[10]

"I like the physicalness of boys," a mother told me. "In one way it drives you nuts that they're walking down the hall putting fingerprints all over, but you know exactly where they are all the time and you know what's happening." A mother often checks on her young son when the house is *too* quiet, frightened that he could be up to some damage and delighted to occasionally find him reading a book.

As much as mothers may wish that we could bring our sons and daughters up in a completely nonsexist environment, we know intuitively, and through observation, that these stereotyped behaviors of boys and girls won't vanish. A broad range of individual differences exists in families, and any mother can tell you how unique each child is, regardless of his or her sex. But biological, family, and cultural influences determine the definition of maleness and sons are not immune to this influence. If mothers are bent on altering a son's masculine nature and want to "make him into what I really want a man to be," they will feel frustrated and defeated. Mothers can and should demonstrate and encourage alternative, less assertive ways of relating to others, but it must be done with full appreciation of their sons' boyishness.

Boyhood

Much gender-related information is firmly entrenched by the early school years. For instance, when kindergarten to third-grade children were asked to remember pictures that they had been shown earlier that depicted men and women in traditional, nontraditional, and neuter roles, they recalled more accurately the pictures that showed men engaged in familiar, traditional sex roles than in either nontraditional or neuter activities. In other words, they could recall the familiar, the comfortable, the pictures that agreed with their version of the world.[11]

Children can describe boys' and girls' behavior very clearly. A seven-year-old girl confided to me that she did not like Ninja Turtles, that boys did. When I asked her why, she replied, "Because Ninja Turtles fight and I don't fight." When I queried further why she didn't fight, she was surprised at my question and had a very simple explanation: "Boys fight, girls don't."

Ninja Turtles and Nintendo have joined the Saturday-morning cartoons that portray the battle between good and evil—

in Hollywood terms. Girls may be amused by these characters and participate in the fun, but the marketing appeal is to boys because girls "don't fight."

We often hear the statement that men don't show their emotions and women do, and research suggests this may be true of children as young as 7 to 12 years of age. In every phase of an experiment conducted by a researcher from the University of Texas, girls displayed more emotions (positive and negative) than boys. Boys adopted a "strategy of inner control" to suppress the expression of their emotions.[12]

"I see all the things about men I would like to see changed," a woman told me, "but I am totally helpless as to how I would make those changes for my sons. I try to make them aware of other people's feeling. I try to make them considerate, but we're working against society. They're getting feedback from other boys and from schools as to what is appropriate boy behavior."

Another woman laughed as she said, "As soon as they hit the school bus at age six, that's it. They learn more on the school bus than anywhere else."

No wonder as a son approaches adolescence, a mother doubts her genetic link with this noncommunicative, demanding, lovable creature. He certainly is not the teenager she was in her youth.

Into Adolescence

As a son enters early adolescence (10 to 15 years old), a mother perceives his development's taking on aspects hers never did. Suddenly, he communicates in strange ways, is fascinated with sex, and can become irritating and uncooperative. She tries to understand what motivates him, why he is ricocheting off the wall one moment and can't move from the bed the next.

Her daughter the same age confronts and criticizes her, but

they have a give-and-take with each other. Although the girl's unconventional stands may hurt and worry a mother, in her heart she understands where her daughter is coming from; her son, however, is different.

"He's reacting to the world as he sees it. He really changed in the last six months," a mother of a 13-year-old told me. She knows from his actions that she is the mother of an adolescent son and she doesn't understand.

Her son's reaction to the world will be pure male as his hormonal and social outbursts invade the household. But this time he is 13 as he asserts himself, proclaiming again as he did when he was 2, "I can do it myself." He has reached puberty and that "special" relationship between mother and son readjusts for the adolescent years.

Memos for Moms

1. Come to terms with your own feelings about having a son and reflect on how these feelings influence the way you raise him.
2. Recognize and value the different ways mothers and fathers interact with sons and daughters.
3. Encourage his father to share in the day-to-day caretaking.
4. Do not give him gifts that foster his natural aggressiveness.
5. Teach him to empathize with others by talking about his and another's feelings, especially after he has had an argument or fight with a friend or sibling.
6. Appreciate his boyishness.
7. Love and cherish a son's uniqueness—even if his adolescent attitudes do not reflect yours and seem incomprehensible.

2

"Crazed with Madness"

Puberty

What Should He Know? • *Hormones*
Timing • *Showing Signs of Manhood*
His Voice Changes • *"My Son Has a Mustache"*
Sperm Development and Ejaculation
And Those Erections . . .
Being Tall Makes a Difference
Becoming "Manly" • *Looking Good*
"He Eats and Sleeps So Much"
Talking About Menstruation
He's a Man • *Memos for Moms*

Puberty sneaked into our family. You would think a mother of four sons would have been aware of her sons' growing interest in sex, a sure sign of male puberty. Yet it wasn't until I discovered stashes of *Playboy* magazines hidden in a crawl space that I realized my little boys' interests had expanded beyond baseball.

At that time what I knew about male adolescent development could be summarized in one word: *nothing*. I could not relate to anything that was happening to them, so I ignored it. I should have talked with Garrison Keillor, the popular host of "American Radio Company" who vividly portrays the maelstrom called puberty: "Adolescence hits a guy like a bad drug experience. You are crazed with madness. Your body is filled with chemicals of rage and despair, you pound, you shriek, you batter your head against the trees. You come away terribly wounded, feeling that life is unknowable."[1]

Were my sons better off because I ignored their "chemicals of rage and despair"? I hardly think so. If they had questions about what was happening to their bodies, they turned to the encyclopedia, to library books, to an enlightened teacher, to a boy at school who was already shaving, or to *Playboy*—not acceptable reading in our home.

Were these sources reliable guides for their young minds?

Perhaps some were, but I missed many opportunities to offer correct information and reassure my sons that the changes happening to them were normal. I now understand how important it is for parents to talk with their sons to help them become comfortable with their growing bodies. Accurate information is available through most schools, but young adolescents seldom attain a comfort and ease with their maturing bodies.

Adolescent bewilderment over bodily changes is an age-old phenomenon. "Sexuality bursts on them like a tempest," wrote C. G. Jung, "filling them with brute desires and needs."[2] But does puberty "burst" on them? Although it may seem to unsuspecting parents that puberty happens suddenly, it actually is a process. Boys' hormones increase gradually until they explode in their bodies during the night and in their fantasies during the day. The boy who may have dreamed about becoming an all-star second baseman now dreams about becoming a great lover.

The years of puberty can seem endless to a boy who lags behind his classmates in development or to the child whose acne-covered face dominates his thoughts and social life. The boy who seeks fame on a sports team now discovers that his early-maturing peers gain the spots and he must wait his turn. Sadly, his turn may never come if all the positions are chosen before he starts growing.

Puberty can be upsetting for boys, yet a Carnegie Foundation report notes that it is "culturally unacceptable to talk about male pubertal changes and the feelings they engender."[3] By failing to acknowledge puberty and its accompanying stress, researchers and educators do a disservice to boys—and to their parents, who are struggling to understand their adolescent sons.

What Should He Know?

"The boys had about five minutes during fifth grade," a junior in high school told me about his complete puberty "education."

"The girls stayed in there an hour." Although at the time he thought the boys were lucky not to have to listen to all that for an hour, now he wonders.

This boy's elementary school experience reflects a commonly held myth that female adolescence is complex and girls need more time with adults to discuss their concerns, while boys are uncomplicated, need less instruction, and are far more interested in what is happening to the girls. These false assumptions shortchange boys when they receive puberty education. Education about sexual intercourse, as distinguished from puberty, will be addressed in a later chapter. It is important to focus first on the changes taking place in a boy during early adolescence. Mothers who understand puberty will have an easier time in their later discussions with their sons about sex and safety.

When mothers ask, "What should I tell my son?" I advise them to tell him everything they know about puberty. And if they know as little as I did, they should go to their local library and become experts. Every boy eventually matures. Mothers who know the facts are a step ahead of their sons—which is not an easy accomplishment during adolescence.

Hormones

During a mother's pregnancy, gonads develop in a male fetus and secrete hormones called androgens that develop the male sex organs of her son. During early childhood, hormonal activity is generally suppressed, but from age seven on, a complicated process of bodily interactions begins. Simplified, the pituitary gland at the base of the brain gradually releases hormones. At first boys do not notice this slow release. But then, sometime between the ages 9 and 15, a boy will detect changes in his body as his hormones begin their work.[4]

The most noticeable developments come when the pituitary gland signals to the testicles to start producing testosterone, the male sex hormone. An increase in his testosterone level indicates that a boy's testicles, penis, and scrotum will start growing and body hair will appear.

Testosterone is blamed for many teenage difficulties, from acne to aggression to impulsivity.[5] Some researchers place responsibility for teenage aggression on "testosterone poisoning." Even if male aggression could be traced solely to testosterone, and even though many women would like to eliminate this aspect of maleness, the fact remains that all boys produce increasing amounts of testosterone during puberty. Without it, they would not mature. Testosterone sets off the process of puberty in a boy and plays an important role in a mature man's sexual activity.[6]

Timing

There is an order to the changes taking place in puberty, but the timing of these changes is unique to each boy. One will be fully mature at age 15 while another may be just starting his growth spurt at that time. Early-maturing boys frequently have an advantage. They attract the girls and the coaches. One boy who attained his adult height in junior high recounted the eighth and ninth grades as the time of his great athletic achievements. Then he told me that by his junior year in high school other boys caught up and then surpassed him. Now he looks back on his junior-high years as his best—a feeling not shared with some of his classmates who recall with dread their awkwardness during those years.

Showing Signs of Manhood

A boy's sexual development remains dormant during his early-elementary school years. A very small percentage of boys experiences precocious puberty, but the vast majority notices changes in their sexual organs sometime between the ages of 9 and 15 (average age of 12 or 13).

Boys, familiar with adult male bodies through public washrooms and communal locker rooms, are not surprised when their testicles begin enlarging, the earliest physical sign that puberty has begun. The testicles are enclosed by a sac of skin called the scrotum, which hangs behind the penis. A boy may be concerned that one testicle seems to hang lower than another, but this is the normal position and should not be a cause for alarm. Some pubic hair may appear and he will start to grow taller.

Another cause for worry is the enlargement of his breasts. This swelling and tenderness of breasts, called gynecomastia, happens to many boys (between one-fifth and one-third). But the increase in breast size is a passing phenomenon for most boys, and a son should be reassured that he is normal. If a boy becomes self-conscious about his breasts, he should talk to his pediatrician, who will confirm that this is a common happening, a temporary imbalance of the hormones. However, if the condition lasts too long or is particularly upsetting to a boy, a pediatrician may recommend plastic surgery. A doctor told me that some boys wait until adulthood and the condition still does not go away. If the parents can afford surgery, this may be an option. But surgery should not be automatic—waiting twelve or eighteen months may solve the problem.

Finding a doctor who likes adolescents and is familiar with adolescent medical problems is crucial. Sometimes a teenager finds himself in a pediatrician's office surrounded by two-year-olds and is embarrassed to ask questions.

His Voice Changes

During the next stage, anytime from age 11 to 16, a boy's penis lengthens, his testicles and scrotum continue to grow, and his pubic hair spreads. A lot is happening to his body—and to his vocal cords.

One mother told me about her son who sang professionally and was being considered for a new show. He had grown three inches and his voice was changing. Sensing a problem with his voice, his mother sent him to a voice coach. The coach taped her son singing some of the required songs and they played the tape on the way home in the car. She reported to me:

"I looked at him and said, 'It sounds terrible.' And when the song was over, I said to his father, who was also in the car, 'He's done. He'll never sing again.' Well, you would have thought I just murdered my son.' He yelled, 'I can't believe you said that. Just forget it. I don't want to sing again.' He was close to tears. I should have been more sensitive."

She is right. She should have been more sensitive. This mother did not pay attention to the fluctuations in her son's voice when he was talking, but singing highlighted his puberty. He was embarrassed and angry and not ready to admit that he was no longer an extraordinary child soprano.

"My Son Has a Mustache"

A son may be four years behind or ahead of his classmates when he decides he needs a shave. And it seems that his classmates can make fun of him either way—if he has a mustache too early, he is teased, or if he can't shave until college, he's embarrassed. Whatever his timing, his parents should not hold up the hairy ideal of the perfect man. Some men have very little body hair while others seem to be completely covered. Either way, it has nothing to do with manliness.

The "hairy man" in the *Iron John* story by Robert Bly symbolizes in the men's movement a return to masculinity.[7] As with Samson in the Bible, Bly attributes great powers to hair. "Sexual energy" emanates from it, he writes, as well as lust for hunting, oneness with nature, hot-bloodedness, "excess" and intuition that leads to wisdom.

Most women would dismiss Bly's exaltation of hair as a flight of fancy. Hair, of course, has nothing to do with sex drive, passion, or superior mental powers. Hopefully our sons will know this, and will find strength in their spirits rather than just in their bodies.

Sperm Development and Ejaculation

As a boy matures, his testicles begin producing sperm. For many boys the sperm in the semen fluid is ejaculated for the first time during the night. He may be completely unaware of this nocturnal emission, commonly called a "wet dream," until he awakens. In a way, this first nocturnal emission parallels a girl's first period, as it can take the adolescent by surprise. A boy may have heard about "wet dreams," but he is still unprepared.

In a small study, researchers Alan Gaddis and Jeanne Brooks-Gunn interviewed boys from age 13.5 to 15.5 and found that most of the boys had learned about ejaculation on their own, by reading.[8] No one had given them literature to read, so the researchers assumed that they obtained their information from adult male magazines. The boys with the most accurate information had talked directly with older men and felt free to report back to these men after their first ejaculation, but none of the other boys in the study informed anyone, peers or parents. This is in sharp contrast to girls, who usually tell their mothers when they have their first period and after a short time share their experiences with friends.

Over half the boys interviewed by Gaddis and Brooks-Gunn had experienced their first ejaculation through masturbation rather than a wet dream. Since the subject of masturbation causes controversy in some families, it deserves attention.

In the past a boy learned that masturbation would cause him physical and psychological harm, sap his energy, deplete his sperm, worsen his acne, and be obvious to others. Now we know that these dire warnings are not based on fact. Masturbation is normal and has no bad effects or telltale signs. Whether or how often one masturbates is an individual choice—some boys and men masturbate often, some less often, and some never.

Nobel Prize mathematician and philosopher Bertrand Russell, reflecting on his adolescence, wrote: "The years of my adolescence were very lonely and very unhappy. . . . My interests were divided between sex, religion, and mathematics. At fifteen, I began to have sexual passions, of almost intolerable intensity. While I was sitting at work, endeavoring to concentrate, I would be continually distracted by erections, and I fell into the practice of masturbating."[9]

Boys who are raised in a religion that disapproves of masturbation may feel guilty or dirty when they masturbate. Offering some words of comfort on the issue, well-known Christian psychologist and parenting author James C. Dobson, Ph.D., writes: "It is my opinion that masturbation is not much of an issue with God. It's a normal part of adolescence which involves no one else. It does not cause disease, it does not produce babies. . . ."[10]

In other words, if a boy masturbates, don't worry. And if boys could talk with adult men, they would soon know that most men masturbated when they were young and many continue to do so into their adulthood.

A mother told me an amusing story. "I caught my son masturbating. It was a shock for both of us. He had been in my bedroom watching TV and I came in calling his name. He shot out the door. I could tell he was flustered and I said, 'What's going on?' He said, 'You know, Mom, you know.' And I said, 'I'm not sure I do know.' But then, so he didn't need to say anything else, I said, 'It's perfectly normal, but I think it would be better if you did it in a room by yourself with the door closed.' "

When I asked her if her husband had ever talked to her son about masturbation, she responded, "I'm sure in his own way he did. One of the things I have noticed with the boys at a certain age is they definitely do need to talk with their fathers more."

And this is one of the areas in which a mother should urge the boy's father or a reliable male relative to talk with her son. She certainly is capable of talking openly with him, but some boys told me they would be embarrassed talking about masturbation with their mothers and many mothers feel equally uncomfortable about such discussions.

"It never occurred to me to talk to my sons," a mother of two boys told me. "I never thought I would have to address things like that." She didn't think her husband had talked to them either because "he's not there. He's not in the car."

And Those Erections . . .

Another common happening that unsettles a boy is the uncanny ability of his penis to become erect at the most unwanted times. It seems to take on a life of its own during early adolescence. In Richard Handy's autobiography he writes: "My eager cock caused me much embarrassment when I was young. One day in math class when I was 14, it unpredictably raised its head when I was called upon to work a problem on the blackboard. To this day, I shy away from writing on blackboards in front of others. . . . I retreated from team sports in the seventh grade, due in part to my apprehension about what it was going to do next."[11]

Spontaneous erections are part of growing up and they do not mean a boy is thinking about sex all the time. They can happen when his mind is elsewhere, even when he's thinking about math. Math teachers must be the only ones who ask students to come to the blackboard because math class is synonymous with embarrassment for many boys.

A mother told me that her sons have a standard comment when they will be alone with their father. "I'll say that I'm going out tonight," the mother told me. "And my sons say, 'Oh my gosh, we'll have the erection-in-math-class talk again tonight.' It goes back to the time when I said to my husband, 'I think you better have a talk with them.' So he sat down with the boys and said, 'Do you ever have funny feelings? Do you ever have erections in math class?' "

This mother went on to say that her sons thought the discussion was hilarious. They believed they knew more about the subject than their father. Now, she said, the incident is a family joke and makes it easier for her husband and her to bring up more serious matters with their sons.

In his book *Fulfilling Lives*, Douglas Heath likens the adolescent boy's preoccupation with controlling his penis with the adult male drive to control appearances, emotions, and excitement.[12] It is hard for women to imagine the impact of an adolescent penis that can cause both anxiety and pleasure and remains immune to thought control. Control, therefore, assumes major significance in the life of an early-adolescent boy. He wants to appear in charge of his body and his emotions. He is reluctant to share his adolescent concerns about erections or masturbation with friends or family. Outwardly, nothing fazes him. He is in control. But the awareness of vulnerability was reflected in a boy's comment: "It's not like you can shape your future," he said. "It's kind of spontaneous. Things can happen."

The size of his penis also may worry a boy. Some erotic magazines—those hidden sources of information—may glorify a large penis, but boys need not be concerned. Penis length varies with each boy and has nothing to do with his height or weight or sexual prowess. I remember wondering why our sons kept going back to a certain page in the book *The Godfather*, until I realized that the whole page discussed the grandeur of an individual penis. A boy can be reassured that his ability as a lover will not be related to the size of his penis, but to his sensitivity and consideration of a woman's sexual needs.

A couple of boys told me that they were too embarrassed to participate in gym class because they were not circumcised. They had not thought much about it until they noticed other boys in the locker room. In some cultures the opposite happens: A boy who is circumcised feels out of place. In the melting pot of the United States, any locker room will expose circumcised and uncircumcised penises, and I think mothers should explain the cultural or medical reasons for circumcision to their sons so they know what to expect.

Being Tall Makes a Difference

Jerry Springer, a morning talk-show host, told his TV audience that he was considered a "nerd" during his high-school years. By "nerd," he meant that he was short—five feet, one inch—when he graduated from high school, and everyone made fun of him. (Now he is a very nice-looking TV personality of normal height.) Appearing on his show that morning were other men and women who also were high-school "nerds."

When they reflected back on their adolescent days, these men and women said that the common reason they were considered out of the mainstream was that they were too short or too fat. Being short particularly made the men feel shunned and disliked by girls. The happiest day of one man's life, he said, was "walking across the stage at graduation."

Unfortunately, our society prefers tall men. I can remember being humiliated in high school because my parents made me go to a school dance with a short boy who was the son of family friends. Going to a dance with a boy as short or shorter than my five feet, three inches did not enhance my desired image. I'm sure he was a "nice" boy, but in my adolescent view, all he was was short.

Because height is determined primarily by a boy's genetic makeup, something he cannot control, mothers should do all they can to build up a son's self-confidence and pride, no matter what his height. Adult height cannot be guessed by looking at a young adolescent. A boy's growth spurt usually begins between the ages of 11 and 16, but he can continue growing until he is 20 and sometimes longer. An orthodontist told me that some boys' jaws keep growing and changing until they are 25.

Some puzzling and, I think, disturbing research suggests that parents—and boys themselves—have higher educational aspirations and expectations for a tall son than a short one. In a Stanford University study, even boys who matured early but were short in stature shared an underestimation of what they could do educationally.

In this particular study, almost four thousand boys between the ages of 12 and 17 and their parents were asked two questions: "Looking ahead, what would you like to do about school?" and "What do you think will happen about school?" Each question was answered with one of the following answers: (a) quit as soon as possible; (b) finish high school; (c) get some college or other training; (d) finish college; (e) go further than college.[13]

More tall boys and their parents chose one of the last three statements. Perhaps short boys wish to abbreviate their education because they, like Jerry Springer's TV guests, are tired of feeling left out. These boys may change their minds about higher education after they leave the dreaded halls and lockers of high school, but for many, the best time in high school may be the day they quit.

"Heightism" also appears in other cultures, as David Gilmore notes in his study of the cultural concepts of masculinity. Gilmore quotes American sources who assert, with regret, that height "affects our social relations, sexual patterns, employment opportunities, political success and even our earning power."[14]

Height can affect a simple interaction between mother and son. A mother told me that her 15-year-old son said to her when she wanted to kiss him good-bye at his school, "If I were tall, you could kiss me. But I'm short, they'll think I'm a baby."

Perhaps a short teenage son needs more attention from both his father and mother to assure him that height has nothing to do with ability. He may not achieve fame as a basketball player, but he can cultivate good friends and accomplish anything he wants educationally, vocationally, or physically. And when he reaches adulthood, his height will not be an issue.

Becoming "Manly"

Consciousness about behaving like a boy rather than a girl heightens during adolescence. Psychologists call this process gender intensification. An illustrative study led by the University of Pennsylvania's Anne Petersen found that middle-school boys, as they progressed through the grades, described themselves in more masculine terms like "self-reliant," while girls used more feminine terms like "yielding"—typical gender intensification.

Not an unusual finding, but what surprised me in this study was the boys' unwillingness to accept male-female equality—even in today's "enlightened" era. "From the sixth to the eighth grades," report the researchers, "girls increasingly approved of male-female equality, whereas boys became less approving."[15]

Perhaps by convincing himself that boys are better than girls, a middle-school boy is boosting his confidence in an effort to compete with the more mature girls in his class. To appear feminine or to like girls as friends may be unacceptable in his school, so he puts girls down in order to achieve status, a destructive habit that some men fail to outgrow. Mothers and fathers should stress that their sons not only treat boys and girls equally, but also acknowledge their individual talents.

Looking Good

Unfortunately, good looks receive undue importance in America and this emphasis can make adolescents miserable. The "perfect" male body, attired only in jock shorts, preens for us on the pages of popular magazines. The perfect skin, small hips, and broad shoulders of a Western cowboy ignite dreams of frontier conquests—in inner cities and suburban villages. But reality strikes. The young reader asks himself: How do I get rid of these pimples? Why do I sweat so much? Should I lift weights? Should I get a nose job?

In a study of sixth-grade students, researchers discovered that physical attractiveness related to how the students viewed one another. Good-looking students saw themselves as more competent and had better peer and parent relationships than those who were lower in physical attractiveness, as measured by face and head photos.[16] Not only does a tall high-school boy have an advantage over his shorter peers, but a good-looking middle schooler also will be more admired and feel better about himself than his less attractive counterparts. No wonder many adolescents think the world is an unfair place.

Boys want to look good as much as girls do—not a revelation to a mother who waits patiently for her son to finish his shower. In our family, acne was more of a problem for the boys than the girls, and this is a common occurrence. Boys seem to be more vulnerable than girls to skin problems. Acne occurs when an adolescent's glands produce excess amounts of oil, which causes pores to block and creates blackheads, whiteheads, and pimples.

Acne should not be ignored by a boy or his parents. Not all skin treatments work, but a combination may help alleviate the condition. Encourage your son to wash his face a few times a day and shower or bathe daily. Shampooing daily decreases the amount of oil around his face and changing his pillowcase frequently helps keep the oil away from the skin. Many boys buy a blackhead remover, which is better than scarring their faces by using fingernails, but they must use caution. It is for blackheads only, not pimples that have developed from the blackheads, and must be applied gently.

Doctors remain undecided about whether or not food influences the skin. However, regardless of his skin's condition, a good diet for an adolescent would *not* include fried or fatty foods. A boy who suspects that diet is causing his outbreak of pimples should keep track of what he eats and note if certain foods trigger an increase in acne.

If, after taking all precautions, acne still poses an embarrassment for a son, consult a doctor. Medications are available and some of them are very successful in eliminating the problem. A doctor familiar with adolescents will understand his concern with self-image and suggest medicine or additional preventions.

The bottom line for a mother is to constantly reassure her son that what is inside him is more important than his looks. But be prepared. He may not believe it since he has to live with the everyday humiliations of not always fitting into the crowd.

"He Eats and Sleeps So Much"

All adolescent boys need more food and more sleep than they did when they were younger. Most mothers gape with astonishment at the size of their grocery bills as their sons demand more and more calories. A family can never seem to have too much food.

And the sleeping habits can drive mothers crazy. An adolescent son may consider the hours before midnight far too important to waste on sleep, but trying to get him out of bed the next morning presents a major undertaking mothers shouldn't have to handle. Giving him his own alarm clock puts the responsibility for getting up on time on him, where it belongs. On nonschool or nonworking days, however, he can turn off the alarm and his body will benefit from sleeping late.

Talking About Menstruation

Boys are curious about the pubertal changes in girls and mothers are the natural sources of information. Because many girls mature faster than boys, a simple explanation of the menstrual cycle can answer questions and clear up misconceptions many boys have. During these discussions, when he is in the fifth or sixth grade, mothers can underscore the importance of not teasing early-maturing girls and reemphasize the idea of respect for girls as equals.

He's a Man

A mother sometimes despairs that her son will be an eternal adolescent. Some boys may continue their adolescent fantasies into adulthood, but at some point a male's hormones reach a balance, he attains ultimate height, and the awkwardness disappears. The little boy is transformed and a young man takes his place in the family. A mother senses a new relationship with her son as he seeks to discover who he is.

Memos for Moms

1. Reassure your son that every boy has his own timetable of growth.
2. Understand the process of puberty so you can explain what is happening to your son in simple terms.
3. Talk to him about spontaneous erections and masturbation so he knows he is normal.
4. Avoid making fun of his voice changes.
5. Remind him that being tall or good-looking has nothing to do with success.
6. Be aware of his need to appear manly and in control during early adolescence.
7. Stress the importance of acknowledging the equal talents of girls.
8. Offer understanding and suggestions if he is concerned about his skin or general physical appearance.
9. Talk with him about menstruation to help him appreciate and respect the girls in his class.
10. Be a source of support during these physically confusing years.

3

Struggling for Identity

Searching for Who He Is

Distancing from Mother • Why Mother?
Mother and Father—Different Roles
Finding Himself Through His Father
Searching for Goals • Looking Inward
Proving His Manhood • Too Risky
His "Persona" • Memos for Moms

Whalen I asked a group of mothers what they liked best about their adolescent sons, one mother answered, "Watching his independence blossom." She welcomed her son's ventures into independence, the hallmark of male adolescence. But when I asked her a few minutes later what she did *not* like about her son, she used quite different words to describe that same budding independence—defiant, obnoxious, distant, inscrutable, disagreeable.

This contradictory reaction to a son's bid for autonomy is normal. Of course, a mother would like to hang on to the obedient, cooperative, fun-loving child of elementary school years. Yes, she loves seeing him grow to manhood—but she is a mother and wants to remain his mother, closely involved with him. He thinks he is a man; she thinks he acts like a child. As one mother said when she tried to explain the dilemma, "He doesn't want to be treated like a child, but he doesn't want to grow up." The other mothers who were gathered to talk about their sons murmured their recognition of the impasse.

Distancing from Mother

Puberty brings a new and often unexpected dimension to the mother-and-son attachment. A mother finds that as her son grows in height and weight, their arguments often increase in number and in intensity.[1] He seems to be flexing his muscles at her expense, to show her who is boss. Mothers can't really understand what is going on. She has not changed. She still loves and tries to understand her son. But the closer she comes, the more he backs off or defies her. "Tell her to relax," a boy told me to tell mothers. "Do something light."

A son may pat his mother on the head and go his way, leaving her frustrated and unable to fathom what is going on in his mind. And that is just the way he would like it to remain. He wants to expand his horizons and doesn't want her knowing his every move. He desires freedom, to stand on his own. Just as he is unable to understand his mother's need for involvement, she is puzzled by his restlessness and detachment.

"I went into recognizable hibernation during adolescence," a man told me. "I was in a cocoon struggling for identity." No one could have broken through that cocoon, especially his mother.

Adolescent researcher Laurence Steinberg suggests that an adolescent son's distancing from his mother follows an ancient pattern that serves an evolutionary purpose, that of preparing a boy to begin his own family. Steinberg's studies looked not at a boy's age but at his pubertal status and found that as a boy moved toward the peak of puberty, the conflict with his mother increased. During adolescence, "mother and sons interrupted each other more [than before], explained their points of view less often, and deferred to each other less."[2]

When a son reaches maturity, the conflict decreases, not because he has more sympathy with his mother but because she begins to treat him like a man. He has emerged from the protection of his mother and does not have to withdraw or protest. Now his mother defers to him.

Few adolescent boys can afford to go out on their own and start families as they might have in past generations. So a boy must construct a sense of separateness from his mother within the walls of the same house.

"My sons have worked overtime to be private," a mother of two sons told me. "As much as I intellectually understand it, it hurts."

Why Mother?

But why is a son's struggle for self-determination focused on the mother rather than the father? A number of reasons may explain why a mother feels the effects of her son's psychological searching. A boy may find it easier to defy his mother because she is more sympathetic, less threatening, and physically smaller than his father. Or he may see her as an all-powerful woman and worries about being absorbed by her. Or a son may be in awe of his father, reluctant to confront him directly, so his mother takes the brunt of his adolescent insurrection. Because he may not see his father on a daily basis, he has no need to quarrel or withhold information from him. Their relationship is uninvolved, flat.

Also, according to Freud, a boy has more of a need to separate from his first love, his mother, before he can establish his own sense of manhood. He wants to identify *with* his father, not separate from him.

I also think that because of her day-to-day involvement, a mother is attuned to her son's activities, but not necessarily to his true feelings. Her desire to have him succeed, to have friends, or to be happy may obscure her awareness of his need to do things his way. He clams up or fights back when his mother becomes too involved. And she misses his impulsive affection, as this mother expressed it to me.

"A good friend of mine told me he has never forgotten the time when my son saw me—when he was eight or nine—and he came full speed and jumped into my arms. No compunction about it at all. And I thought about that so much this spring and how that spontaneity is not there in the same way. Every once in a while he will give me a wink or something, but it's like those hormones have kicked in."

The decrease in physical affection and the increase in bickering happen in every family, and these changes do not mean a boy loves his mother less. He may only want some distance to find out who he is. She, on the other hand, wants to know what he is thinking, what he is doing, how he is feeling. She feels an overwhelming responsibility for his development and wants to be reassured that she is doing a good job.

A boy reacted to his mother's encroachment when he told me, "When she asks over and over, it gets on my nerves. She keeps asking and asking, it's really annoying."

Many men can remember well their mothers' attempts to probe their adolescent minds, but their outer shells were difficult to penetrate. Instead of continually asking how he feels or what he thinks, a boy suggested that mothers stop interrogating and start listening by remaining quiet but attentive. Eventually, he said, a son may open up. By waiting for him, she is respecting his personal boundaries.

Mother and Father—Different Roles

Many sons voice a closeness to their mothers and some can articulate the unique contribution of their fathers to their upbringing.

"My mother is very outstanding," a boy said. "She cares a lot about me and my sister. She not only cares, but listens to our problems and wants to know about our problems . . . but sometimes she gets too involved and will say, 'You didn't tell me that.' My dad is different. He's not home a lot, so he doesn't know a lot about what is happening. But I don't know—he just seems to know what to do. It's up to me if I want to talk to him."

A son may not admit to his mother that he feels strongly connected to her even though he knows she would like to hear it. An admission of affection may be embarrassing. A boy demonstrated his ambivalence about his mother when every time he said something positive about her, he countered with a "but."

When I asked him, for instance, what he liked about his mother, he replied, "Honesty. She really tells you how things are. But she is too overprotective, worries about everything. I think it's great that she cares so much about, me but I think she gets too worked up. Sometimes it's crazy, but she's a mother, so she has the right to do it."

This boy could understand his mother's care and concern and appreciated both qualities. He also spoke clearly about his father's influence.

"I'm closer to my mom than my dad," he continued. "But I do a lot of things with him. We go fishing, go to the beach, go crabbing. We spend a lot of time together. But I look at my dad in a different way than I look at my mom. I think of my dad as on a higher level. I don't know if that's fair to say. My dad is more strict. He's there for me and I could talk to him, but I don't feel so comfortable talking to him."

This boy's response matches the research that suggests that as a boy advances through adolescence he moves into a more equal relationship with his mother, not his father. Control of the family is now shared by three people: father, son, and mother.[3] Mother has transferred some of her power, Father has not. "It's a constant power struggle between my son and me. He will not do anything till he wants to do it," a mother moaned.

"I treat my mother in a more equal way," a boy said. He thinks of his struggle with his mother as a contest between equals. He often tries to wheedle his mother to join his side as he confronts his father, and sometimes a conspiracy of silence forms to exclude his father from the reality of the boy's life. "Don't tell Dad," he pleads.

"The key word in our house is *control*," a mother of a 16-year-old said. "He doesn't want to be controlled by me."

Even the word *control* can bridle an adolescent boy. To be controlled by a woman, especially his mother, is unacceptable, not manly. He may say he wants to be independent, but in reality, he needs his family. The notion of *inter*dependence, a realization that we depend on one another throughout life, must replace the inflammatory "control" issue.

Parents depend on each other and each parent fills a role in helping a boy validate his distinctiveness and uniqueness. His father usually challenges him with demands about goals, ambitions, school achievement, commitment, and loyalty. His mother, on the other hand, often sensitizes him to others' feelings, his own motivation, his inner strength. A parent can contribute to either role or provide both roles, but a son needs both voices.

"She's more concerned about helping me than punishing me," a boy told me proudly.

These boys were lucky because both parents were available to them on some level. Some boys aren't as fortunate.

Finding Himself Through His Father

"The essential goal in becoming a real man is to liberate one's self from the previous identification with the mother," writes psychiatrist Willard Gaylin in his book *The Male Ego*. "To be a real man, we must stop being a 'Mama's boy' since a crucial stage in male development demands abandoning the primary identification with the mother."[4]

But to be a "real man," a boy needs a model, and many sons have no male to turn to. If an adolescent boy does not have a strong father or father figure, can he become a "real man"? Obviously, the answer is "yes." Many boys have matured into fine men without a father's guidance. Strong, confident mothers can raise strong, confident sons, and that is what this book is all about. However, I am convinced that today more than ever adolescent boys desperately need their fathers' attention.

Often while interviewing boys, I would seethe with anger against the unknown father of the young man seated across from me. Sometimes I would come home and tell my husband that I would like to throttle all fathers—to wake them up and force them to listen to their sons' longing for them.

Robert Bly calls this longing "father hunger." A boy becomes finely tuned to his mother's body and rhythms before and after birth, but as he moves into adolescence, Bly says, he must now retune himself to his father. "Slowly over months or years," he writes, "the son's body-strings begin to resonate to the harsh, sometimes demanding, testily humorous, irreverent, impatient, opinionated, forward-driving, silence-loving older masculine body. Both male and female cells carry marvelous music, but the son needs to resonate to the masculine frequency as well as to the female frequency."[5]

The son who cannot satisfy this hunger will feel a "bitter, unexpungeable shame" about his condition and try to replace the missing substance. To help men find their masculine frequency, Bly convenes them around meeting halls and camp fires to recreate a rite of passage into manhood. He encourages men to unleash their masculinity, their "Wild Man" pulsations, and to bond with one another as brothers and fathers.

When I first encountered Robert Bly, I was both amused and offended by the banality and artificiality of camp fires, drums, and savage cries. I was annoyed by his inability to recognize that the age of the noble savage was over, and I was frustrated by his adolescent expectation that reenacting ancient myths would bring inner harmony. What I thought men needed was more connection to their feminine qualities of nurturing and peace-making, not less.

Now after interviewing many boys, I have come to understand Bly's fear that a strong active male spirit is losing value in our culture and that passivity is replacing it. And I applaud his clear call for men to mentor adolescent boys. I agree that a young man must know himself as a man—in the company of men—and that his mother should welcome his masculinity.

But I strongly disagree with Bly's contention that a boy must sever his ties with his mother in order to connect with his father and establish his maleness. A son's longing for his father does not preclude a strong attachment to his mother. He needs attachment to both parents to instill the inner strength necessary to assume responsibility and to acknowledge dependence. Interdependence is real life, not a mythic epic.

Boys do crave the companionship of their fathers, and they don't even have to talk to each other, an arrangement women have trouble understanding. Companionship for father and son could mean fishing next to each other, walking in the park side by side, watching a football game together. Or it could mean real mentoring, tutoring a son, coaching him to catch and throw a ball, to draw an artistic line, to play a musical instrument, to hang a picture. It means praising his accomplishments, encouraging his endeavors, inspiring and supporting him after his failures.

In Andrew Malcolm's absorbing book about his youthful relationship with his father, he writes:

> I don't know how it happens, but there was a moment early in the life of boys in my generation—I imagine that it's late on a Saturday morning—when somehow even the most mundane mutterings of Dad became anointed as the Voice of God. What moms say are The Rules, or at least Her Rules. But what dads say is The Gospel. Most of the time these men don't even know when it happens themselves.

One minute they are mere mortal men who blow their noses
like everyone else; the next they are forever Dad, Voice of
Experience, Judge Advocate, Platoon Leader, Chief Guy,
Head Coach. This aura is enduring, waterproof, and resilient. It resists time and rust, though not resentment.[6]

What an enviable opportunity for fathers. A boy is looking to
him, idolizing him, wanting him as a mentor. A father doesn't
have to prove himself to his son, he just has to be there, physically
and psychologically. His son is waiting.

Andrew Malcolm's experience contrasts to that of a 17-year-
old boy I interviewed. When I asked him how he could improve
communication with his father, he responded, "I would have to
forgive him for the last seventeen years and I don't see that
happening. I've gotten so used to the way it is that it probably
would be strange if it was different."

And this young man was living with his father, not his mother.
They shared the same roof, but not their lives. He felt betrayed by
his father's pursuit of his own interests and his consequent indifference to his family. He had lost his trust in men.

When I asked another boy how his life had changed since his
parents were divorced, he replied, "It didn't affect my life 'cause I
never saw him anyway." I heard this theme over and over—"I
never saw him anyway."

When I asked for advice to give fathers, a boy offered, "Tell
them to get more involved with their sons. When my dad worked
in the city, he was never home. Now he has moved his work closer
and I see him. I have a lot of friends where no one is around. The
father has to get more involved."

Psychologist Guy Corneau verifies his suggestion: "The lack of
attention from the father results in the son's inability to identify
with his father as a means of establishing his own masculine
identity. A son deprived of the confirmation and security that
might have been provided by his father's presence is unable to
advance to adulthood."[7]

I think Corneau's words are too harsh. A boy can advance to adulthood without the attention of his father, but the path is harder and a mother must act even stronger. She must maintain both roles mentioned above and it is not easy.

Although the thought of a substitute father may disturb women who are confident, knowledgeable mothers, I think the idea should not be disregarded. Most mothers appreciate any help in raising a son. The most logical choice would be an uncle or close male relative who will remember a son's birthday, include him in holiday trips, and cultivate his interests in typical male activities that his mother may not find very entertaining. If a mother does enjoy sports like fishing or football, then she could ask the favored man to join her and her son in these activities. I don't think the relationship between a son and a male relative or friend will happen automatically. A mother has to talk frankly with the adult male and solicit his help in providing a strong male image in her son's life.

Searching for Goals

Besides identifying himself as a male, an adolescent son faces an additional task of figuring out what he will do in life, how he will support himself when he leaves the security of family.

"I have a lot of personal problems concerning my future and my goals," a 15-year-old boy wrote for a creative writing class I taught in a shelter for homeless teenagers. "I have a hard time deciding what I want to be. Sometime when I'm trying to come up with something that I really like or want to be, it gives me a headache. I know I have said I want to be a professional basketball player, but I'm not too serious about it. Although I wish I was serious about it because if I was, I would know that I have one particular profession to strive for."

This teenager's struggle with goals is essentially male and his writing could not be mistaken for that of a girl. He never mentions a person or a relationship and is concerned only with doing something, proving himself. Girls in the shelter wrote about friends, family, and problems with relationships. Although the chances of this young man's becoming a professional ball player are slight, his agony is real. He must find something to do so he can be someone. How sad for him that his personal struggle is intensified because he lacks a secure home life.

In my book about adolescent girls, I departed from the work of Erik H. Erikson, who wrote extensively about adolescent development. Erikson's research into human development was based primarily on male experiences and did not, in my view, pertain to young women. But his insights depict accurately a main feature of the adolescent male turmoil. Erikson thought that the adolescent's primary task was to create a stable sense of self and a purpose in life. Only then would he be ready for the next stage of development, that of making commitments and finding intimacy.[8] Erikson felt that a boy who did not achieve identity by the end of adolescence would extend his restless search into adulthood.

In contrast to Erikson's theory based on the male experience, a girl's identity and sense of self develop primarily *through* relationships and may not gel until after adolescence. Because of the interconnection she feels between herself and others, a woman can spend a lifetime defining herself in terms of her relationships at a particular stage in life. As Carol Gilligan from Harvard suggests, adolescent girls and women tend to remain far more tied to family and friends and frequently base decisions on their relationships. They do not separate relationships and goals.[9] Females do not think of goals now, relationships later, but intertwine them throughout their lives.

The teenager who suffered headaches when he pondered his future knew that his self-esteem depended on his ability to work toward a goal. He did not identify himself as a son, a brother, or a friend, and therefore had trouble articulating who he was. His doubts about himself were confirmed because he could not answer his own question: What will I do?

This boy's dilemma deepens because of the lack of employment opportunities for young men. Even if his education has prepared him for employment, the current emphasis on individual choice and self-fulfillment can make the process difficult. In past generations, a boy's choice of job or career was influenced by family expectations and community values. A boy knew what was expected of him.

Now many communities cannot agree on a common standard of responsible adult male behavior, so a boy cannot measure himself against an accepted criterion of male conduct. When society tells him that anything goes (even doing nothing or being supported by others), parents must step in early and provide a foundation of expectations, teaching and showing him the work ethic they expect him to uphold. He may not agree with them, but at least this way he knows where they stand. A wide range of career choices excites the imagination, but choosing a job that will support him economically and psychologically can be daunting. One boy may suffer headaches, but another may turn to drugs or alcohol.

Looking Inward

The relationship to his mother can affect the male quest for identity, and recent research is confirming that a strong attachment to Mother helps a boy's knowledge of self. One study verified that both male and female college students who reported that they were *attached to their mothers* showed higher levels of "identity achievement."[10]

In addition, this research found that the closer sons were to their fathers, the more satisfied they were with life in general. Although daughters typically were more attached to their mothers than sons were, both sons and daughters reported being more connected to mothers than fathers, regardless of whether their families were intact. The many adolescent boys I interviewed confirmed this intimate alliance with Mother. They may want to be recognized as themselves and maintain distance, but they are close and attached to their mothers.

When I asked a handsome 17-year-old what he thought about the most, he said, "The future. For instance, I sometimes think about someone very close to me dying, like my mother. I can even start crying about it. And I think about what would happen if I moved out of the family, were on my own, and what would I do to support myself."

In contrast to the boy with the headaches who had no family support, this young man thinks of himself as a family member, a son, close to his mother and concerned about being on his own. He associates the loss of his mother with being forced from the security of home—a dramatic image of his need to distance himself from his mother, yet remain attached.

The prospect and excitement of becoming self-reliant consume an adolescent boy and can take priority over his emotional attachments. He conceals his affection from his mother because of his strong and necessary desire for autonomy.

"I'm excited to get away," said a high-school senior. "I'll kind of miss my mother, but not my dad. He has a new life, with a new wife and another son. I will have a new lease on life, so I want to get away and get on with it."

When pressed further, though, this young man disclosed his ambivalence about leaving his mother and his younger sister. "Sometimes I wonder what my life would be like if something happened to my sister," he worried. "I wouldn't want to deal with it. I think about that a lot." Although appearing nonchalant at first, he was deeply attached to his mother and sibling. This is not a boy unconcerned about relationships.

His friend, who seemed equally indifferent about leaving his family, confessed, "I'm really worried about my brother because

I'm not sure he has sense. He goes to a big college with drugs and it scares me a lot. I worry that he gets out of control."

The boys I interviewed were struggling to balance their sense of responsibility and love of family with their need to appropriately move away from their mothers. Most boys understood that these conflicting feelings were normal and would not stop them from entering the next phase of life.

Their mothers may lament their departure, but a strong mother welcomes her son's transformation into adulthood, even if it hurts. "The more intense the relationship with a son, the uglier is the breaking away," a mother said candidly about her son's noticeable change in attitude as he prepared to leave for college.

When Susan Harter of the University of Denver examined conflicts in adolescent self-portraits, she asked young people to describe what they were like with parents, with friends, in the classroom, and in romantic relationships. Harter discovered that girls reported more contradictory self-attributes and conflict than boys at every grade level. Harter suggests that a boy "forges a path of independence and autonomy in which the logic of his moral and social decisions takes precedence over an affective empathetic response to others with whom he has formed emotional bonds."[11] In other words, he moves out and on because he knows that is what he should do.

Proving His Manhood

As a boy shifts his social preferences away from his family and seeks more time with friends, his mother worries that he will do all the things she has dreaded. He will take risks he is not prepared for. His impulsiveness will get him into trouble, and authorities (police and school officials) will overreact to his exuberance for adventure.

The serious areas of drugs, alcohol, and early sexual activities will be discussed in later chapters. Now, however, I want to concentrate on why ordinary boys seem unwilling to lead normal, quiet, steady lives during early adolescence.

"I tried to get away with as much as I could," a young man told me. "When I would sneak out of the house during the night, I always imagined what I would do if my mother or father were sitting on my bed when I crawled back through the bedroom window."

"I've seen signs of rebelliousness I never saw in my girls," a mother of a 13-year-old told me. "This wanting to be independent creates a real defiance. And the way he is wearing his hair . . . It is completely shaved on one side, but he pushes the longer side over when he wants to cover it up."

When I later discovered some of the risks our sons took in their early-adolescent days, I was grateful that they made it through ninth grade, much less high school. They jumped in front of cars at night, walked the railing of a high bridge, skied off cliffs, swam way beyond the ocean barriers, fooled around on the edge of roofs, and did everything too fast or with abandon. They didn't seem to care what would happen to them. Sometimes they didn't think beyond the immediate moment (perhaps most of the time).

When one of my sons was in middle school, he and two friends carefully planned and executed a shoplifting spree in a local store. Meeting me downtown, however, was not in their plans. When I asked them what they were carrying, their short life of crime came to an abrupt halt. They hadn't thought about getting caught, by the shop owner or me. To them it was a game, a risky adventure, a dare. To me, it was clearly wrong.

At other times I marveled at how they extended themselves beyond their physical limits. Were they competing against one another to show who could think up the most daring exploit? Perhaps, but from discussions with other mothers, I am convinced that many boys enjoy taking risks simply to prove their manhood, their courage, or their recklessness.

When I recently asked another son why he did so many crazy

things in middle school, he replied, "It was adventuresome. You would dream up something and say, for instance, 'Wouldn't it be great to take the skateboards down that steep hill and up that ramp to see how fast we can go?' "

He said it was like an "adrenaline pump." His group of friends got "fired up" about doing something daring and they enjoyed talking about it after they survived the exploit. And the daredevil stories entertained them for years after. In the middle of our conversation he advised mothers to read Bill Waterson's cartoon strip, "Calvin and Hobbes." Five-year-old Calvin, he said, typified the young male adolescent.

My son also mentioned two kinds of risks. One is a dare to do something you don't want to do, to prove to someone else you are not afraid. This is more scary than fun, he said, and in some neighborhoods this risk can lead to serious injury or death.

The second type of risk is an escapade you and your friends think up; you may be nervous about executing it, but the excitement and thrill override all hesitation. The camaraderie and fun are what count—our son thrived on the exhilaration and so do many young adolescents.

Most mothers did a few daring things themselves during their teen years, and some may have gone over the edge during the sixties and seventies. But activities like bungie jumping, car racing, rock climbing, or gang rituals typically attract young males, causing mothers bemusement or terror.

Willard Gaylin, writing in *The Male Ego*, reminds us of ancient rituals during which boys proved they were capable of joining the adult world.[12] The elders conducted the initiation, teaching them respect and responsibility as men. They didn't have to show off to their friends to demonstrate manliness, as American boys do; they had to show their elders.

Learning how to hunt and provide food was essentially a male role in these societies. Since industrialization has replaced the hunt with mass-produced foods and supermarkets, the food-provider has lost its gender affiliation and we no longer have rites-of-passage rituals for young males. Gaylin writes: "Since ritual and ceremonial rites of passage have been attenuated or abandoned, and manhood is never completely defined, one must probe one's manhood almost daily."

What a strain it must be to probe your manhood daily. Women don't have to "prove themselves." Mothers don't have to "make" women. But boys think they have to be made into men—if not through ritual, then through the daily defense of their manliness.[13]

Many boys create their own initiations, a modern version of the hunting and war ritual. "My thirteen-year-old had four friends spend the night and they played war. They had infrared hats, camouflage. They played in the dark, leaped from the trees, genuine play."

In some neighborhoods, the war games are real. The allure of gangs and the presence of rival factions feed into the adolescent urge for ritual, friendship, and excitement. This is not "genuine play" but survival, where newly acquired skills are used to duck bullets, avoid dealers, ignore insults, and elude enemies. Not a safe way to ritualize manhood.

Some discover more acceptable challenges, like racing with bikes or motorbikes to reenact the adolescent ritual. Two boys I spoke with got their "kicks" by motorcross racing on Sunday mornings and training during the week. Racing not only gave them the status they sought but helped them overcome or ignore their personal problems.

As one boy explained: "When my parents were getting a divorce, I won a lot of races. When you're winning, you're on a high and that helped me a lot. I don't know what would have happened if I didn't have racing."

A mother laughed as she related the junior-high exploits of her now-young-adult son. Among his many daredevil feats was "proving himself" by hanging from an interstate bridge over a river below. Now her son's wife shudders when she envisions her two young sons imitating their father's youthful adventures.

The big thrill of another man's early adolescence was scaling three stories every week to the roof of a movie theater, lowering himself into the men's room, and then walking into the theater to see the movie—free.

Many fathers can relate personally to similar antics, but a father's tendency to accept risky behavior as normal is not often shared by a boy's anxious mother. She wants her son to stay out of trouble, not create it.

When I asked a man in his thirties to describe some of his early-adolescent escapades, he said he didn't have any. Interestingly, he added that he regretted this because he thought early risk-taking would have freed him from unnecessary anxiety and enabled him to take more business and personal risks in adulthood. Taking risks when he was young, he said, would have made him more confident about taking chances as he grew older.

Too Risky

These young-adolescent adventures may provide men with many evenings of fond recollections and hearty laughs and prepare them for adult decisions, but some young sons can't move fast enough or they get left behind during a daring feat, affirming a mother's worst fear.

An eighth-grade boy was killed by a train while he and his friends were taking a shortcut on their way home from the movies. The experience traumatized not only his family but his classmates who routinely ran across the tracks and climbed up on the platform. A mother whose son was with the boy when he was killed told me that her son now needs more affection and reassurance than her other sons and is reluctant to go away from home. The horror of watching a friend die has removed the excitement of exploration and temporarily halted his quest for independence.

More boys than ever witness the deaths of family or friends in

American streets, and these deaths are not all caused by their own risk-taking. Death by accident or homicide stalks neighborhoods. Stray bullets from drive-by killers or gang crossfire can abruptly end the life of an unsuspecting youth. The long-term effect of ever-present and violent loss on young people is not fully known, but the increase in adolescent depression and suicide tells part of the story. Loss of family and friends delays the resolution of the main adolescent task of defining oneself and planning for the future. How can a boy plan when he doesn't know whether he or his friends will make it until their twentieth birthdays?

His "Persona"

When life seems overwhelming to a boy, he may resort to an unrealistic view of himself. By assuming a mantle of distinct originality, he can imagine surviving where others have fallen. This attitude may seem irrational to a mother who wants her son to be practical and cautious, but a boy needs to reassure himself that nothing can happen to him. If he believes that dangers are lurking behind every street corner, he will never develop the confidence needed to overcome his inner fears.

He builds up his defenses by convincing himself, like a two-year-old, that "I can do it." This self-assuredness allows him to envision himself as an individual with a purpose. I don't think a mother should be too concerned with this maddening egotistical attitude. Underneath the swagger lies inner doubt and skepticism about the surrounding world.

One woman feared that her son would reject traditional life options merely because they are traditional. "I want him to make the right choices for himself, not for the persona he is developing," she said. "He is becoming too much of a free spirit, a person who will question everything, convinced he is right and we are wrong."

Her son's skepticism makes her worry. "He's everything I didn't marry my first boyfriend for," she reminisces. "He is the son I thought I would have with the wild-haired hippie. I swung to the other extreme and married a very responsible man, thinking he would be a better role model. The kernel of me that is *not* Mother just loves this kid. The kernel of me that *is* Mother is worried about whether or not he will be able to get a responsible job and be able to support himself."

The gleam in this mother's eye revealed her deep love for her son, but she finds his self-assuredness unsettling. He has to prove his uniqueness to set himself apart, to show that he is not his responsible father, he is not the former boyfriend, he is himself.[14]

As her son questions, challenges, and eventually listens to others' ideas and beliefs, he will overcome his need to construct a fortress of skepticism. He will recognize other people's experiences as legitimate (including his parents') and other viewpoints as being worthy of his consideration.

I think involving sons in community functions will open their minds to the needs and experiences of others. Boys can volunteer to play with children in day-care centers or work with youths in community recreation programs. They can assist the elderly in their neighborhood with shopping or home maintenance. A personal involvement or commitment to a younger child or older person will help a son shed his egotistical "cocoon" and emerge from hibernation.

A son then will realize that "independence" is a myth, that we all depend on and need one another, that interdependence, not independence, is what he is seeking. He does not need to separate from his mother or others to discover who he is. He can be recognized and cherished as an individual with his own personality and goals within his family.

Memos for Moms

1. Understand a son's need to emotionally step back from you as he enters puberty.
2. Remember that this distancing does not mean he doesn't love you. He wants to remain attached.
3. Wait for him to open up. Interrogating him about his thoughts and feelings doesn't work.
4. Realize that he wants to share in the decisions that affect him.
5. Give him options so he can make choices and have some control over his own activities.
6. Respect his desire to spend time with his father and don't try to control the activities they do together.
7. If his father is not available, ask a male relative to provide adult male companionship.
8. Don't begrudge his admiration of his father or father-substitute.
9. Encourage him to think and talk about his goals, his future.
10. Appreciate his adolescent exuberance for adventure.
11. Be grateful that he doesn't tell you everything.
12. Reduce his preoccupation with himself by suggesting community activities where he can volunteer to help a young child or elderly person.
13. Stress that interdependence, not independence, is what works in the real world.

4

"Should I Tell Him
I Love Him?"

A New Relationship

The Dilemma • "No Problem"
Mother's Admiration • Maintaining the Boundaries
"Unconditional" Love? • Father's Affection
Mature Dependence/Interdependence
"He Thinks He Hears What I'm Not Saying"
Enhancing His Maleness • Single Mothers
Stepmothers • But Should I Tell Him I Love Him?
Memos for Moms

I remember the day I realized my oldest son was a man. A sophomore in high school, he and some friends were heading out the door to an athletic event. They were full of energy, enthusiasm, and masculinity. It suddenly dawned on me that I no longer was the mother of a child, but of a captivating and sexual young man. He was my child, but he was distinct. He was from me, but he was not me. I loved him deeply, yet I knew in my heart that I would have to use this maternal closeness to liberate him (and his younger brothers) and send him on his own path to manhood. Our bond would be an affirmation of his maleness, an acknowledgment that he possessed depths I could not comprehend, an inner energy descended from my husband and my male genes that I could never fully grasp.

This awakening of a mother to a son's sexuality may occur at any time, often causing confusion and a blurring of boundaries. Sometimes a son or mother's privacy is invaded and secrets are shared that do not belong to each other. Or his raw virility so alarms a mother that she builds barriers, leaving him to struggle without her support.

A son can gasp under the weight of a mother's intrusion into his inner life if she tries to mold him into the man she wants. Some men, driven by their mothers' ambitions and desires, realize in midlife that her ambitions are not his. At a conference I attended, a 40-year-old man spoke of his recent emergence from the domination of his all-powerful mother. But his honesty is the exception. Most men refrain from blaming or crediting their mothers' influence, leading to a silence about themselves.

Although a mother often is unconscious of her influence, there is no doubt that she can inspire and motivate a son or overwhelm and discourage him. By listening to boys and men and reading men's lives revealed through their writings, I have come to understand the extraordinary power a mother possesses.

When Russell Baker decided to write his autobiography, he realized, "I would have to start with my mother and her passion for improving the male of the species, which in my case took the form of forcing me to 'make something out of myself.' Lord, how I hated those words. . . . She was realistic about the difficulty. Having sized up the material the Lord had given her to mould, she didn't overestimate what she could do with it."[1]

"You don't want to hear about my mother," a man told me, revealing that he still struggled with his feelings about her. Mothers, perhaps with the exception of Mrs. Baker, are usually oblivious to the force of their words and actions, unaware that their sons are absorbing them.

Most mothers aren't even conscious of a son's curiosity about her body. A mother commented, "I have a seven-year-old who is handicapped and I guess I continue to do things with him because it is quicker and easier for me. I take showers with him and I happened to mention it to a man friend and he told me I was ridiculous and shouldn't do that. So the next time we were in the shower, I really looked at my son and this guy was absolutely right. There was my son looking at me, a different kind of look, and it made me feel uncomfortable. He may be delayed and he may have problems, but I told myself that this kid is too old to be in the shower with me. Someone out of the family had to show that to me."

If a boy is not openly curious about his mother's body, he may admit his fascination with another authority figure. "We were at an awards dinner," a mother told me. "A teacher was speaking and my sixteen-year-old son said, 'Mom, do you know I did nothing but stare at her boobs during seventh and eighth grade? We used to talk about them all the time. We had signals and could tell when it got cold by her bosoms." The teacher, according to this boy's mother, doesn't have big breasts, but her male students noticed every change in her nipples.

"I remember when my sons turned thirteen or fourteen they continued grabbing me," a woman said when she was describing her sons' physicalness. "It was their way of starting to feel females."

Another mother told a funny story about emerging from the shower and opening her closet door. "There were five neighborhood boys staring at my stark-naked body," she related. "No one moved. I started screaming like a maniac and they ran out of the house. I could have killed my son. I didn't see them for weeks. I don't think they planned it—it was too contrived for a boy." She may not think it was planned, but I wonder.

Mothers, in turn, often admire their sons' bodies. When I asked a mother what she liked about her son, she answered, "I like his muscles, his maleness." Another woman said frankly about her three sons, "I am in awe at how well turned out they are—what beautiful specimens of malehood."

"It seems like he grew up overnight," a mother said with a touch of embarrassment. "When I see my son in his underwear, I am in shock. I want to say to him, 'Get some clothes on.' I have a seven-year-old, too, and it's like night and day."

Her friend commented, "The emotions don't match the body. I have this little boy in a big boy's body."

Attentive mothers and alert sons sense this new stage in their relationship and try to accord each other some privacy.

The Dilemma

When a boy develops an intrigue with women's bodies, his mother or sisters may satisfy his curiosity at first, but in a short time, his interest in them wanes. He discovers girls and forbidden girlie magazines. This is a healthy sign. A mother may protest that girls are chasing him or he is too young to be attracted to girls—and she may have good reason to want him to slow down—but the recognition of his masculinity isn't confined to her observations. The girls in his class also appreciate his attractiveness.

A mother, aware of her son's sexual drive, said he was "pretty disgusting" to her between the ages of 16 and 18 and she had her own unique explanation for his frustration. "This child could not grow up and break away," she said. "Until he had his first sexual relationship, he was furious with me. I think it was because biologically he knew he was ready to take the plunge, but emotionally he wasn't and I was the one and only female he knew best and I reminded him of how inadequate he was feeling. It was a pretty rough time and there wasn't anything I could do or say."

Some sons, awkward about their newfound masculinity in relation to their mothers, are either confused or afraid. "Mothers have to realize that their sons are men and treat them differently," a boy pleaded to me three or four times. "They should remember they are male."

All boys respond differently to their mothers, but each one faces a similar dilemma. How can he return his mother's love and, at the same time, deny her the psychological intimacy she may desire?

Nancy Chodorow, a well-known psychoanalyst, writes, "Masculine personality comes to be founded more on the repression of affect and the denial of relational needs and a sense of connection than [does the] the feminine personality."[2]

Jonathan Rutherford, describing the workings of a men's group in his book *Men's Silences*, agrees with Chodorow that men lack a "language of feeling" that would help them articulate both their affection for and their withdrawal from their mothers.[3] The men in his group, organized to combat sexism against women, could not talk about their own mothers, the first women in their lives.

This paucity of emotional vocabulary, evident in some men more than others, could have originated in a boy's early childhood when his needs were satisfied so quickly that he did not have to articulate his inner distress. In his boyhood, adults did not teach him to regard another's feelings or pay heed to his own. It solidified in adolescence when he learned anew that too much joy or too much grief would draw his mother's attention, pulling her too close, detracting from his male image.

"No Problem"

A boy's dilemma in discussing his mother became apparent as I did research for this book. When I interviewed girls for my book "*Don't Stop Loving Me*," I typically would ask a group of them whether they had any problems with their mothers. I didn't have to ask another question. They immediately talked with animation and passion, criticizing their mothers, praising them, hating them, loving them. But I quickly learned in interviewing boys that they became reticent or evasive in a group, reluctant to talk about their mothers. So I scheduled one-on-one meetings and conversed with them about their activities, social life, family life—and still I had to work in my questions about their mothers. If I asked them directly, for instance, if they would want to change anything about their mothers, most would say, "No."

"I don't have a problem," one boy told me. Later he mentioned that his mother had left the family to pursue a life of her own in another state, yet he still would not say anything disloyal about her. A boy wants to distance himself from his mother during adolescence, but distancing is not the same as criticism. He may set limits on her intrusiveness, but he has a hard time articulating his feelings about her. His tendency is to accept and protect her.

In some neighborhoods, to say anything negative about another's mother is to provoke a fight. This devotion to Mother permeates the adolescent male community, regardless of neighborhood. Sons know their mothers are their interceptors, their protectors, and they reciprocate. "I bond with my mother," a boy said, reflecting the feelings of many.

"She understands me, doesn't get too involved," said another.

"My mom, she's easy to talk to, gives me what I want," said a third. "Dad says it's too expensive, Mom says, 'Buy it.' I don't know how to put it. She's nicer, I guess."

Mothers admit they succumb to their sons' charms. "I have a soft side," one mother said with a smile. "He tries to play on it."

"My son has the wit and sense of humor and charm to take you all around the room and get his way in the end," another mother said, with the other women in the room laughing in agreement.

A woman in the same group confessed that her husband had to point out that she was always rescuing her son. "I can remember sitting my son down—he had refused to do a drawing for a book report—and handing him the paper and crayons. My husband said, 'Do you see what you're doing? He's in junior high and you're still doing his work.' Thank God for my husband," she added jokingly. "He has no feeling or emotions for this child."

Another woman agreed: "My son puts me on a pedestal because my husband is so hard on him, yelling at him. I'm always confirming and consoling, but I think his father is a better parent because he is teaching him, giving him instruction."

Boys somehow sense that their mothers are on their side, pulling for them, wanting them to succeed. They repay her solicitude by remaining uncritical sons—keeping their negative thoughts to themselves or focusing on her good qualities when speaking to others. A son may argue with his mother as he reaches puberty, but he stops before the words become too personal and hurt. He has too much to lose.

"Men's perceptions of their mothers were idealized or out of focus," writes Rutherford. "For their attachment to this maternal fantasy precluded a real relationship with an actual woman. At an unconscious level, masculinity was organized around sustaining this fantasy of the mother."[4]

A strong, healthy relationship between mothers and adolescent daughters develops in spite of (sometimes because of) disagreement and confrontation because they can both love and disagree with each other at the same time. A son often doesn't understand this. He wants to maintain his mother's emotional support, so he accepts her with all her imperfections. Another son may think that criticism or disagreement will provoke a mother's wrath to such a point that she will become a formidable opponent or a cold stranger. A boy is cautious. Although he needs to distance himself from his mother in order to confirm his adolescent manliness, he wants her on his side. Remaining uncritical guarantees that she will remain his booster.

No wonder a mother who is openly dethroned by her adolescent daughter exalts in this acceptance from her son. "We tend to prefer people who prefer us," writes author Carol Klein. "A son who knows he is a mother's fondest triumph will behave in a way to foster that evaluation. Her unconditional admiration erases the need to argue or rebel."[5]

I think a son who conceals his "need to argue or rebel" in order to maintain his relationship with his mother is doing a disservice to both of them. Not only will she miss out in knowing her son's true feelings or his real activities, she may reinforce his belief that uncommunicative men are the most acceptable. A son must learn that relationships involve an exchange of ideas and emotions, and that most women prefer men who communicate.

Mother's Admiration

Although sons may talk hesitatingly about their mothers, mothers have no trouble expressing their feelings for their sons. Some glow when they talk about them and this glow may disturb their daughters, some of whom wonder if they are admired in equal fashion. A young Yale University student, Jenifer Braun, wrote this poem called "MotherDaughterSon" while she was in high school.

When we carpeted the dining room
>*my brother was seven*
>*I was eleven*
my mother spent days emptying the hutch
wiping, wrapping, packing away
her bridal silver, bridal china.

I bridle up inside me
red stomping horses who roll their eyes
when she pours over my brother's life
like she poured over gilt-edged, lily-colored tea-cups
that day they carried carpet through the dining-room door.

All women with sons are like this.
Sons break their mothers' hearts as easily as china.
I have seen this, sitting in the car with her
after his team lost, or when he didn't make the team.
She bruises up around the eyes and
I cannot touch her.

Not that I haven't stolen her clothes,
or nagged and whined and been forgiven.
Not that I haven't woken to find the dress laid out for me
>*smoothed and hemmed and perfect*
while every wrinkle absent in the sleeve

reproaches me from her forehead, later
over midnight coffee.
There are many debts and they are all mine.

But, selfish still, I wish I knew
if she pours over me, too, like her china and her sons;
if I could break her heart like he does.

A mother-son bond as intense as the one Jenifer so powerfully portrays in her poem can obstruct a mother's realistic view of her son, hindering her ability to act as his parent and guide. A mother whose son had been suspended from school many times took his side on all the issues, blaming the school and the police for causing his problems. When I asked her to describe her son, she said, "He has what every girl dreams of, the nice muscles, the nice shoulders. My neighbor says he is a hunk and I have to agree. He can say anything he wants to me and he knows that and he'll protect me. I could walk down any street and have no worry. He's big and very confident."

Some mothers speak longingly of their desire for even more closeness with their sons. "Our relationship is tension-free," a woman said of her 15-year-old son. "My only desire is to hear more of his personal life and share more."

Another woman laughed as she said possessively, "I'll break the legs of any woman who tries to get him." Then she went on to tell me how her own mother-in-law had "emasculated her husband and worshipped her son." She thought mothers of her mother-in-law's generation revered their sons too much, not realizing she herself fell into the same mold.

I remember getting frustrated with my own mother-in-law's telling me repeatedly what a wonderful son my husband was and my smiling husband agreeing with her. I knew he was not always the perfect son, but she remained blissfully ignorant while he savored his favored position.

A mother of a 21-year-old told me he had been a wonderful,

sensitive, communicative child until the age of 15, when suddenly he didn't tell her anything. "When he was home, he really wasn't home," she said. "I missed him and waited for him to return to his original skin." It took him until he was 21, but she never stopped adoring him.

A mother of a 15-year-old actor said proudly, "When I talk about him, I hyperventilate because I'm always trying to figure him out and I can't. I think he's an unusual child."

Because of this maternal blind spot, a mother may unwisely cover up for her son, providing protection—from his father, his teachers, his girlfriends—freeing him from responsibility, hard feelings, and tough choices. She becomes his emotional sponge, isolating him from his and others' true feelings.

Quite surprising to me were the few mothers I interviewed who seem to know everything about their sons' lives, creating what I call a "new intimacy." For instance, a 15-year-old boy shared with his mother his first sexual experiences, telling her not to "tell Dad." One mother interceded with a girlfriend on behalf of her son, intercepting a telephone call from her 16-year-old son's girlfriend to tell her how much she had hurt her son's feelings. His girlfriend wanted to break up with him, and he had revealed his "unbelievable hurt" to his mother. She stepped in to lessen his pain.

Another mother related her 18-year-old son's anguish at not being able to have an erection and his jubilation when he finally "did it" with his girlfriend. She beamed with pride at his confidence and trust in her as she told her story to a group of women I was interviewing—who knew her son.

These examples represent extreme involvement with a son's private life and are not typical. Perhaps these sons were assured that as long as they talked—the "let it all hang out" mentality— life with Mother would be easier. These boys were not seeking their mothers' advice or wisdom, but their approval.

One problem with candor and full disclosure, though, is that it may foster the expectation that a son can do anything he wants.

He has won his mother over by reverting to the little boy who pleases her by telling all. So he confesses that he skipped school, cheated on a test, got drunk, smoked pot, is sleeping around, and she listens like a same-age friend. Her ambition is for excessive communication, not high standards of behavior. Some boys can carry this habit into adulthood and do whatever they want, knowing that their revered male/son status will guarantee forgiveness for any actions. They are the eternal adolescent males.

Maintaining the Boundaries

If becoming too intimate with her adolescent son threatens his authentic adult maturity, how can a mother and son show affection for each other and respect the boundaries of their lives?

There is no question that mothers should love, challenge, and direct their sons, but does confiding all to his mother make a son the "new man" and prepare him for living with another woman? Or does Mother's complete acceptance make it difficult for another woman ever to replace her?

Conversely, does concealing his feelings and activities turn him into a Neanderthal holdover, making it impossible for him to live with any modern woman? Neither extreme, true confession or stoic silence, respects the boundaries or realities of today's families.

Because boys are faced with social pressures and family conflicts never faced by young people before, it is absolutely crucial that a balance be maintained between too much and too little involvement. With the advent of instant news and instant gratification, along with the possibility of death from sex, boys must feel free to talk to worthy adults. Usually his mother is the most reliable, concerned adult he knows, so she—and his father—should always be available as guides and counselors.

Friendship with Mother, however, is not what he desires. "You do not have to be a friend *of* your child," a woman told me, "but you should be a friend *to* your child." The distinction is important. An adolescent boy craves same-age friends so he can talk without fear of recrimination or lectures. He wants to confide in other adolescent boys and girls because they share the same worries, the same despair at family situations, a similar discomfort with their bodies, and an equal dismay at school grades or unfair treatment.

He doesn't need another buddy, but a strong person who can guide, listen, empathize, and help him make decisions, not make decisions for him or protect him from the consequences of his actions. He should be aware of his mother's high standards and behavioral goals and realize that when he violates them he will not receive an understanding embrace, but advice and consequences.

When he has serious problems (drug or alcohol use, pregnant girlfriend, sexually transmitted disease, doubts about his sexuality, failing in school, worry about a friend, suicidal thoughts), he can talk with her and elicit her guidance. He should know she will *not* cover up for him but will help him sort through his confusion and make good decisions.

"She's definitely helpful if I have problems," said a 17-year-old. "I'd be nervous talking about anything major, but she'd be the one I'd talk to."

When Erik Erikson spoke about the necessity of sons "separating" from mothers in order to achieve their identity, I think he observed a lack of boundaries in his clients. A son does not want to lose his basic connection with his mother—nor she with him. However, he must have a sense of his own individuality so he can lead a mature life.

Some sons can feel as though the world should be beholden to them because they are "the man." "He feels he's the man," a mother declared. "Everything has to be done for him. His father was a cop and he was the same way. He provided, so we did everything for him. My son wants me to prepare his bath and do everything for him, get his bowl for cereal in the morning. He will work, but you have to pay for it. I feel sorry for his wife." This woman's son is 10 years old and both she and her 20-year-old daughter play into her son's "manly" domination of their home.

By allowing her son to get away with his demands, his mother perpetuates "the man" myth. I feel sorry for this boy's future wife because his expectation that the male of the house will be waited upon is not realistic. When a mother respects her son's individuality, privacy, and his ability to assume responsibility, then she is a strong mother.

"Unconditional" Love?

I think the term "unconditional love" is misunderstood. If a son thinks that anything goes because his mother loves him, he is not experiencing unconditional love, but parental neglect. To love a child unconditionally means to be committed to him forever. The mother-son bond is established at birth (or time of adoption) and never changes—a son cannot choose another mother and a mother cannot claim another son. A committed mother does not abandon a son if he gets into trouble, but gives guidance, sets limits, establishes clear standards, and teaches survival skills. She wants her son to achieve a strong sense of himself and his abilities. Unconditional love does not entail coddling or emasculating a son and refusing to hold him responsible for his actions. It means being tough when necessary.

Psychologist Jack Kornfield recalls friends' asking an old Tibetan lama how to raise a child to become a spiritual, wise, compassionate, and fine person. "You have the wrong idea," the wise man cautioned. "He will be whoever he's going to be. If you want to raise somebody properly, raise yourself. You can do your own practice with a sincere heart and let him feel that from you."[6]

A mother who raises her son with a sincere heart will not turn him into her male confidante, molding him into the desired man

she could not find, or into a robot who has so successfully con-
cealed his emotions from her that in adulthood he finds he has
none. She will find the happy balance.

Father's Affection

I shared, for one brief day, a hospital room with a 16-year-old girl
who welcomed high-school friends throughout the day. They
ignored me—so I, feigning indifference, listened in on their conversations. Her friends at one point talked animatedly about how
wonderful a boy's father was. Intrigued by their enthusiasm, I
realized with a start that the quality they admired the most about
this man was his custom of hugging his adolescent son. Not once
did they mention his job, status in the community, the type of car
he drove, trips he took, or athletic talents; they talked only about
his ability to show affection to his son. The other boys gathered in
the room openly envied the boy's relationship with his father. I
was so struck by this that I immediately repeated the conversation
to my husband, who had been raised in a family where the father
only shook hands with his sons. He and our sons have benefited
from my roommate's small talk.

Nowadays more fathers are involved with their children from
birth, and hugging and touching a son do not run counter to their
definition of male. But the small number of studies that look at
touching between father and son suggests that as a son approaches
adolescence, the relationship changes and he receives fewer affectionate touches from his father. In one study, for example, researchers found that during preadolescence, both fathers and sons
initiated hugs, kisses, and pats on the back or shoulder, but these
interactions became less frequent as the son grew older.[7]

Hopefully, fathers in the future will continue hugging their
sons well into their adolescence, because that is when boys need
many reassuring embraces from their fathers. My teenage hospital

companions confirmed the rewards of a natural, comfortable, physically affectionate father-son attachment. They loved a hugging father.

Mature Dependence/Interdependence

"Satisfactory mothering comes from a person with a firm sense of self and of her own value," Nancy Chodorow writes in her book on feminism and mothering.[8] A woman who values herself is not completely dependent on others nor is she fully independent, relying on no one. Instead she realizes that each person needs others and hopes her sons will appreciate their *inter*dependence.

Many women—and men—raised in an atmosphere of individualism and competition mistakenly believe that they don't need anyone. They are the superwomen and supermen who never seek emotional support because they fear a revelation of vulnerability. If they do acknowledge any dependence, they worry that they may be exposed as weak and give someone else power over them.

Mothers in this competitive pattern don't seek the wisdom of husbands, mothers, grandmothers, colleagues, or friends to help them balance their busy lives. Adult men, in this mode, think that if they work harder, they will be happier and prove their independence and malehood even more. But they both are lonely, unable to understand why they are not content.

I think many generations of women and men have been hoodwinked into believing extremes. Years ago, most women thought that being completely dependent on a man was their only option, and men accepted the burden of supplying a woman's financial security and psychological happiness. She was "the heart," in charge of the family's emotional well-being. He was "the head," the leader and authority, and the roles never blurred. Father's talents within the family and Mother's talents outside the home went underutilized and unrecognized. They may both have worked outside the home, but in the home, the domestic lines were clearly drawn. Thankfully, that era has passed.

Then we swung to the other extreme—complete emancipation from each other. Women could do it by themselves, produce children, raise them, and support them physically, psychologically, and financially. Men were superfluous or inadequate. The ancient masculine maxim of "Procreate, protect, and provide," the backbone of most societies, became unwelcome. Women were independent. Men were independent. Children were lost. Hopefully, we are coming to the end of that era, and a period of partnership and interdependence has arrived.

More than thirty years ago, Harry Guntrip elaborated on the connection between independence and maturity. "Maturity is not equated with independence, though it includes a certain capacity for independence," he wrote. "The independence of a mature person is simply that he does not collapse when he has to stand alone. It is not an independence from need of another person with whom to have a relationship: that would not be desired by the mature."9

Mature dependence, or interdependence, is demonstrated by a person's ability to give as well as receive, to recognize one's own vulnerability and to willingly work, love, and play as partners. Whether a wife or husband works in or out of the home is not the concern; the core of the relationship builds on their ability to acknowledge and support each other.

A man's ease with admitting dependence on others develops primarily (though not exclusively) through his relationship with the first woman in his life, his mother. A boy can depend on his mother without confiding everything in her—a distinction some mothers find difficult to understand.

During the course of interviews I conducted for this book, I found that boys hold a deep respect for mothers who possess a strong sense of self, an inner value, a confidence in themselves as mothers. One boy explained, "As I got older, I took more responsibility for everything. I think it's because she is more secure with herself now. We're closer now because she is more confident in herself. It's not just my relationship with her. It's her."

"She has the most inner strength I have ever seen," stated a boy whose mother fights cancer. "She'll be fine for a couple of months and then down. But even after an operation, she'll be up quickly and walking around. She is a really warm, funny person, but has a quick temper and gets on my tail if I don't do something right. You have to have that faith in your children and she has it in me."

A strong mother radiates confidence in herself and "faith" in her children, knowing that maturity means interdependence.

"He Thinks He Hears What I'm Not Saying"

Sometimes a boy becomes so used to repressing his own thoughts that he thinks his mother is doing the same thing and reads something into what she is saying. One mother reported, "I think he cares that I'm listening to him and want to hear his point of view. I want to give him my opinion and yet I have to listen objectively. I think boys are very good at listening to body language. He is sensitive to my voice. He thinks he hears what I'm not saying."

She explained that she often "puts a bracket around what I say," afraid that if she is direct, he will turn away. She has her opinions but bites her tongue, "brackets" them, puts them on hold. Rather than knowing what his mother thinks, her son has to figure it out. No wonder her son "thinks he hears what I'm not saying." Her bracketed, unspoken lines may be the crux of the message, so he is alert to her voice and body language in order to get the real meaning behind her conversation.

In a convoluted way, this women has identified one of the common problems between mothers and sons that will be addressed further in Chapter 6. "This growing up was tricky business," Andrew Malcolm writes about his mother. "Learning all the different feelings you were supposed to show instead of the ones you were really feeling. Control and camouflage yourself—with women anyway."[10]

No wonder many boys don't confront or argue with their mothers as daughters frequently do. They have a hard time reading their mothers' coded messages. What you feel is not what you say. We give that message to both sons and daughters, but daughters tend to ask for clarification and reasons, while sons just put it on the back burner, figuring this is just something else they can't understand.

If mothers want direct responses, they should be candid and clear in their discussions. But often a mother is not raised to be straightforward, so she turns to the indirect approach to get beyond a son's enigmatic know-it-all smile. He thinks that if she knows what is behind the smile he is in for trouble, so he responds code for code. An impasse is reached.

This type of family interaction often leads to a continuation of male-female stereotypes, which doesn't help a mother guide her son and leaves him with a vague notion that he'll never understand women anyway, so why try?

A study conducted in Texas confirmed that interactions within a family influence a son's concepts of a woman's role. The researchers examined the dynamics between a group of seniors in a Texas high school, their siblings, and their parents as they planned a fictitious two-week all-expense-paid vacation—including a day-by-day itinerary and activities for each day.

Mothers in this study who not only requested information from their sons but acknowledged their ideas and agreed on some of them had sons who could compromise, state another's feelings, and respond to requests for information. These sons exhibited a give-and-take with their mothers and later indicated higher admiration for and acceptance of strong, direct women than did sons who had less interaction with their mothers. The study concluded: "These findings are consistent with previous research that suggests that maternal warmth appears to play an important role in males' identity development and sex role development."[11]

Perhaps a son who seeks direct communication and thinks he is blocked from an honest exchange with his mother will come to the conclusion Andrew Malcolm did, that control and camouflage are more effective than listening, disagreement, and compromise. Most mothers need to remove the brackets so their sons know what they're saying.

Enhancing His Maleness

Oscar Wilde wrote in *The Importance of Being Earnest*, "All women become like their mothers—that is their tragedy. No man does—that's his."[12]

Although few men want to become "like" their mothers, many men yearn for some of their mothers' qualities. Similarly, many women would like to adopt some of their fathers' positive traits. Often, these cross-gender attributes are acquired later in life when each feels confident enough in his or her own sexuality.

Expecting an adolescent, however, to become a completely individuated person, comfortable with all human qualities, may be too much to hope for. Most mothers don't want to detract from a boy's newfound masculinity, but they do want him to be more sensitive and responsible. I think a mother can accomplish this and enhance her son's maleness by showing pride and comfort with her own positive traits. As one mother told me, "You never want to subtract from children, you always want to add to them."

A mother can add to her son's appreciation of women—and his own feminine side—by showing him that she likes being able to empathize with others, to have insight into feelings, to express joy, anger, affection, frustration, and love. She can teach him that love is a springboard to maturity and can be communicated through many emotions.

Single Mothers

Single mothers, whether divorced or widowed, face additional problems in maintaining boundaries and expressing affection. A son can become overprotective. "He is overly mature and concerned about everything," a widowed mother of a 14-year-old told me. "We lost my husband two months ago and he has taken on the male role. I wish he would lighten up. He's telling me what to do. He is very tall and his voice is changing. He's helpful, but he's so strong that if he pushes you, it hurts. So I tell him to keep away. He's growing too fast. He wants to be the head of the house. He asks me what I did today and wants to tell me what to do." Perhaps her son's attitude reflects his dread of losing both mother and father through death, and he wants reassurance that she will not disappear. But sons of divorced parents can suffer the same worry and become overprotective.

"Now that I am a single mother, our relationship has changed," said another woman. "My son has been very responsible, but mixed into all of that is the sexual thing. He is more aware of my dating, what I'm wearing, he comments on anything suggestive. He asks, 'Who are these people you're dating?' He has something to say about all of that. He has a pretty strong personality and he's assuming the father role, the man of the house. Also, he's a teenage boy who is in love and discovering his own sexuality."

Other sons can do the opposite and become completely uninvolved. "He doesn't want to be told anything," a divorced mother said of her 15-year-old. "He seems to be better with my ex-husband. It was reversed for many years when he was better with me. I suggested he go back to therapy, where he went a few times when we were getting divorced. He told me not to waste my money, that he would just sit there. 'I'll talk to my friends,' he said." Most likely his feelings about his mother are evolving and he doesn't know how to handle them.

In her acclaimed book, *Second Chances: Men, Women, and Children, a Decade after Divorce*, Judith Wallerstein writes that after divorce, mothers and sons "are caught in a powerful psychological dance in which they are mutually drawn close to each other and then pushed apart, back and forth in a classic pas de deux."[13] A mother wants a boy's support as an ally, but realizes that her closeness may be detrimental to him as a male adolescent. So they both are confused.

What a boy does not want or need is to be thrust out on his own. More boys felt "pushed out" than put upon in Wallerstein's study. A mother may dislike a son's similarity to his father or she may fear too strong an attachment to him, so she turns aside. But adolescent boys want to remain connected to their mothers and need reassurance that they are valued by them. A boy can worry that the departure of the dominant male from the family may contaminate his mother's feelings about him.

Just when a boy needs a strong mother, she may back down, bemoaning the lack of an older male to discipline or guide him. She may insist that he live with his father—depending on the willingness and availability of the ex-husband, custody may provide a good solution or cause further anxiety. Boys do need their fathers, but if a father has found a new life that does not include his first family, a son will be disillusioned.

Most boys I interviewed would not admit, at first, to hard feelings about their parents' divorce. One boy who was the oldest of four children said his parents' divorce had not affected his life. "Nothing's changed that much. She wants me to be a good example to the younger children, but I'm not usually. She knows. She understands. She runs the whole show. There's nothing I can really do about it, so I accept it."

Later on, he admitted that when he was told about the divorce, "I was sad and upset and mad. I don't know, I had a lot of mixed emotions. I didn't really know what to think of it. It was kind of hard not having my dad there for Easter, but then, I don't know, it got to be an everyday routine."

But it was not an everyday routine. Still further into the interview he commented that they were not doing too well financially. "We've just done our bills," he said in a fatherly way, "and we're trying to sell our house because we have a pretty big house and it's too expensive to keep up, so we're not doing too well right now. She's kind of stressed."

This young man, who at first said, "Nothing's changed," revealed that a lot *had* changed, but not even his friends knew his concerns. Financial matters bothered another boy whose two brothers, because they got into trouble, lived with his father while he remained with his mother. "Sometimes she will bring up the money situation," he said. "It's not that she can't afford things. But when she pays she thinks my father should be paying more. When I hear one side of the story and then I hear the other side, I don't know what to believe, so I just try to block it out."

Sons of single mothers often block out their anger to avoid conflict in their families. In a study led by Judith Smetana of the University of Rochester, researchers found there was less conflict between adolescent and parent in their sample of divorced families than in their sample of married families. Although this finding can be interpreted as good news for divorced mothers, the results should be examined cautiously, according to the researchers. Less conflict may reflect less interaction or involvement, and "moderate levels of conflict may be necessary for healthy adolescent ego and identity involvement."[14]

Single mothers must table their anxieties, reassure themselves that they are capable parents, and call on all available resources to reinforce their confidence. Mothers who consult with and give encouragement to one another help not only one another but also their sons. Most research has found that adolescent children from divorced or remarried families have problems adjusting to their new status and tend to act out many of their problems.[15] Parenting a son by oneself is not easy and mothers need constant inner renewal—and friends—in order to remain strong.

When single mothers remarry, their problems are not over. A

son may resent a man's replacing his father or himself as the "man" of the house. A stepfather has to win a son to his side, and until the younger male can trust the older man to be supportive of his interests, he will not cooperate willingly.

When I asked a 17-year-old boy what advice he would give to parents, he said, "If they get a divorce, don't put the kids in the middle. I don't think parents realize it's a hell of a lot harder on the kids than it is on them."

Stepmothers

Often an adolescent boy finds himself with an attractive, younger stepmother who is willing to befriend him. One boy clearly articulated his confusion about the role of his stepmother: "My dad is fifty and my stepmother is thirty, so she's from a totally different generation and so are her perceptions of teenagers. She scares my dad 'cause she tells him what she did as a teenager, and so he automatically thinks I'm a drug addict, and every time I talk to him he asks if I'm on drugs. My stepmother helps in some ways because she has an understanding, yet in other ways she's, like, extreme."

Some boys told me they could talk to their stepmothers about their sex life and get advice. "If I have a problem, I go to my dad's soon-to-be new wife," said one. "She's about twenty-seven and she has talked to me about sex. It just popped up and she makes sure my brother and me use condoms." This boy prided himself on having access to a young woman confidante. Yet stepmothers must be as careful as biological mothers in maintaining generational boundaries. Although they may not be a generation apart in age, they are a generation apart in status and must keep in mind their position as stepmothers.

The majority of research about stepfamilies concentrates on a mother's remarriage and the assimilation of her new husband into the family. Since most children do not remain with their father, a stepmother's contact with his children often occurs on weekends and holidays. A stepmother must recognize that a boy's biological parents are primarily responsible for his behavior and her role is to support her husband's commitment to his family. A new wife may at first resent the time her husband is devoting to his own children, but his children will benefit from her love and attention as well as his. Her husband, hopefully, will treasure her understanding.

For both parent and child, successful transitions to the remarried life do happen. Researchers followed one family who effectively integrated a son into the remarriages of both his mother and father and cited some of the helpful patterns: "clear generational boundaries between custodial mother and son; adequate problem-solving ability; a quality father-son relationship with regard to visitation, communication, and limits . . . and the renegotiation of a different relationship between former spouses, new spouses and all family members."[16]

But Should I Tell Him I Love Him?

As I indicated above, a son longs to be reassured that he is loved by his mother, not for some vague heroic image of malehood, but for himself, a growing and frequently confused young man. When he realizes that his mother values his masculinity, his differentiation from her, and his uniqueness as an individual, he will not be uncomfortable when she says, "I love you." He knows she says it as a concerned and loving parent.

He then will feel freer to voice his feelings and acknowledge her good qualities as well as her idiosyncrasies, knowing that she will not encroach upon his independence but guide and encourage him toward interdependence. He then can willingly acknowledge, "I love you, too."

Memos for Moms

1. Be aware that you may be surprised and attracted by your son's masculinity.
2. Realize that he is conscious of his own sexuality and curious about women, including his mother.
3. Respect his privacy of thought—and space.
4. Appreciate the fact that boys can feel protective of their mothers and are reluctant to criticize, but encourage a freer exchange of emotions and viewpoints.
5. Admire your son for who he is, not for a fantasized image of the perfect male you would like to create.
6. Encourage his father to hug him.
7. Loving a son unconditionally means guiding him, setting limits, encouraging him, remaining committed. It does not mean covering up for him or rescuing him from the consequences of his own behavior.
8. Becoming too close or too distant is not what he needs. A son needs a mother to maintain a healthy balance of attachment and individuality and love.
9. Be direct with a son so he doesn't feel the need to conceal or camouflage his feelings.
10. Value your own feminine traits so he will want to emulate your qualities of care, compassion, and nurturance.
11. Build confidence in your parenting abilities.
12. Tell him you love him.

5

"My Mother Would Kill Me"

Strong Mothers

Boys' Pride in Attentive Mothers • Theories and More Theories

Authoritative Parenting • Highly Demanding Moms:
Make Sons an Integral Part of the Family
Impart Family Values
Set Clear Standards
Monitor Behavior
Supportive, Not Punitive

Highly Responsive Moms:
Foster Individuality
Foster Self-regulation
Encourage Assertiveness
Remain Committed

Memos for Moms

When I asked a boy how he had avoided the trap of drug dealing, he replied, "Most of the people I grew up with are drug dealers, but they know how I am and they respect me for that. I don't mess with it. My mother would kill me. A couple of years ago they wanted me to go in with them, but I said no and they said all right."

I wanted to hug him—and his mother—because he stated so clearly what many men have always known: that behind a successful man stands a mother who didn't give up. This boy, about to graduate from high school, is a success. He has come through adolescence with goals for his future and a knowledge of who he is—thanks to his mother.

Some adult men may react against the suggestion that their mothers made a difference in their lives, but when grown athletes turn to the television cameras and say, "Hi, Mom," one has to suspect that they are really saying, "Thanks for sticking with me and pushing me. I would have stayed out with the boys, skipped school, and just hung out if it hadn't been for you. I knew you wanted me to make it."

Strong men can break down when they talk about their mothers. A woman told me that the only time she sees her husband cry (a "tough" inner-city cop) is when he is thinking about his mother, who died many years ago. I watched an induction ceremony into the Baseball Hall of Fame and the players fought back tears as they saluted their mothers. One star was too emotional to continue speaking. I don't think he was crying crocodile tears; they seemed to come right from the heart. These men were grateful to their mothers.

Boys told me time and time again that they needed their mothers' prodding. "My mother's straight with us," said a boy from a family who lived in a high-crime area. "She stays on our back about everything. She pushes us to do better. She helps out with homework. She feels that way about everyone in the family."

When I asked a mother from a similar neighborhood why some mothers give up on their sons, she replied, "To keep peace. But it hurts kids inside if you don't take the role of authority and they will get you back. A lot of parents feel that if they don't let the kids have their way, the kids won't like them. Who cares if they like you? They will like you more if you're tough when they're young and then you can become friends when they are older."

Mothers everywhere are challenged by adolescent sons who take risks and experiment with whatever the neighborhood is offering them. But women who successfully raise children in crime-infested neighborhoods merit special accolades and deserve recognition. Inner-city boys who survive adolescence with a strong sense of themselves credit their mothers.

"All my friends—their mothers are protective," said a boy during an interview at a housing project community center. "The streets, the environment, are too rough."

"My mother looks after my best interests," his friend said in a later interview. "She works and I work after school. As soon as I get my paycheck, she makes me put my money in the bank and I help her pay rent. She tries to teach me responsibility."

Not all urban boys live with single mothers; fathers also wrap a protective buffer around their sons. "My father puts restrictions on me," a boy said proudly. "You can't have your kids running off like crazy people all the time. Restrictions are good, but if you make them too strict, that isn't good because kids are just going to find a way around it. They'll try to sneak out of the house when you're sleeping."

He's right. Mothers and fathers have to "restrict" their sons in such a way that they won't sneak out of the house at night, yet let them know that certain behaviors aren't permitted. And if parents don't give up, they will be rewarded.

A 17-year-old self-styled "tough guy" told me how his parents kept after him. "It was good 'cause I needed discipline and I was tired of getting punished, tired of being stupid, tired of being the tough guy. I knew both my parents loved me and I changed. To tell the truth, I've never seen my father so proud of me since I made the big turnaround. Like when I handed him my report card, he looked so proud. I feel real bad now 'cause I know all the bad things I was doing. My mom was going back to school and my father was working three jobs. Now I realize they were really trying to do things for me and that's why they punished me so much."

Other people, like his older cousin, also influenced this boy, who now wants to continue his education in a community college, but it was his mother who made the biggest difference. "I didn't get into drugs on account of my mom," he told me. "If I had done that, she would have been kicked out of her apartment and that wouldn't have been fair to her. Even if I had given her the money [from selling drugs], it still wouldn't have been right. The whole family would have been kicked out."

Boys' Pride in Attentive Mothers

I was surprised that wherever I interviewed boys, from inner city to suburb, they expressed pride in their mothers' hands-on parenting when it existed and decried its absence when it didn't. Although they admit that if Mother becomes too involved ("enmeshed" in psychological terms) they turn away, they still welcome her attention. Even if a boy tries to avoid Mother's interrogations, as all sons do, he acknowledges that she probably has good reasons for her inquiry. Often a boy could look at his mother objectively and appreciate her concerns.

At first I thought the boys' comments were just reflecting my built-in belief that adolescents desperately need attentive mothers and perhaps my questions were leading them to the "right" answers. But enough boys spoke so convincingly that they confirmed my conviction and I recognized the truth in their remarks. Adolescent boys want their mothers to care.

"My mother's supportive," said a boy. "She's always interested in what I'm doing. She gives me certain guidelines to go by."

I asked another boy, who seemed to have a good sense of himself, what mothers should do and he replied, "Give him a lot of trust and tell him, 'I'm trusting you,' because you feel bad if you let your mom down."

Not all mothers happily anticipate parenting an adolescent son, because they cannot see the immediate effects of their mothering skills. And most mothers are surprised when I tell them that their sons appreciate their interest and concerns. The boys usually don't show their appreciation. In fact, they may tell their mothers to stop treating them like babies or they may just ignore them, but hands-on parenting does work.

Theories and More Theories

We have seen many shifts in psychologists' perceptions of adolescents and the appropriateness of their behaviors. Theorists at one time thought that adolescents needed to separate from parents, join with their peers and lead autonomous lives, for only then were they ready for adult responsibilities. We now understand that adolescents without guidance are not happy and lives of freedom can be dangerous. Boys need adults to guide them through the pressures society is inflicting upon them at too young an age.

A counter-theory then appeared in the adolescent literature. These researchers considered any type of normal adolescent behavior dangerous and advocated tighter restrictions on young people. Adolescents who wanted to spend more time with friends or explore new ways of thinking or acting had to be controlled because the risks were too great.[1]

Mothers and fathers who are in the midst of trying to raise teenagers can be bombarded with these extreme ideologies. Television, for example, often portrays one extreme, in which the typical American family is one in which the adolescent dominates the home and sets his own standards. And the other extreme advocates completely limiting children's activities with the dire warning that an adolescent's natural desire to explore will condemn him.

Neither theory makes sense to parents who can observe their adolescent children and know that neither complete independence nor complete control will work. Mothers often just intuitively guide adolescents through a trial-and-error process with love and trepidation, hoping and praying they will turn out all right. A discipline measure that doesn't work is thrown out, but the boy—or girl—knows his parents care.

Now new research is pointing to a more realistic view of child rearing in which neither extreme control nor extreme freedom plays a role in preparing adolescents for adult life. And I think this research can, at last, offer guidance to parents.

Authoritative Parenting

After examining questionnaires answered by ten thousand ninth through twelfth graders from socioeconomically and ethnically diverse groups, a highly regarded research team wrote: "Regardless of their ethnicity, class or parents' marital status, adolescents whose parents are accepting, firm and democratic, earn higher grades in school, are more self-reliant, report less anxiety and depression and are less likely to engage in delinquent behavior."[2]

Could a mother ask for anything more? If she is accepting, firm, and fair, her son will be self-reliant, less anxious and depressed, and earn higher grades. Other studies show he will be more likely to resist drugs less likely to suffer from alcohol abuse, and less likely to engage in delinquent behavior. Most mothers would say, "Yes, yes—give me the magic parenting formula and I'll drink it, what is it called?"

Coined by Diana Baumrind of the University of California at Berkeley, the magic formula is called *authoritative parenting*. Authoritative mothers and fathers *know that they know more* than their children. They not only are the responsible adults in the family, they are the parenting specialists. Authoritative parents are highly demanding and highly responsive with their children, and researchers have singled them out as the most successful types of parents.[3]

Sometimes a mother will complain that parenting a little boy was easy compared to mothering an adolescent. She could test a disciplinary action with her child, and if putting him in his room didn't work, she would try something else the next time. But to authoritatively mother a young man, that's another story. How can you be the voice of authority when he's so big?

I remember my own frustration when my big and strong 13-year-old son was playing his records (no CDs then) very loud in the living room. I asked him to turn the volume down a few times, but he continued, telling me that I should appreciate great music—the louder, the better. Well, loud music was not my idea of great at six o'clock while I was fixing dinner for a hungry family. So I very calmly walked over to the record player, removed the record, and broke it over my knee with great flourish. Needless to say, he reacted. He lifted me up with both arms and I thought for a minute he would fling me out the large window next to us. Then he put me down, with admirable control. The incident marked a turning point for both of us. I realized that I would have to find other ways to parent an adolescent boy, and he realized for the first time that he was much bigger than his mother.

Many boys recognize the irony of a small-size mother monitoring a big son's behavior. As one boy told me, "It's scary for a mother once your kid gets twice the size of you." When seven-foot, one-inch, 303-pound Shaquille O'Neal was interviewed shortly after signing a lucrative basketball contract, he said the best thing that ever happened to him was having his mother and father telephone to say they loved him (an ingredient in authoritative parenting). I'm sure his parents also pushed him out on the playground when he was young and taught him to respect coaches and teachers.

Highly Demanding Moms Make Sons an Integral Part of the Family

Most sons are not seven feet tall, but even five-foot sons can cause consternation when they begin demanding adult rights. Although mothers may think it impossible to be demanding with their adolescent sons, Baumrind's research shows that highly demanding mothers let sons know that they are an integral part of the family, no matter how large or small they are. That awareness of interdependence is the first ingredient in a successful family.[4]

In successful families, a son knows that he matters; his mother needs him, depends on him, and reassures him that he is not an overgrown appendage that just happens to be living in the same home. He realizes his mother counts on him, not just for helping out, but for his ideas about family events or activities, family get-togethers, Grandmother's birthday, trips, financial problems, decisions to move, decisions about his social life. In other words, he participates in family discussions and his opinions are encouraged and appreciated.[5]

A mother with a very busy household told me she sits down with her children on Sunday nights to discuss everyone's activities during the coming week—what nights she will be at meetings, what special homework assignments are due, what school events a son wants to attend. Sound advice from a busy woman. Some families review the television listings on Sunday and decide on the programs they'll watch during the week, but this family's weekly planning sessions let the children know that their mother is interested in what is happening in their lives.

In a recent newspaper article about runaways, a police sergeant was quoted as saying, "Kids today don't communicate with their parents and the parents don't worry about their kids until something drastic happens. You would be surprised by the number of cases we have where the parents don't know very much about their children's habits or friends."[6]

Trucks used to rumble down highways with the slogan "Make Wednesday Night Spaghetti Night" emblazoned on the side. If mothers adopted "Make Sunday Night Information-Sharing Night" as their credo, that same police sergeant might not feel that "society is degenerating." Parents and children in highly demanding homes know where their children are.

I asked a high-school exchange student from South America how he compared American families with those in his own country and he replied cautiously: "American kids are freer than in my country and sometimes the parents here don't care about them. Parents here pass a week and don't see their kids, and American kids stay away from their parents. I say to a kid, 'How is your father?' and he says he doesn't know. He hasn't seen him in two weeks. When I ask why, he says his dad starts work when he's asleep. They don't have time to be together. They don't have time to talk about anything. They take a picture and put it on a wall and say, 'That's my family.' I think in my country the family is closer, we talk together. Mother is Mother all over the world and Father is Father. They need to get a kind of love and I think they've lost that here in the past years—the kind of son to mother, mother to son, son to father, father to son. They have to find that again. They have to spend more time."

This young man's view of American families may be shaded by the length of his stay and his selection of friends, but his message gives pause to all adults concerned about adolescents.

Highly Demanding Moms Impart Family Values

Sometimes a mother thinks because she and her son live in the same house, he will soak up her values through osmosis. But often an adolescent boy doesn't assimilate what his mother thinks he does. Only verbal communication guarantees that a value is conveyed, perhaps not heeded, but articulated. Of course, a mother's example of honesty and moderation delivers a powerful and lasting moral, but boys sometimes assume that because a discussion wasn't held or a warning given, anything goes. As one mother said, "They are so literal. Things are black or things are white. You have to spell it out for them."

News articles and broadcasts offer many opportunities to talk about values. A mother might ask a son what he thinks about a certain issue. Political problems are human, moral problems: the homeless, teen pregnancy, gay rights, military intervention, immigration policies. Almost all national issues contain a moral component that is exciting to talk about—not fight over. A son needs to hear a mother's side of any debate. He may not agree with her, but they each should know what the other thinks about issues.

In a study about early-adolescent moral development, a Harvard researcher found that parents who communicated intentionally and easily with their adolescents and who understood and supported them stimulated their ability to reason morally. These family attributes also had a "sleeper" effect and predicted more mature moral judgment in later adolescence and early adulthood.[7]

Popular television shows marketed to young teenagers promote their own values each week and may not reflect a mother's way of thinking. If a mother watches teenage television programs with her children, she will have a better understanding of their pressures and intrigues—and an opportunity to give a pitch for her opinions.

Many families race through busy days and weeks without time to spare, but a mother who plans and insists on family dinners is a determined parent who knows that dinners unite a family and dinner conversations can convey values. One woman called me frantically; her son's therapist had convinced her that she, her husband, and children had to start having family dinners. She was desperate because in her fifteen years of marriage, neither she nor her husband had prepared a family meal and they didn't know where to start.

A family dinner remains the most accessible family ritual, even if it occurs only one or two nights a week. Some families substitute a weekend brunch for a weekday dinner. Researchers have found that an adolescent's attachment to his family is highly correlated to his participation in family rituals including dinner, weekend activities, vacations, annual celebrations, religious celebrations, and cultural traditions.[8] During these family occasions, adolescent children discover what is important to their parents.

One father participating in my parenting workshop spurned the idea of family meals. He could remember his father leaning over the dinner table and smacking him, everyone yelling in persistent arguments, and no fun. He thought the idea of family dinners was crazy and certainly not important anymore—a throwback to the fifties.

I disagreed with this father. So many distractions disrupt contemporary family lives, that I think families need more time together than ever before. Since everyone has to eat, dinner seems the most natural occasion to catch up with children—as long as an effort is made to keep the meals pleasant and informative.

Highly Demanding Moms Set Clear Standards

Along with letting a son know he is an indispensable member of the family and conveying her values to him, an authoritative mother sets clear standards of behavior with her son, always including him in those decisions. To set down rules without an adolescent's consultation invites noncompliance from the start. Authoritative parenting is not the same as authoritarian parenting, in which a son has no input and is just told what to do. That will work when he is very young, but as he matures, he wants input into the discussion about reasonable hours and expectations.

"Let him know the rules before he goes out so he knows what he has to fulfill before he gets into trouble," one boy told me. "If he doesn't know the rules, if you haven't told him, then you can't get mad at him."

Discussing rules with a son before—and during—his intense social phase is wise advice from this 16-year-old. Adolescents often are far more reasonable than parents give them credit for, and parents are more open-minded than adolescents believe. A passionate discussion about conflicting standards should be encouraged, not dismissed because a parent decrees, "I said so."

Mothers must be flexible and willing to compromise as a son grows older. Many high-school seniors told me their curfews were, "Come home at a reasonable hour," and they complied. One boy contended that a mother should be "tough" until a boy is 14, then "slacken off." He and his friends got into the most trouble in middle school, not an uncommon happening.

Each mother must judge her own son. Some boys are less social and don't need many limits. Some may not like taking risks, so discussions aren't as frequent or heated. Each boy has his own personality and his own network of friends, so even in the same family, talks about behavior will vary with each child. What remains constant are the family standards and expectations.

Highly Demanding Moms Monitor Behavior

One mother told me that when her son was in high school he started acting strangely, not quite himself, a little too laid back and relaxed. She suspected he was doing drugs, probably marijuana. With great trepidation, she later told me, she handed him a small paper cup and asked for a urine sample. He ranted and raved, yelling that she didn't trust him. He never gave her the sample, but from that day on, his behavior changed and he became himself again. He knew she was on to him. When she asks her son, now in his twenties, about that incident, he smiles, and she knows she was right. She's a perfect example of a highly demanding mother who monitors her son's behavior.

A mother often has to struggle to differentiate between normal and abnormal adolescent actions. But following her own instincts, as the mother above did, will serve her well. Often a mother can sense that something is wrong with her son, something is bothering him, or he is acting unusual. She should act on those impulses, questioning him or observing him closely. Professional drug therapists claim that it can take parents three years to detect a child's drug use. If there is a suspicion, ask. In three years it may be too late, and it certainly will be more difficult to help him.

A study examining 699 adolescents and their families looked at the effects of parenting practices on adolescent drinking, delinquency, and other problem behaviors. "The findings confirm that parental support and monitoring are important predictors of adolescent outcomes even after taking into account critical demographic/family factors, including socioeconomic indicators, age, gender and race of adolescent, family structure, and family history of alcohol abuse."[9]

In this study, the adolescents whose behavior was monitored by supportive parents were less likely to drink regularly, use illicit drugs, cut classes, or get involved in other deviant behavior (described as minor offenses like breaking curfews or arguing with parents, as well as more serious ones like having sexual intercourse, beating up someone, or running away from home). The support and monitoring helped adolescents across all sectors of the population, whether from intact or single-parent families.

One boy commented about his mother: "She has set us up with enough morals so none of us lie to her. You try, but you always get caught. I don't know how she always finds things out, but she does, so most of the time we end up telling her."

When I wrote my book for mothers of adolescent daughters, *"Don't Stop Loving Me,"* I particularly emphasized *vigilant trust*, a concept I developed to describe just the type of supportive monitoring mentioned above. Because girls accuse their parents of not trusting them more than boys do, I addressed the issue frequently. Trusting adolescents is believing that they are capable of successfully winding their way through the adolescent social scene. But a safe journey to healthy adulthood does not happen automatically. Mothers must become aware of the local social scene; discuss their expectations of behavior with their adolescents; listen to their ideas; set guidelines for them to follow; then trust the adolescents' judgment; remain vigilant, monitoring their behavior; give consequences when trust is broken (which will happen); and then reinstate trust. This eight-step process of trust, vigilance, and reinstatement of trust may have to be repeated over and over again, but it does work. Eventually, the young person will become trustworthy.

"If a kid does well," one boy said, "it's because they're mostly influenced by their parents. If I break their trust and I've done it, they punish a little. I understand because they're disappointed."

Another boy said, "Parents should say, 'If you come home drunk, you won't sleep here.' My parents said that to my brother and they followed through. They follow through on everything. It's good for parents to back up their demands. My parents are straightforward."

Highly Demanding Moms: Supportive, Not Punitive

A mother who has worked out reasonable social standards with her son, is vigilant, and confronts him directly when she suspects he has broken her trust, should be congratulated. But where can she turn when she discovers that he has violated the rules that he helped determine?

In Diana Baumrind's research, successful parents used what she calls "supportive rather than punitive" methods to bring him back to reality. To ground a son for months at a time will only build resentment, and soon a mother will back down just to get him out of the house. "If parents punish and punish, a kid will rebel," one boy told me.

A reasonable consequence ties the punishment to the deed. If a boy has been drinking, a mother could take away the car keys for a couple of weekends or keep him home from a few parties, but not the whole year. If he crashes the car, let him work off the repair bill (and save your insurance policy). By the time he has paid off the debt, working for minimum wages at a fast-food restaurant for example, he will have learned his lesson about driving carefully.

Letting a son experience some of the pain that others have suffered may help his adolescent mind realize the consequences of his actions. For instance, take him on a tour of a jail or sign him up to help out in a hospital with victims of drunk driving. A few hours in a jail won't hurt him and a court appearance may scare him into honesty forever.

Hall of Fame relief pitcher Rollie Fingers told a story about starting a fire in his house when he was a boy. His father, who knew the county sheriff, took Rollie to jail and left him in a cell for three hours to think about his actions. He said he never played with matches again and he gained a new respect for his father.

Two of our sons went out on Halloween night with a friend and his BB gun. Their friend shot at a passing car that happened to belong to a policeman on his way to work. When we received a phone call from the police department to come and retrieve our sons, we were quite distressed. But the experience of appearing in court on "conspiracy" charges was something neither they nor my husband and I will ever forget. They learned that even if they didn't "commit the crime," participating and not stopping a dangerous action deserved consequences. We learned anew that parenting takes patience, love, and vigilance.

In some communities, parents go to great lengths to cover up their sons' minor or major offenses, trying to erase them from the "police blotter." They deny their sons the consequences of their actions, thinking they are doing him a favor. Covering up for a boy, however, is not a gift. Years later, he may still think he is beyond the law, exhibiting a Michael Milken mentality in which he thinks he can outwit the authorities—a fatal fantasy not limited to businessmen.

One boy related his parents' discipline methods: "One time they told me not to go out," he said, "but I went out and they telephoned home and I wasn't there. I came back and they wouldn't let me in the house and they had a friend pick me up outside the house and I spent the night there. The next day they picked me up and I said, 'What's happening?' and they asked me what I thought they should do, that they were really disappointed. I was trying to argue, but they gave me that disappointed thing and I felt bad."

When I asked him if the grounding worked, he said, "Oh, yeah. I think parents need to gain respect from their children 'cause I see a lot of kids that don't respect their fathers and mothers. The parents say, 'You're going here,' and they're like, 'No.' They totally don't respect them."

Some mothers may find that just talking tough works. Telling a son frankly that if he comes home drunk, he can stay home for a determined length of time. If he fathers a child, he can support the mother and child. If he does drugs, he will be sent to a rehab center. Each mother has to judge her own son, his honesty, reliability, and good sense. Most sons cooperate because they have had input into the rules, and when they do break them they are aware of their parents' disappointment.

The youngest boy I interviewed, a 13-year-old, told me, "Mothers should sit down and talk face-to-face with their kids so they won't be hoodlums. They should stop [physically] punishing them so much." Evidently his mother was physically punishing him, a method I strongly discourage.

Some boys would be really strict with their own children. When I asked a boy who had been in considerable trouble what advice he would give a mother, he said, "Lock him in a room with a teacher. It's high school and junior high where most of the trouble comes from. Sometimes it's even elementary school when they start coming in with a bad crowd. Parents should show them who they don't need to be with. It's nice to have friends, but at a certain time you have to back off from them."

Highly Responsive Moms Foster Individuality

Diana Baumrind's research shows that successful parents were not only highly demanding, they were highly responsive to their children. Their sons were assured of affection and attention and could disagree with, even criticize their parents without the fear of losing them. And their parents cherished their individuality. Mothers know they react differently to each child. Some boys bounce from the crib to school to college, nonstop motion. Others assess the world more calmly, weighing each step. Some draw accurate representations at age four while others the same age can't manipulate a regular pencil. An authoritative, highly responsive mother relishes these differences.

"Just be supportive of your son," one boy told me to tell mothers. "Let them be who they want to be. Let them become individuals and support them in what they want to do. I'm very different than my parents in lots of ways. I think that should be allowed. It makes for a stronger individual, I think."

This junior in high school said his parents said he could go to any college he wanted, but "I want a school with a film major. My mom says that's okay, but my father is saying that I can do film courses over the summer. I think he knows I could never do that, but I'm still looking at the schools he wants me to." He was a quiet young man who showed great respect for his parents, and I hope he can satisfy both his dream and his parents' hopes.

Often adolescents who have witnessed the disintegration of their parents' marriage may hesitate to dissent or argue for fear that the remaining parent, usually the mother, will walk out. I think a boy should be reassured that he can disagree with her without fear of abandonment.

One boy disagreed with his parents all the time. "We fight about everything," he told me, "work, going out, school, grades." When I asked him if he would like his parents to back off, he answered, "It's kind of necessary or otherwise I'd sort of slack off." Most boys, however, don't like confronting their mothers, but they do want to speak out, have their opinions count, and be recognized as unique.

Highly Responsive Moms Foster Self-regulation

Self-regulation means stepping back as much as possible and letting a son wake up by himself, do his own laundry, arrange his transportation, do his homework, and be a responsible member of the family. But the goal runs deeper. Mothers want their sons to act responsibly at all times—at home, in school, out at night. However, he will never learn responsibility if he is not given any. A mother who cleans her son's room, washes his clothes, and does his homework is not preparing him for adulthood.

One mother told me that when she was a young bride, her mother-in-law visited and was aghast at seeing her son making the bed. She exclaimed to her new daughter-in-law, "I did not raise my son to make beds." This woman responded, "My mother didn't raise me to make them either." I doubt if many mothers cling to that outdated attitude, but some adolescent boys still expect more maternal service than their sisters.

Most boys are realistic about doing their share of work, even if they cooperate begrudgingly. "Give kids responsibility and they will be okay," one boy told me when we were discussing responsibility. "It's like respect. If you want respect, you treat them more like adults. Respect them and you'll find they'll do it [be cooperative]. Kids that are treated like kids are rebellious to authority." An interesting and perceptive observation from a 16-year-old. The more responsibility mothers give their sons, the more responsible they will feel.

A woman came up after a talk I'd given and told me that her husband treasured the hard work that he, as an adolescent, had put into his family's restaurant business. The experience made him feel wanted, important, and responsible. She thought her own son missed that because they could afford cleaning help, a car wash, dishwasher, and all the modern conveniences. She wondered if her son was missing an important element of belonging and responsibility. I advised that she begin having her son pick up his own room and do his laundry and not to let anyone else do it. She should talk about responsibility in a positive, upbeat manner, letting him know that she wants and appreciates his help. Boys also like to take charge of their lives, particularly their bedrooms.

A mother whose son refused to accept responsibility for doing anything for himself said, "My son felt homework was an offense to his freedom. We could set rewards with him, anything. Nothing worked. When he got to high school, we decided it was time to end the conflict between us. He couldn't understand going from me nagging him all the time to saying, 'It's your choice now.' He ended up going to summer school. I don't know what happened then. Either it was summer school, which he loved, or something clicked with his hormones. This boy is an incredible new child this year. We don't have to wake him up. Last year I would tell him that if he wasn't up at six-fifteen, he wouldn't get breakfast. I set the rules, but then I had to take a walk so I wouldn't give in. Now it's all changed."

This mother—and her son—have both benefited. "It's almost like setting a pattern for life," she continued. "You're not going to be there all their lives, and in high school when they're old enough they should know what you expect and what society expects. But it's really hard to back off."

Another woman told a story of her friend, whose high-school senior son delayed filling out college applications, postponing time and again the laborious process. At last his mother told him that she would not talk to him about it again and she didn't. It nearly killed her, but she did not give in and the next fall he watched his friends go off to college while he went to work. The following fall, however, he joined his friends in college, a year late but after he had acquired responsibility and self-regulation.

Highly Responsive Moms Encourage Assertiveness

If a son asks his mother to talk to a teacher on his behalf about what he perceives to be an an unfair grade or mistreatment, a mother should beware. High-school teachers often are subjected to parental fury because they have attempted to teach a boy honesty and accountability. One teacher told me a father even threatened to sue her because she accused his son of copying another's paper.

I suggest to parents that they tell their sons to argue their own case with a teacher or person in authority. It will be a good experience for them, and a mother can coach him on the best way to present his argument.

It may seem strange to say mothers should encourage their sons to be assertive when many women think men are too assertive, but assertiveness and aggression are not the same thing. Assertiveness implies stating positively what a person believes in. If a son thinks he has been mistreated, then he must assemble his facts, keeping track of specific incidents, and present them forcefully and respectfully to the teacher and then to a superior if the teacher will not listen. A boy who responds aggressively by yelling, swearing, or insulting a teacher will not win his case and will get deeper in trouble.

Boys often don't know how to state their feelings or opinions without appearing defensive or aggressive. Mothers perform a great service by teaching them how to argue assertively. The four-step problem-solving technique that I explain in Chapter 7 will help him organize his approach.

Highly Responsive Moms Remain Committed

Adolescents who know they can count on their mothers to be loving, responsive, and committed are lucky. A mother of four sons revealed her good humor as she described her 13-year-old to me: "He taps the creative side of me and there are things in him that I just love. But he is the one who can bring me to the mat. I come down to being a real two-year-old with him. Sometimes we have a real battle."

Recounting an argument they had the day before, she said, "I could have killed him. There are times when we go head-to-head. My husband thinks that if you fight it means you don't love someone, but I think if you go to the mat with someone, it means you care."

Her enthusiastic, loving humor was contagious and I think the other women in our discussion envied her ease and comfort with mothering. When her 13-year-old is older and bigger, he may not want to "go to the mat" with her, but then again he may, because he realizes his mother's great vitality likes being challenged.

I think boys and their mothers can discover admirable and fun qualities within each other. An authoritative mother doesn't have to be drab, tedious, or wearisome. She can be fun, witty, and entertaining—or serious and reflective—as well as highly demanding and highly responsive. She can be herself and her sons will love and appreciate her.

Memos for Moms

1. Remember mothers do make a difference in their sons' lives.
2. Regain confidence in your parenting. A mother is a parenting authority and knows more than her adolescent sons.
3. Remind him that he is an important, integral member of the family. Make Sunday nights an information-sharing night so each family member knows where the others will be all week.
4. Include him in family discussions. Welcome his ideas.
5. Make sure he knows your family values. Speak them clearly and live them.
6. Arrange family meals.
7. Set clear standards and expectations for his behavior. Ask for his input.
8. Be vigilant and monitor his social activities.
9. Make the consequences of his wrongdoing teach a lesson rather than punish.
10. Enjoy his individuality and let him disagree without losing your affection.

11. Let him do as much as he can for himself, including taking care of his room and doing his laundry.
12. Encourage him to assert himself when he thinks he is being treated unfairly. Teach him how.
13. Remain committed to him and have fun.

6

Mother-Talk, Son-Talk

Communicating with a Son

Boy/Girl Differences • *How Adolescent Boys
Communicate* • *Boy-Talk* • *The "Cool Pose"
Sons Who Won't Talk* • *Modifying the Pattern
Stereotypes?* • *Memos for Moms*

A re you trying to tell me something?" my son asked me one day. "If you are, why don't you just say it?" I was relating a detailed story about a friend's son who was involved in a drunk-driving accident. My son immediately knew that I was cautioning him, in a round-about way, about the dangers of drinking—and he was right.

I, like many women, had learned to express my concerns obliquely, presuming that a listener would pick up the intended message and I would not have to be explicit. So when I told my son the accident story, I was hoping he would absorb the implicit message and I wouldn't need to spell it out. But he was impatient with my strategy. He informed me that if I wanted him not to drink, I should say so frankly, directly, and pull no punches. Direct and explicit communication is what he wanted and understood.

"You have to be so direct, so literal with boys," one mother said. "I came home from work late and dinner needed to be put together. My son was watching the tube. I said to him, 'The dishwasher could have been emptied,' and he replied, 'You didn't tell me.' I told him, 'I didn't think of telling you, but I was at work and you were home, maybe you could have thought of it yourself.' "

Mothers hope sons will react to unspoken messages or obvious situations (like full dishwashers), yet adolescent boys comprehend direct transmissions only. Subtleties fly right past them or are

112

misinterpreted. Maybe mothers and sons, like many men and women, exist on different wavelengths. Perhaps if they understood each other's speaking style, they would communicate better.

In his wonderfully titled book, *Men Are from Mars, Women Are from Venus*, John Gray discusses how easily adult men and women can misread each other.[1] At first I thought his interplanetary analogies applied only to adults, but as I began to examine mothers' conversations with sons, I realized that this pattern of miscommunication between men and women often begins in adolescence—between mother and son.

My sons became skillful in interpreting my underlying messages, but they were not always right. If I had learned earlier to speak precisely and directly, they may not have had to struggle to figure out exactly what I meant. This practice of one person speaking indirectly and the other looking for hidden meanings can become a habit. Gray gives many examples of such discussions: For instance, if a woman says, "Nothing is working," she may be looking for sympathy or a helping hand. But a man may interpret her statement as "She's blaming me." If she asked directly for help or if he understood the meaning behind her words, their communication would be less muddled.

When a boy told his mother to stop being so "nice" and just tell him what she wanted, she was hurt. Having been raised to couch her requests, she was surprised at her son's objection. Men and women seem to possess unique ways of discoursing, and the recent influx of books on communication between the sexes confirms the need to understand the two dialects.

Boy/Girl Differences

According to Deborah Tannen's book, *You Just Don't Understand: Women and Men in Conversation* (at one time on both the hardcover and paperback best-seller lists), men and women communicate differently from early childhood onward.² Intelligent men and women presume they can talk and listen to each other without misunderstanding, and many possess that ability. But Tannen does not believe that accurate communication between the sexes happens naturally; it must be worked on.

When discussing adolescent communication with a group of women, one commented, "With my daughter, I feel she's concerned with how something she says is received—if it hurt someone. But when I tell my son he's really hurt someone's feelings, he's totally surprised."

"I find boys—and men—don't talk about their feelings that much," said another mother. "I don't think in the end they're less sensitive. I think it's more they don't think about it."

"But you know where you stand with boys," protested a third mother. "When they're mad, you know it. They're physically mad as well as verbally mad. It blows over quickly and I like that. They don't hold on to it as long as girls do."

A boy's anger can dissipate quickly and mothers are relieved, but if a boy will not discuss why he is mad or even acknowledge his furor, he has missed an opportunity to learn how to handle similar anger-provoking situations.

While looking at tapes of boys and girls talking with each other, Tannen observed that girls talked to enhance their relationships; she called their talk "rapport talk." The girls shared similar experiences and confirmed one another's feelings. When a girl told a friend about her difficulties with a boyfriend, for instance, her female companion expressed sympathy and told of comparable dilemmas to let her know she wasn't alone. However, the conversation kept returning to the girl's problem with her boyfriend so the girl who initiated the conversation knew her friend was listening.

The boys also talked about themselves but engaged in "report talk," negotiating "status" by relating their own experiences and seemingly dismissing the importance of the partner's story. They engaged more in a story-for-story can-you-top-this type of conversation rather than sympathetically responding to one another's experiences. They were listening to one another, in their own way, and seemed happy with the conversation, but a girl in that situation would not have thought her friend was listening.

This boy/girl difference also was found in a study that looked at same-sex friendships of eighth-grade boys and girls.[3] The researchers found that both boys and girls felt emotionally close to friends with whom they had shared some feelings or secrets. The pathway to closeness for boys, however, came through experiences they had shared together, not exclusively through talking. Many studies have suggested that it is through "doing" that boys meet, make friends, and develop intimacy and closeness, while girls meet and know one another through talking.

It is natural, then, for mothers to want to talk with sons to get to know them better. Although sons talk to mothers more than fathers, they may retreat after saying very little, leaving mothers unsatisfied. Men and women, boys and girls, often speak the language of their gender, their "genderlect," and overspeak (speaking too much) is not in most adolescent boys' genderlect.

Another boy/girl distinction becomes apparent in the classroom. Since most girls enjoy talking privately, chatting and gossiping about personal matters with friends, they often lose their voices in a classroom setting. Because boys prefer talking about impersonal issues, they tend to speak out in class more than girls, asking and answering questions. Women's groups are addressing this issue, encouraging teachers to demand more class participation of their female students.

Although these gender distinctions are apparent to mothers and fathers, understanding and appreciating the differences are not always easy.

How Adolescent Boys Communicate

A therapist who works frequently with adolescent boys told me that he often plays board games or tosses a ball with them rather than requiring them to talk immediately. The pressure to talk about feelings is often an added pressure to an already overburdened youngster. If direct eye contact or direct questions do not initiate any "feelings" response (as with this therapist), a different tactic has to be used. Once a boy feels he can trust the therapist, he opens up.

When I interviewed boys for this book, we sat at angles to each other, never face-to-face. One of the most productive sessions took place when a boy and I sat side by side, turned slightly toward each other, at a long computer table. He did not need to look directly at me and I didn't ask him to change his position. He glanced around the room while he talked candidly, and directly, to me. Another boy fiddled with his shoelace while he was telling me how his father had betrayed him.

I was constantly aware of the boys' energy as they slouched in the chairs and kept their hands occupied with hats, pencils, or whatever during an interview. Because they knew I would not reveal their names or where they came from, they felt free to talk, but it was not always easy for them to overcome their innate dislike of discussing personal issues.

When I interviewed 13- and 14-year-old boys, our exchanges were endearing but monosyllabic—not much material for me when I transcribed them. The older boys found their voices and were animated when we talked about their activities, although less lively when we discussed their feelings.

Because I had lived with four adolescent sons, I was not surprised at boys' combining movement and conversation. Advisers to youth groups know that when they schedule activities, whether it is hiking, basketball games, or helping an older person fix up a house, boys show up and talk while working. Boys are less willing to participate in the group discussions about relationships, especially ones that have no interactive exercises.

Boys also get more impassioned when they are actively engaged. In a study that asked boys and girls about a wide range of emotions (interest, joy, surprise, shyness, guilt, sadness, fear, anger, disgust, contempt, shame, and self-hostility), boys reported that their activities and achievements brought forth the most emotional responses, while the girls said their relationships with others activated emotions.[4] When the boys were asked in the same study to recall particular emotions they had felt during the last week, month, or year, they could not remember having experienced any. But when they were asked the same question on a daily basis, they admitted feeling these emotions.

Boys certainly feel emotions, but this study shows they either don't dwell on them (as mothers realize) or they don't recognize them enough to recall them. The fact that they feel the most animated and the most emotionally involved when they are actively participating in a happening suggests the importance of after-school and weekend activities. Talking just doesn't do it for them.

Boy-Talk

One evening I heard four adult men rave about how much they liked a certain radio talk show, so the next morning I tuned in and couldn't believe the inane, pun-filled one-liners masquerading as conversation. I wondered if I was listening in on a locker room conversation. As I thought back to the previous night, I realized that the males I met that evening sounded just like the radio talk-show host and his three regular male participants. These men were caught up (at least for one night) in adolescent banter.

Boys tell me that the insulting comments they pass back and

forth are fun and are not to be taken seriously. They like jokes, put-downs, and sarcasm, a uniquely adolescent male characteristic that is often difficult for mothers—and girlfriends—to understand. In one way, I used to envy my sons' freedom to jest and rib one another and their friends. They seem to have such fun. When they were with girlfriends, however, they restrained themselves. They must have realized that girls did not prize their continuous one-liners and could be hurt by their sarcastic remarks. Their earthy, ribald humor remained confined to male friends.

Trying to explain this phenomenon, one boy said, "Guys are kind of one big happy family. You don't have to be an actual friend with someone. Everyone sort of jokes around. I have one person I could call a best friend, but I joke around with everyone else."

Outside of the school halls, boys talk with their mothers more than their fathers, and what they converse about is different with each parent. "My sons talk to their father about politics, more impersonal stuff," said one mother. "They'll talk to him when it comes to fixing the bike. They talk to me about what's happening to them."

In a study that examined adolescent relations with mothers and fathers, researchers asked boys what they did with their mothers and with their fathers.[5] Boys reported that 48 percent of the time spent with their fathers involved homework help, getting advice, or learning a skill. Twenty-five percent of the father-son time was spent in conversations about common interests or practical matters, and 17 percent of their interactions were shared recreational or work activities.

The numbers were reversed with their mothers. The most common interaction between boys and their mothers was conversation (42 percent), talking about their fathers, problems with siblings, how well they were doing in school, views on religion, and attitudes toward marriage. A boy rarely talked about any problems he was having with his mother, his views on sex, or his views on society.

Mothers and sons spent 25 percent of their time together on homework or advice sessions. Mothers spent 15 percent of their time together "nurturing" a son—cooking for him, taking care of him when he was sick. Only 2 percent of the boys reported sharing activities other than talking with mothers, although when asked what they *enjoy* doing with their mothers, the boys said they liked going places with her—like shopping.

This survey reflects what some boys told me. "I can tell her almost anything," a boy said. "She won't react. She will first try to handle the situation and then deal with me later. If I have a problem, I try not to tell her at night 'cause she'll stay up all night thinking about it and then in the morning she might be exhausted, but she'll have the solution."

Because a son feels comfortable talking to his mother does not mean he will tell her everything, reveal his emotions, or talk about personal matters, and a mother must be prepared to accept this from an adolescent boy. If he does fully open up, she should be thankful and respect his disclosures.

One boy identified the biggest roadblock in communicating with his parents. "Basically I'm afraid they'll tell their friends," he confided. "My dad has a huge mouth and my mom has a mouth, too. They try to be more than a parent. They try to be my friend and find out what's going on. That annoys me because I know that they know everyone in town and they'll probably tell most of the stuff I say. So whenever they ask something personal, I try to answer something that satisfies them but doesn't even come close to what they want to know."

When I asked him if his evasive responses were deliberate, he replied, "Yeah, so they don't find out what is happening." When I inquired further if he was happy with that arrangement, he said, "Well, I'd rather be able to tell them stuff, but I can't trust them 'cause I've told them some stuff and it's come back to me."

When boys build up the courage to divulge their concerns to their parents, parents must respect that confidence.

The "Cool Pose"

"Don't confuse a boy with the disguise he wears, the armor he wears in public," the head of a boys' school warned me. The "armor" an adolescent boy wears can interfere not only with a mother's understanding of her son but also get him into trouble with school or police authorities.

Richard Majors studied the "cool pose" of inner-city youth and found "that the essence of cool is to appear in control, whether through a fearless style of walking, an aloof facial expression, the clothes you wear, a haircut, your gestures or the way you talk. The cool pose shows the dominant culture that you are strong and proud, despite your status in American society."[6]

One inner-city mother worried about her son's pretense of indifference, his "attitude," combined with a sharp tongue when provoked. "He's strong-willed and my concern is that he will be misjudged by adults because he is outspoken," she told me. "I don't consider him disrespectful. He just says what is on his mind—to anyone. It's that he knows he is a valuable person and wants to be heard. When I warn him, he says he has to say things. I get concerned that he will meet an adult who will think he is a threat."

Majors and this mother are concerned about the defensive pose of black inner-city young males, but many youths of the dominant culture, as noted by the head of the boys' school, are assuming an impenetrable shield to protect themselves from revealing the fears of their troubled lives. A boy will let down his guard and express his true feelings when he feels secure with an adult who will not reveal or ridicule his legitimate fears. Mothers must be able to see through this "cool" pose and offer their sons a safe environment to say what is "on his mind."

Sons Who Won't Talk

"I adore Arnold Schwarzenegger," a well-built boy said. "He doesn't say much." Ahhh ... the stereotypical male: a strong, silent, macho man—the model for many youth. Some boys don't have to go to the movies to observe this stereotype; they find it in their own families.

"My father is withdrawn, unemotional, you know, like most men," one boy told me. Still another boy spoke of his silent role model: "Dad is a very quiet person. I hardly say anything to him. We have nothing to talk about. I'll be in my room when he's home."

An adult man told me of his great relief when during a family gathering no one pressured him to talk, so he relaxed, remained silent, and enjoyed himself. He was articulate in his profession, but not in his home. Some boys experience the same relief their fathers do if they are not forced to participate or speak out about personal matters.

"Be sensitive to a kid's feelings," one boy told me to tell mothers. "If he doesn't want to talk about an issue, don't keep bringing it up. Bring it up once, talk about it, then stop."

When I asked him what a mother should do if she doesn't get a response, he replied, "A son should tell his mother that he'll try to explain it the best he could and try to answer her questions, but he doesn't want to talk about it. A mother has to know how to be sensitive. Mothers always need to know more. They can't seem to know enough."

In many studies, early-adolescent boys spend more time alone than girls do. They are more inclined to "do household tasks, homework and watch TV in solitude."[7] The need for a son to distance himself from the rest of the family does not mean he doesn't like them. There are times when he just has to be by himself and not talk—frustrating for a mother who likes conversations.

"When we have a problem, just let us go," one boy cautioned. "It probably won't last long. If we're moody for a long time, then you should talk to us. But, you know, basically leave us alone."

Newspaper columnist Austen Ettinger revealed a male's abhorrence of discussing personal issues when he claimed to have found the secret to a happy marriage: not let it all hang out and not to talk everything through.[8] Ettinger says that because "lengthy examinations" of his and his wife's feelings only produced worse feelings, they have eliminated those discussions. They now substitute "silence for communication" and depend on their deep "common interests to soften the anger before it becomes irretrievably encrusted." They decided that few issues were more important than the relationship, so "why give them significance by giving them focus?"

Ettinger reports that when the air is clear of such "verbal weapons" as irritation and anger, he and his wife can have an open and sharing relationship. An intriguing thought when one applies this concept to a mother/son relationship. Many boys will mentally (or physically) withdraw if they continually face verbal barrages from their mothers. As Deborah Tannen points out, "Trying to settle the problem through talk can only make things worse if it is ways of talking that are causing trouble in the first place."[9]

In a discussion about communications, one woman expressed the same fear of excessive and open talking that the columnist did. She said, "I think we're getting a backlash. In my family, we couldn't say anything and now I think too much communication is a dangerous thing. We don't have a balance yet. Maybe in the next generation we will."

A mother who wants her son to be able to communicate feelings as well as facts faces an uphill, but not impossible, task. I think first she has to acknowledge that her son has an inner core that belongs to him alone. That inner self must be respected. An adolescent boy who retreats from his mother's probing is afraid or can't articulate what he is feeling and would like to leave well enough alone—for the moment.

Both Gray (*Men Are from Mars, Women Are from Venus*) and Tannen (*You Just Don't Understand*) refer to men's silence as an essential part of their communication style. Gray talks about the need for men to go into their "caves," to have time to reflect. He says that men process information differently than women and need to "mull over" and think about what they have heard before they speak about it. Women have more of a tendency to think out loud, talking through an issue so it becomes clearer to them. Each way has value and needs to be recognized.

Tannen observed that men often withdraw when problems arise or, conversely, when everything is going well they remain silent, equating silence with intimacy. They think words are superfluous and don't hold a relationship together. Most women would react just the opposite in each situation. They would talk through their problems and share intimacy through conversation, the "glue" of relationships.

A mother can be puzzled when her son begins this male pattern of struggling with a problem by himself, thinking his situation through in the privacy of his room rather than discussing it with her. When he has arrived at some sort of action, he may share it, but some boys—not all—need quiet in order to resolve their difficulties.

One mother told me that when her son broke up with his girlfriend, she asked him how he was doing and he replied that he didn't need to be counseled. He clearly wanted time to himself and wanted her to know he was okay and could manage. His way of telling his mother not to worry was hurtful because she thought he, like she, would like to talk about it.

Tannen points out that when men don't say anything, it does not indicate that they aren't thinking. When a son is taciturn, it may not signal an empty brain (as some mothers suppose), but a mind that is occupied with information or emotions that he doesn't want to express or doesn't know how to express.

Modifying the Pattern

One mother spoke with frustration about her boys: "No matter how much you try and invest in them and think they're going to be different from a lot of men, they seem as they get older to fit the prototype of men. Even though they have been exposed and we have consciously set as a goal that they are going to be more sensitive than other men and be able to say what is on their minds—even though we have coached them and encouraged that, it seems so many boys don't have that skill. It seems that boys are always competing against each other. They're getting feedback from society, not us, about what is appropriate boy behavior."

Although some mothers desire to change all men, most mothers' ambition is to communicate well with their sons—better than previous generations of mothers and sons. The intensity of the lives of this generation of adolescent boys compels them to let off emotional steam, and mothers hope the release will be healthy. Talking with Mother is one way to reduce the stress—not the only way, but one way.

The mothers I interviewed do not want to turn their sons into women, into female companions with whom they can "rapport talk," but they want their boys to have the capability of understanding the emotions that propel them. To ignore those emotions or be unable to define them denies a son access to a rich part of his inner life.

But how can a mother modify the typical male communication style to help her son become more responsive to the emotional needs of himself and others? First, I think it is necessary to understand the present pattern of male silence and female conversation that I have just described. Then a mother can adopt alternative ways of communicating with her son that will help him look into himself, while keeping in mind that he is young and incapable of being perfect.

Mothers also must be aware of an adolescent's strong need for connection, for relationships. He may have a different way of expressing this need, but the desire to have his parents recognize him and love him is as strong in boys as it in girls.

Listening versus Hearing

For an adolescent son to talk, someone must be listening. His friends usually listen without injecting admonitions, judgments, or lectures. That's why sons often prefer talking with peers than with parents. Even boys who told me they could talk openly with their mothers hesitated when I asked them if they could go to them with serious problems. If mothers want sons to confide, then, they have to examine their listening skills.

"My kids are so used to my talking at them," one mother said with appealing honesty. "They have to listen to me so much, and as soon as they have five sentences out, I have an opinion. I'm already talking again. It's easier to be conscious of it than to act on it."

After a while sons can anticipate their mothers' responses. My sons often baited me to see how I would react to an outrageous comment and then they would laugh because I said exactly what they thought I would say. Their sense of humor allayed my chagrin at responding in such an obvious "motherly" fashion.

Listening is a skill, particularly between generations. When a mother knows so much more than her son, she wants to jump in and offer advice before she hears the whole story. "I think it's hard to be a mother, easier to be a mentor," one mother reflected. "A mother is so involved, she has a hard time listening. A mentor can just listen."

A mother should not always assume that she knows what her

son is talking about. The expression "I know how you feel" does not sit well with an adolescent boy who thinks his feelings or experiences are unique. A son doesn't believe his mother could possibly know how he feels—she is of a past generation. So just listening or nodding in agreement would be more helpful.

When a son says, "No problem, Mom," or "It's okay, Mom," believe him. He doesn't want to talk at that moment or he honestly believes he can handle a situation. If a mother senses a serious problem underneath the nonchalant attitude, she should plan immediately how and when she will approach him. When a mother and son are alone and relaxed, he is more likely to open up. And if a mother has told her son to come to her when he has problems, she must not be too busy to listen when he decides to talk.

The art of listening to an adolescent was described by Paul Swets, a researcher in effective communications, as the ACE Model: Attending, Clarifying, Evaluating.[10] When a mother (or father) "attends" to a son, she eliminates unnecessary distractions such as TV noise, listens to his exact words, and notices his body movements (is he nervous, sad?). He realizes he has her full attention.

"Clarifying" a son's message means making sure a mother understands what he is saying, by his standards, not hers. If she doesn't grasp the situation, she should use some clarifying responses such as: "So what you're saying is————, right?" or "Tell me more about it so I understand," or "Will you give me an example?"

After attending to her son and clarifying his message, a mother can then "evaluate" what he has told her and decide how she will respond. She may need more time to think over a request or she may require more information. Perhaps she doesn't have to respond at all; she only needs to listen.

"When my son hears himself talk about a problem, he usually solves it by himself," a mother told me. "All I have to do is listen."

Boys can sense whether a mother is a willing listener or is just hearing his words. If he and she are in the same room but are not connecting in their conversation, he may not repeat his effort. Moments of intimate discussions with any person, male or female, are to be cherished.

Requesting versus Nagging

"My mom bugs me so much," one boy complained. "It really doesn't help." When I asked him what his mother should say when she wants something done, he replied—seriously—"I don't think I'd have her say anything. I'd rather have her say nothing."

As much as this boy would like a biological mutation, mothers and sons cannot communicate by osmosis. Mothers request favors or tasks from their sons and usually want them accomplished quickly. To avoid delaying tactics or stubborn refusal, a mother must plan her strategy, deleting words that irritate.

Many parent/child communications "experts" advocate stating a situation and expecting a child to cooperate. However, I have never found that to work. Boys just don't get the message. Instead of saying, "The garbage is full," as these writers suggest, a far better approach is to say, "Would you take out the garbage?" In *Men Are from Mars, Women are from Venus*, John Gray, discusses ways to "motivate" a man to cooperate. Although some women may consider any technique of conversation a form of manipulation, I disagree. Mothers want their sons to know how to cooperate and offer support.

Gray suggests "five secrets to correctly ask a Martian for support": appropriate timing, nondemanding attitude, brevity, directness, and correct wording. I thought his advice sounded so reasonable that I am applying his suggestions to adolescent males. This technique can be implemented in any situation.

Appropriate Timing. If a son is in the middle of a phone conversation with his girlfriend, that is not the time to ask him to take out the trash. Ask later when it will not disturb his train of thought. Or if he is in the middle of a homework assignment, say, "When you're finished with that subject, would you take out the trash?"

"Most of the conflict with my mother stems from normal mother nagging," one boy reported. "She has a knack for bringing up things at the wrong time. Like, 'Why don't you clean up your room?' when I have to work on something important. I'd say that's when the conflict begins."

Nondemanding Attitude. If a mother's request reflects her impatience or the fact that she keeps making demands ("Take out the trash. Do your homework. Clean your room. Get off the phone"), he soon will tune her out, knowing that she never appreciates anything he does, anyway, and her demands will keep coming no matter how he reacts.

Be Brief. A mother doesn't have to list the reasons for a request. Mothers have many legitimate reasons to request a son's help. She doesn't need to explain that the dog will get into the trash, the mice or rats will have a field day, the smell is obnoxious, the sanitation crew comes in the morning. A simple request is all that counts: "Would you take out the trash?"

Be Direct. A direct request, as discussed above, is appreciated by boys who cannot read their mothers' inner thoughts. A statement is a statement; a request is a request. Mothers often hear the refrain "You didn't ask me to do that." A mother may have asked him, but he didn't hear her. "Would you take out the garbage?" is direct, and adding a "please" makes it sound even nicer.

Correct wording. One of Gray's most original contributions to the understanding of "genderlect" was pointing out that questions introduced by "could" or "can" are requests for information, not action. If a mother asks a boy if he "could" or "can" take out the garbage, he may reply appropriately, "Yes, I have two arms and two legs and I can lift a trash bin and bring it outside." His mother has asked him only if he is capable of executing the task. Using "would" or "will" to preface the request legitimizes the question: "Will you (would you) take out the trash?" He will not misinterpret her appeal.

Conversing versus Interrogating

"Instead of bugging them," advised a junior in high school, "maybe mothers could turn the questions around to something positive, like asking how your classes went or if you did anything interesting. Mothers maybe could spur your interest in class—you know, help your motivation in some way."

Mothers often interrogate sons about their social life or school life in a negative way, demanding information (Where were you? Whom were you with? Who else was there? Were the parents home?), and sons frequently develop amnesia, divulging no information about their night life or school.

I discovered that boys seldom ask questions of their parents and, consequently, know very little about their mothers' or fathers' activities. One boy told me that his mother had returned to school, but he could not recall or did not know where she went or what she was studying. Many boys could barely describe their fathers' work. They knew the city he worked in but everything else was vague. "My father commutes to North Carolina," a boy from New York State told me. When I asked him if he and his father ever talked about his job in North Carolina, he said, "Yeah, I ask him how his week went and he says, 'Fine.'"

This lack of knowledge about parents stems from the demise of the art of conversation. When parents and adolescents converse only about rules, regulations, and adolescent activities, sons—and daughters—are missing opportunities to know their parents as real people.

Sometimes mothers and fathers have to take the initiative and begin sharing experiences with their sons, telling them what they did at work that day, describing whom they saw in the store, relating a telephone conversation they enjoyed, talking about family and relatives—just as they would with a same-age friend. A mother may not recognize sports heroes or the latest rock video or even be aware of the latest teenage fashions, but she can share what is happening in her life. Then her son may share his life with her more easily. The need for interrogation lessens.

Sincere and positive inquiries into sons' activities can indeed "spur" their interest as it did with the boy mentioned at the beginning of this section, but be prepared to hear the unexpected. Confused about answering questions truthfully, one boy said, "I'm too honest. People tell me the truth is not always good and I say the truth is always good. But when my mother asked me if I liked the dessert and I told her it was awful, she was so mad. I said I was sorry, but she said next time you have to think first. That kind of thing happens to me all the time. It's hard—you never know what people want you to say."

This boy faces the dilemma of learning how to respect others' feelings while remaining true to his own. If he had said, "I liked last night's dessert better," he would have been truthful yet considerate of his mother's efforts. An honest exchange of conversation will help a boy grasp what is important in his mother's world and she will discover what matters most to him.

Negotiating versus Controlling

"He doesn't like to take orders," the mother of a 16-year-old lamented. Another mother nodded her head in agreement. "My son's always negotiating with me. He doesn't accept anything."

Boys negotiate because they don't want to feel controlled by their mothers. As early-adolescent boys lose control of their bodies during puberty (those penises that spring to action), control becomes a central issue, the plague of mothers. Boys want to make decisions, call the shots, have power.

That's why successful "authoritative" parents allow sons to have input into their rules and regulations, not allowing them to take charge and run the house, but listening to and respecting their opinions.

Boys love negotiating and are more apt to cooperate if they have bargained a bit. For example, a mother wants her older adolescent son to come home close to midnight. First, she must realize that an absolute time is often unmanageable and a challenge. Even if there is nothing to do, he may wait until the designated hour to walk in the door. To arrive home before the deadline is embarrassing—his parents will think something is wrong and start interrogating him.

A curfew discussion should start with an underlying assumption that he will be home at a "reasonable hour." Then mother (father) and son can discuss a reasonable hour (taking into account community standards for teenage activities). He undoubtedly will choose a later hour, say 1 A.M. They then can negotiate until they arrive at a mutually agreeable hour, say between 11:45 and 12:30. Although a mother may think the haggling isn't worth the effort, it is. He will cooperate more willingly if his viewpoint is respected.

I believe a son is more willing to accept nonnegotiable messages like "I don't want you to take drugs" if he has been able to influence less crucial decisions like curfews or household responsibilities. Given choices, the time or type of chore, boys often work out a schedule that satisfies everyone.

"My 14-year-old son has set up a system," one mother told me. "He is to keep his room clean, do his own laundry, and is responsible for some part of the dinner. Then he can choose what part of the house he wants to clean. Right now he cleans the living room, vacuums, et cetera. He receives a weekly allowance for these jobs. But I need more work done and he needs more money, so he told me to put a list on the refrigerator and when I think of something to write it down. It's not a big list, but it is there all the time and on Saturdays, he'll take something from it. Then he told me that he was tired of weeding—one of my requests—so he rewrote my list and started it with things he won't do—for the time being."

This mother later acknowledged that she has lowered her standards of cleanliness when it comes to her son's room. It has to be in some order but he has control over his sanctuary—his cave.

Another mother commented, "In order to give him control, I must give up some of my own. It's not as critical as I once thought it was to have his room cleaned once a week." She also had "lowered her standards."

Another woman agreed on the value of allowing a son to plan his own chores. "If you tell them what to do, they feel subservient." And then she added, "If I make up stuff for my sons to do, they will fight me tooth and nail. But if I need something, they are really there. They can sense the difference. They know if I'm making up work or really need a hand." Smart sons, wise woman.

"You know what I find so interesting living with men," said a mother of an all-boy family. "They don't like to be told what to do. If I asked a girlfriend to do something for me, she'd just do it and vice versa. Men do not do that and I think I've finally realized where it comes from. It goes back to Mother and that control thing. Men like to do things their own way, not to be told." I suggested she use the "would you" technique.

Stereotypes?

Are mothers reinforcing male stereotypes when they consciously work around their sons' style of communication? I don't think so. I have observed and listened to enough mothers and sons to appreciate the universality of these male/female differences in Western culture. Neither style of communication is better than the other—only different. A well-balanced person, male or female, will cultivate both aspects of his or her personality.

Extreme, stereotypical ways of communication are not productive. If a girl dwells on her emotions to the exclusion of acting on or solving a problem or cannot speak out publicly, she is stunting her overall development. And if a boy never examines his feelings or the effect of his statements on another, or is tongue-tied in private conversations, he is denying his rich inner life.

Mothers who face reality realize that what motivates one child to action may not motivate another. If her adolescent male child will move and accomplish something—anything—when she listens rather than hears, requests rather than nags, converses rather than interrogates, and negotiates rather than controls, they both will be winners.

Memos for Moms

1. Speak clearly and directly to an adolescent son. He has trouble interpreting unspoken messages.
2. Recognize the difference between boy-talk and girl-talk.
3. Remember talking is not the only way to form close bonds. Enjoy being with him.
4. Be aware that "doing" things with a son may help him relax and feel more comfortable talking about feelings and personal matters.
5. Appreciate that most boys enjoy talking with their mothers, but don't expect them to disclose all you want to know.
6. Respect his confidence in you if he does open up. Do not repeat to others what he has told you.
7. Don't take his silence as a personal rejection. He may need time to himself.
8. Listen to a son attentively and make sure you understand what he is saying. Ask for clarification if you are uncertain.

9. Make direct requests. Use "would" or "will" instead of "could" or "can."

10. Converse with him about your everyday life. He may reciprocate and learn the art of conversation.

11. Be willing to negotiate with him. If his ideas about rules and regulations are respected, he will be more cooperative.

12. Realize that effective communication skills require practice—and more practice. Be patient. Sincere attempts to listen rather than hear, request rather than nag, converse rather than interrogate, and negotiate rather than control will be rewarded.

7

"Why Do They Fight So Much?"

Boys and Violence

Proving Himself • Fighting Back
Fighting with Toy Weapons
Fighting with Real Weapons
"I Turn My Fear into Anger"
The Economic Factor • The Media Factor
Violence Turned on Himself: Suicide
Releasing Stress • Problem Solving
Memos for Moms

When I stopped in traffic one morning, I noticed two small red-haired boys pounding each other with their backpacks, wrestling each other to the ground, yelling at each other—and loving every minute of it. Their big grins told the familiar story of little boys who love to roughhouse.

As I recalled the incident to a group of mothers gathered to talk about daughters, we all agreed that little girls would not have been laughing. Girls would not consider wrestling each other to the ground, especially in their school clothes, fun. In no other interaction do the differences between boys and girls become more apparent than in fighting, wrestling, and aggressive behavior. Although girls show up in the reports of teen violence more frequently than in the past, the preponderance of fighting is carried on by boys and men.

Because a son enjoys the rough-and-tumble play of early childhood does not mean that he will turn into a street thug. When my sons were young, I thought they would never take their hands off one another. I used a standard phrase, "No roughhousing in the living room!!" They tackled one another at every opportunity, and the ensuing free-for-alls could drive me up the wall. The noisy melees erupted so often that I reached a point—for my own sanity—that I didn't notice. Although most of the roughhousing was in fun, some was not. I once thought that two of my sons would never understand each other or would kill each other before they reached adulthood. Thankfully, during their middle-school years they grew to appreciate their differences and became the best of friends.

"When we were young," a senior told me, "my brother and I used to compete a lot. Then about eighth grade we decided if we really fought we might kill each other. Now we talk rather than try to pin each other down. In fourth grade we would see who could give the other one a dead leg, but in eighth grade we thought, 'What's the point?' "

When I asked him what happened in eighth grade, he said, "I guess we figured out that fighting didn't solve anything and left things worse off. When you're little, you always have to be the winner. When you're older you think, 'Who cares who has the TV clicker?' "

Most of the time the grabbing and wrestling that go on between brothers and close friends are their way of having fun. Any mother can talk about her son's rowdiness. As a mother who had only sisters told me, "I don't think I'll ever adjust to their fighting all the time."

A son's natural physicalness can be a positive and enviable trait if he develops less fear of physical harm, an ease of movement, and a comfort with his body. One high-school boy described his student lounge: "There's a lot of wrestling, macho stuff, but we do everything in a humorous way. We play around and punch each other in a relaxing way."

This natural "playing around," however, can turn into a competitive, defensive, unemotional drive for superiority, to win in all cases. And a boy who is not "relaxing" but taking his anger out by bullying and tormenting others is not having fun and neither is his victim. I don't want to dampen the exuberance of roughhousing that seems central to young males' relationships, but I think boys should see the disadvantages of this physical play as well.

Proving Himself

"A man has to do what he has to do as a matter of obvious principle; and that means defending yourself when threatened or challenged. A brave scrapper is praised as a man 'who can take care of himself' while a failure is ridiculed as a 'chicken-shit bastard,' a 'mark' or a 'boy.' "[1]

Although one might think this quote comes from an adolescent boy, it was written by anthropologist David Gilmore while discussing "manhood codes." Comparing anthropologists' reports of the Micronesian island of Truk, some Mediterranean cultures, western sections of Canada, and parts of the United States, Gilmore continues: "What is so striking is the sense of masculinity as a pose that is deeply conflicted, pressured and forced, a mask of omnicompetence and an almost obsessive independence."[2]

Is this "pose" an essential part of masculinity, reaching back to the primitive times when a man needed to protect his family from the wild? How ingrained is this need to appear "omnicompetent"?

Although we may not know the answers to these questions, we do know that in many societies boys have to "prove" themselves to be considered men. Since most Western societies do not provide universal rites of passage into manhood, we must examine how our culture defines manliness and look at what our sons have to "prove."

Fighting Back

Every boy at some time has an object taken away from him or is attacked by another child. Should he hit back? In a study that looked at the consequences schoolchildren expect when they defend themselves, researchers from Florida Atlantic University found that a boy (the average age of boys in the study was 10.6 years) does not expect parental disapproval when he fights with a boy who has provoked him.[3]

Parents want their sons to retaliate. We often hear a mother or father tell a son not to let another boy get away with hitting him, to "stand up for yourself." This parental attitude of revenge lets the boy know that it is okay to "even the score" with another boy who crosses him—even if it is unintentional. He is not taught to turn the other cheek or to resolve the dispute peacefully.

In the same study, boys felt less guilty and upset than girls when they acted belligerently. Still other research suggests that a boy's self-esteem actually may increase after he gets into an altercation.[4] When boys find little disapproval for exchanging blows and feel better about themselves when they do, we should not be surprised at their behavior.

A mother told me about her son and his cousin. "My fourteen-year-old son is older than his cousin by three or four years but they are the same size. My son would never hit him back because he naturally avoids confrontation. We raised him that way. But one day his cousin hit him and really knocked the wind out of him. I got upset and said I really have to draw the line. My sister-in-law says my son is a wimp if he is going to take it. I got annoyed at her attitude. I think that's how parents come across to their kids. She wasn't telling her son not to hit. She was encouraging him; telling her son that if my son was going to take it, give him more."

In adolescence, this "manly" attitude can become a way of life. When I asked one boy why he fought so much, he replied, "If you bump into me, I'll hit you." This boy did not take time to determine whether a person bumped him accidentally or deliberately. He considered any bump a threat and he felt the need to strike back. He had learned his lesson on manhood well and was developing a reputation for constant defensiveness and explosive behavior.

"My son would take a challenge on and not be afraid of anyone," one mother said proudly, but then admitted, "But he's tired of hearing gunshots. I'm working on the whole family moving for his safety. Anywhere you go, there's problems, but for him to be able to live free, I think it's best."

Another boy, wearing a leather jacket, a long heavy metal key chain, and multiple earrings, told me that his group engages in lots of fights because of . . . skateboarding. "A lot of people hate skateboarding and make fun of us," he said. "Then when we catch them, we start with them, and they always chicken out. We ask them if they have a problem and they'll say no and try to get out of it. We'll say okay and then wait and get them in school. We fight in school."

Principals in schools from diverse socioeconomic neighborhoods have told me that student confrontations have increased during school hours. In a quiet Massachusetts community, three boys entered a school and knifed a student to death because he had insulted one of their mothers. One principal commented that not only was the rise in fighting upsetting, but equally disturbing was the lack of any effort by other students to stop the violence. If they don't fight in school, they arrange meeting places where they can do so after school.

When I interviewed a group of mothers from an inner-city school, they were rightfully concerned about the retaliation mentality they see in young people. Many of their sons had been challenged to a showdown.

"I tell my son," one woman said, "it's better just to walk away and if they want to call you chicken, ignore it. If you know who you are, you don't have to prove yourself. The older he gets, the more he believes me. Now he is talking to other males who feel secure about who they are and that helps. My father was a very strong man who was in World War Two and the Korean War, so he knows about courage and living and dying. He didn't have to put his hands on anyone to prove who he was. He let his actions prove it. He didn't make an appointment with someone to hurt him. He used to say if they're going to hurt you, they should hurt you right then and there, because being forewarned is being forearmed. It takes more courage to walk away."

If we train our sons to defend themselves physically rather than walk away, we are creating a world of revenge and retaliation, a world of violence. And if we insist that they fight back, we are encouraging them to use weapons as well as fists—because weapons can guarantee success.

Fighting with Toy Weapons

"I refused to buy my sons guns," one mother told me, "but the minute they found sticks, they started shooting with them." Yes, little boys like to play cops and robbers, their version of hide-and-seek. They inevitably invent their own weapons. But when parents give a son a gun, they send a message of approval: It is okay to play with weapons.

Even squirt guns, which were once considered harmless, have been transformed into mighty weapons of power. Many schools have banned them because of serious injury to students. In addition to guns, many toys marketed for boys advocate belligerence and intolerance. Myriam Miedzian, in her revealing book *Boys Will Be Boys: Breaking the Link Between Masculinity and Violence*,[5] describes the story line of some militant playthings. A Transformer robot named "Rampage" tells its users that "those who conquer—act, those who are conquered—think." In other words, the thinkers lose. Miedzian also quotes the marketing theme of Rampage: "Barrels through life with an uncontrolled fury. Has difficulty talking coherently for more than a few seconds before violently lashing out at anything near him, *friend* or foe" [my emphasis]." Some teachers fear that Rampage is sitting in their classroom or roaming the halls of their school—which is why the school has a metal detector and security guards.

Although an isolated Rampage image may not damage a boy, a barrage of violent images will affect him. A continuous stream of barbarouslike toys, serial-murder trading cards, and video games that exterminate the opponent will convince a young boy that bad guys get attention.

Mothers usually control the purse strings for guns and games and should search out entertainment that encourages cooperation, fun, and healthy competition—where winning does not mean annihilation.

Fighting with Real Weapons

When I asked a mother from an inner-city school what she worried about most, she replied, "He could catch a bullet at any time. We live on the top floor and we hear gunfire from the roof. He knows what streets to avoid."

"Nowadays, you get fourteen-year-olds saying, 'I'm going to shoot you,' " a tough-looking high-school boy told me. "They may be just talking big, but if I hear a fourteen-year-old say that, I keep on walking. I don't want to get involved in that."

The fact is the 14-year-old may have a gun. Gunshot wounds rank as the "second-leading cause of death among high school age children in the United States and they are increasing faster than any other cause among both blacks and whites."[6]

"If a person has a weapon," one mother told me, "the choice to fight or not to fight is taken away because then you are a victim, not an equal opponent."

According to the American Medical Association, deaths and injuries from guns now constitute a public health crisis. Researchers found that one-third of Seattle high-school students had "easy" access to handguns, and 6 percent of high-school students reported they had brought guns to school.[7] As one boy told me, students carry handguns to "protect" themselves. They are not,

however, protecting themselves from criminals, but from peers—
at school, on the street, or at a social event.

In rural communities, suburbs, and cities, boys face an increasing chance of getting shot in retaliation if they look at someone the wrong way, bump into them, make a nasty comment about their appearance or their family, or cross a member of the drug world. Or they can be shot accidentally by standing at the wrong street corner or by playing dangerous games.

Where are teenagers getting these guns? It's easy. Firearms can be ordered from catalogs, purchased directly without a security check, bought on the black market, exchanged for drugs, or taken from home. Ask a teenager where a gun can be obtained and he will tell you.

Guns can provide turning points in young lives. When I asked a boy what key event turned him away from being a real troublemaker, he responded, "A friend of mine got shot when we were in junior high. I was very close to him. I was going to go to a party with him that night, but it turned out that he and some other guys were going to go out and rob some people and the gun went off and killed him."

An FBI study found that in the 1980s the number of murders committed by youths with firearms rose 79 percent.[8] "Guns aren't just for gangs or drug dealers," a youth in our nation's capital told a reporter. "It's everybody who's looking for a reputation. The more powerful the ammo somebody's got, the more respect he's got."[9] Another lesson in manhood that we are giving our sons: The more powerful you are, the more respect you will have.

Guns, especially handguns, should be removed from all homes with adolescent boys. It could save the life of your child or someone else's child. In a New York area suburb, two boys shot and killed each other using a handgun belonging to the father of one of the victims. In suburban Chicago, a father also owned the gun that killed his son in a fatal game of Russian roulette.

Even the slightest possibility that a son can get hold of the family gun should provide enough reason for parents to turn the weapon over to the police for proper disposition. Adolescent boys are the most likely to show off and kill someone unintentionally, and if an adolescent is drinking or doing drugs, the chances of his mishandling a weapon are even greater.

The American Medical Association reported that many homicides and suicides are impulsive, involve a handgun, and occur in or near home.[10] In Louisiana, a confused homeowner shot to death a Japanese exchange student who knocked on his door for directions to a party. Guns are not needed to protect a home, as most homes are robbed when no one is there and the chances of killing an innocent person are high.

If a family lives in a neighborhood where gun-carrying is common, parents should search their son and his room and remove any gun. Many schools now have metal detectors to ensure safety, and mothers and fathers must act as the metal detectors in their homes. The strong message must be: *No guns allowed.* Parents who think removing guns from their homes is extreme need to realize it could save the life of their child or their neighbor's child.

"I Turn My Fear into Anger"

"What tees you off?" I asked a handsome well-built senior who had a reputation for a violent temper. "School," he responded. "If you don't get the grades they want, they don't care about you. It's the attitude. I don't count. I'm just another person in the class."

The answer was not what I expected, but the tone of voice and his fear of no one's caring about him were. The survivor of a bitter divorce, he would not blame his parents for his anger. "The divorce really got me mad at the beginning, but now I've learned how to deal with it. You can't get angry." But he *was* angry and he took it out on his teachers and in sports, but not on his mother or sisters with whom he lived.

"If you lose your cool at home," he told me, "you kind of lose their respect, so I don't get that angry at home."

So how does this boy get rid of his stress? Football. "A lot of things get me angry in football and that's what fuels my playing. The angrier I get, the better I play. If I'm not angry, I can't play any sport. *I turn my fear into anger.*"

Turning "fear into anger" is what fuels many boys, from inner city to outer suburb. Their fear can take a variety of forms—the fear of failing, the fear of getting attacked, the fear of losing a father through divorce or a friend through death, and the fear of growing up and putting it all together. Rather than talking through their anxieties, these boys think that real men get angry or act indifferently.

"This place [school] drives me out of control sometimes because you get so much stress built up," the senior continued. "I used to lose my cool completely, but now I just blow it off and that really pisses the teachers off."

If he doesn't have an outlet for his stress, an adolescent boy may just "blow it off" by driving his parents and teachers wild. He doesn't want to appear weak and ask for help, so his mask of indifference conceals his inner turmoil.

A boy's fear may be aggravated by moving into a new school area and having to "prove himself" once again. "When we moved into a new neighborhood," one mother told me, "my son fought every day for a month to assert his manhood. Every day he fought the baddest guy on the block, and they fought until they were too tired and they both had black eyes. They wound up sitting on the curb and my husband went down and talked to them and now they're best of friends."

And in another neighborhood, a woman told me, "My son is afraid to wear expensive sneakers because he is afraid he is going to be beat up. That's primary in a lot of areas in his life—getting beaten up. When he first went to junior high, he spent the whole first five months biting his nails before he went to school and he wouldn't tell me why. Someone accused him of something and a gang was going to get him. He found some people to protect him and it goes on to this day and he is in tenth grade now. You could say they are a gang but they don't call themselves a gang, but he is afraid. I know that."

Another boy has a unique way of working off his stress. When I asked him how he got rid of his fear and anger, I was surprised at his response: "I go home and get a baseball bat and beat up a tree. I really pound on this tree. I don't like dealing with my problems at school. People just get me madder."

Initially this boy told me he had no problems at home, yet later in the conversation he said his mother has been sick since he was 13 and has been hospitalized frequently. Because of her illness, neither his mother nor father can attend any of his school events. Yet there is no lack of love in his family. He told me, "I have no problem with my parents. We don't argue, we talk. They tell me, 'When you have a problem, come and talk with us.' "

Out of love for his family he does not want to burden them with his problems. His mother's illness is enough for the family to cope with, and since he won't talk to a counselor, the tree becomes his release.

When I asked another boy who was described to me as "out of control" how he handled stress, he struggled to define his new attitude. He had outgrown acting out his anger, he told me. "I go work out, take a run, exercise, listen to music. If someone gets me angry, I try to think good things about them, not negative. Because if they say something negative about me, they're the ones that have the problem. There's nothing wrong with me. I don't have to worry. It's very hard, very hard, but it's better to walk away than to get into trouble."

He credits his mother with convincing him that he will feel "better about myself" if he walks away from a confrontation. "It doesn't make me feel like a wimp 'cause I know I could do something. But," he reiterated, "it's really hard." This boy has learned, hopefully, that retaliation does not make a real man, and walking away does not make a wimp.

The Economic Factor

A series of studies that examined the connection between economics and family life found that economic hard times influenced the relationship between a mother and father. The resulting tension between them changed their way of parenting and made a boy's problem behavior more likely.[11]

An adolescent boy is stressed more by the marital conflict that financial strain can bring than by the prospect of less money. His father may become irritable, his mother depressed, and he gets into more trouble and more fights.[12]

And in mother-only homes, where the income is usually lower than in two-parent homes, the economic tension may be even more pronounced. A mother, overwhelmed by hand-to-mouth living, may be too exhausted to pay close attention to her adolescent son and remain unaware of his anxiety about their finances. He then may turn to acting out his worries.

In a divorced family, the strain between the spouses over child support can escalate during adolescence. An adolescent who requires more spending money may have to work rather than study, and as a result his grades may be affected. In addition, Judith Wallerstein in her study of divorced families found that many adolescents could not afford to attend college even though their fathers were capable of paying their tuition.[13] Often a father has assumed a financial role until his son (or daughter) reaches the age of 18. However, when the child applies for student aid, his father's income is figured into the financial aid package, making his son or daughter ineligible for a grant.

Although poverty can cause conditions that lead to violence, many poor families, whether they're headed by one parent or two, maintain a secure, strong relationship with their sons. They discuss their problems as a family and try to work out a fair distribution of their income. A sense of attachment and commitment can reassure a son that their economic problems can be handled. It may be tough but together they will manage.

Some sons, however, regardless of their parents' relationship, react strongly to not having enough money. One boy told me that his father had lost his business and his parents had to "cut him off." "I started going crazy. My parents wouldn't buy me anything, so I was mad all the time, I'd cause trouble and cut classes." He admitted that he had been spoiled and previously had bought anything he wanted.

Many boys, in average homes, wealthy homes, or poor homes, get everything they want. And they may die while protecting their possessions. A 15-year-old boy shot two acquaintances to death, reportedly in a quarrel over a bracelet. "He was a good dresser," a classmate said of his dead friend. "A lot of people were jealous of what he had—Polos, Guess, and Fila shirts."[14]

In a middle-income suburb, a 13-year-old felt the stress of having to "look good." "If you wear a brother's hand-me-down," he told me, "they'll look at you like you're dirt." This son of a single mother was transferring to a school where a dress code removed the stigma of dressing in second-hand clothes.

Many inner-city schools are switching to uniforms to avoid confrontations between students and to control the competition of expensive jewelry and clothes. Teachers want to focus on learning, not on who dresses the best.

Because parents usually don't share money problems with children, a son may see only the resulting discord or depression. Adolescents possess an uncanny ability to pick up undercurrents in a home. If hard times hit a family, parents should include their son in discussions of what the family plans to do.

The charade of pretending everything is all right in a home that is beset with unemployment, divorce, sickness, alcohol abuse, or drug abuse confuses a child. He may resort to hitting a tree, but he also may turn to more harmful aggression, inflicting harm on himself or others.

Because boys are taught that "boys don't cry," a natural release of stress is lost to them. A mother told me that when she informed her adolescent sons that it was okay to cry, they stared at her blankly, as if she had lost her senses. "But I told them," she said, "it's healthy. It's okay. If you hold it in, it does more harm inside. I said it's like gas, you have to release gas. It's a natural function. You can't stop certain things that are natural to people." Adolescent boys can understand that analogy.

The Media Factor

In all homes, television and movies that glorify violence exert a profound influence. Parents must work hard to overcome the pervasive media message that the tough guy wins through belligerence and aggression. When my sons were young, I limited their Saturday-morning cartoon viewing because I thought those shows were too violent. Now those programs seem mild compared to the fare offered daily to young viewers.

Recently researchers have been discovering a close link between the increase in violence among children and adolescents and television viewing. A recent study reports that children as young as 14 months imitate what they see on television. And in surveys of young male prisoners, 22 to 34 percent had consciously imitated crime techniques learned on television.[15]

"Violence is glamorized on TV," said a mother who lives in a violent neighborhood. "The street may introduce him to something he saw on TV and he says, 'Oh, that's not too bad. I saw it on TV.' When they watch movies they see them die in glory and everyone is saying, 'That's my man.' I'm afraid of that attitude because it's not glory on the street. On the street it's bad."

One study followed 875 boys and girls for twelve years and found a significant link between violent television and aggression. The link goes two ways. "Aggressive children watch more violent TV and violent television makes them more aggressive."[16] By age

30, the young men in the sample who had watched the most television had committed more serious crimes, showed more aggression while drinking, and administered harsher punishment to their children than those watching less television.

"The current level of interpersonal violence has certainly been boosted by the long-term effects of many persons' childhood exposure to a steady diet of TV violence," Dr. Leonard Eron told the Senate Committee on Government Affairs.[17]

Violent TV cartoons that are used as baby-sitters for young children endanger their mental health, and violent TV shows marketed to adolescents promote the unbridled violence we see in our homes and in our streets.

Mothers can monitor television shows since the TV usually is centrally located and has an on/off button. Also, members of Congress are calling for television manufacturers to install electronic chips that would allow parents to control the incoming channels. Mothers should ask for information at their local television stores about control devices that are now available. Families that allow boys to have televisions of their own are making a mistake. Discussions about TV programs will never take place if a son is choosing his own shows and viewing them in his own bedroom. There are good shows on TV that adolescents can watch, and if there is a question about a show, the family should watch it together.

Families should have rules about how much and what type of television can be watched. Some families sit down on Sunday night and decide what shows they will view that week. That does not guarantee that if the parents are out, a son will not watch the most gruesome murder movie of the week, but the message he receives from his parents is the important one—viewing of violence is not tolerated.

The inhumane treatment of other people is not an ideal to be viewed, laughed at, or imitated. A constant diet of violence can make a boy less sensitive to the suffering it causes. TV is not the only media villain. Slasher-type movies make killings seem like everyday occurrences, not something unusual. Movie-goers are no longer shocked.

After he had killed six women, Nathaniel White told reporters that he had committed his first murder after seeing the movie *Robocop*. "I did exactly what I saw in the movie," he said.[18]

When the chief of police of a large city asked a 15-year-old why he had just committed murder, the boy replied, "He deserved to die."[19] That line could have been taken right from a Rambo movie.

Often adolescents will say they are going to one movie and end up at another. But that does not mean that parents should give up on banning movies that depict men in macho, aggressive, and violent ways. Besides teaching their sons critical viewing skills, they must advocate for movies that show men who strive for nonviolent solutions to problems.

Violence Turned on Himself: Suicide

A son who thinks no one is interested in listening to him, who feels extreme anxiety and stress, and who has access to guns or drugs may fall victim to his own violence. The suicide rate among adolescents and younger children has tripled in the last three decades. As the overall suicide rate in the United States declined, the rate increased among young people ages 15 to 24. Each year over half a million young people attempt suicide. The dramatic rise in adolescent suicides coincides with the "striking" increase in the use of illegal drugs.[20]

But drug use is not the only factor contributing to adolescent suicide. A mother whose son had committed suicide told a reporter, "There are as many reasons for suicide as there are kids who commit suicide."[21] Depression and fear about one's sexual orientation are major contributors.

A son who alternates between depression and hyperactivity,

who has "difficulty concentrating, racing thoughts, irritability and impulsivity" may be at risk, according to a University of Pittsburgh study of the life histories of youthful suicide victims. Substance abuse can add to that risk by making an adolescent more depressed and removing the inhibitions to self-destruction. The research also found that behavioral disorders, such as the tendency to frequently get into fights, can also be related to suicide. A combination of depression, drugs, and acting-out behavior can unbalance a boy and lead him to kill himself.[22]

The availability of a loaded handgun enhances the chances of a successful suicide. An in-depth study of seventy adolescent suicides reported that 60 percent of the deaths were attributed to self-inflicted wounds from handguns. Children of law-enforcement officers accounted for a "disproportionate" number of these tragic suicides because of the availability of guns.[23]

Although theories abound for the current increase in adolescent suicide, I want to discuss an area not frequently mentioned: a feeling of not being attached to a parent.

A study at Boston University compared three groups of students: students who had a history of thinking about or attempting suicide; students who were depressed; and students who had no history of depression or suicide attempts. Those students who had contemplated or attempted suicide rated their parents as not emotionally available to them. They had "significantly less trust in the availability, accessibility, and responsiveness of their parents to their emotional need states."[24]

When a son does not believe that his parents really love him or are committed to him at all costs, he can become overwhelmed. Many families with suicidal adolescents tend to be families that avoid issues of conflict and cover up their feelings. This avoidance may lead a boy to conceal his problems, turn increasingly inward, and feel more hopeless and depressed.

A mother can often spot a change in her son's attitude about himself. He may lose his inner confidence, or be unwilling to look her in the eye or talk about why he is upset. Even his way of walking can convey the attitude of "I'm no good." When a mother notices this attitude, she should immediately assure him that she would like to hear about his troubles and listen in a nonjudgmental way. Telling him only that he is fine and everyone else is wrong will not change a son's attitude about himself. His dissatisfaction with himself or with events in his life must be heard from his perspective and be respected as his experience.

Sometimes parents of suicides will report that they did not know anything was wrong with their son. Often a boy does not know how his failure or his feelings of inadequacy will be taken, so he keeps his disappointments and heartache to himself. Then a deeply disturbing event—the loss of a loved one through death, divorce, or romantic breakup; a major disappointment or humiliation; the shame of something being uncovered—triggers this vulnerable adolescent into attempting to take his life.

Some boys drop hints like "You won't have to bother with me much longer." Anytime an adolescent talks about everyone's being better off without him, parents must pay attention. If he is entertaining suicidal thoughts or even hinting at them, he should be seen promptly by a professional who works with adolescents.

Releasing Stress

A mother who encourages her son to accept others, not to always stand tough, to like himself, and trust his instincts will be teaching him real survival skills. A father who does not use force with his son, who does not condone violent behavior, who demonstrates cooperation and gives unconditional affection to his son also will be a strong influence in teaching him how to be a man and to live nonviolently.

"A man who thinks raising his children is 'women's work' is a man who is unwittingly pushing his own son toward violence," wrote Thomas Blackburn in *The National Catholic Reporter*.[25] The idea that only women can nurture and only men, through confrontation, can solve problems produces an uneasy truce in families. Boys must see cooperative problem solving from both their mothers and fathers. Conflicts about custody or parental shared hours can cause pain to a son, as can constant hostile arguing within a family. Even a father who is separated from his family can remain a strong positive influence in his son's life.

And it is all right for boys to be afraid. When I was discussing violence with a group of mothers, they were concerned about some boys who swore they would never be caught "off-guard" again after a friend had been killed by a rival gang. "The fear has not left them, but they only act tougher," one mother commented. "I know a lot of parents who teach them that it's wrong to be afraid," said another. "These boys act so macho they're paranoid. They say they're never going to be caught off-guard again. But you can't go through life like that. You should be afraid."

Many boys do not realize that they may bring additional stress on themselves by their macho attitudes. One mother told me she took out a mirror and asked her son to look into it and make the kind of face he made in class. He quickly realized why the teacher acted negatively to him. His face said, "You can't teach me anything—just try it."

That same defiant look can cause fights. A boy who told me he was always fighting now says he has given up the "tough guy" role. "Today," he said, "if I bump into someone, I say I'm sorry, and if someone bumps into me, I say, 'No problem.' People treat me with so much respect these days. I say hi to everyone even if I don't know them. I used to think it was a joke when my teachers in middle school would say you should respect everyone. I used to think no one was going to respect me unless I fought. I got tired of that kind of life. I didn't feel like a real human being when I was playing that kind of life. I felt like a bum."

This boy has learned to cope with others, has earned their respect, and now realizes that he doesn't need a defensive posture in order to feel like a man. He expressed real surprise that others now respected him, and he felt truly proud of this accomplishment.

Other sons describe different ways to handle their stress. One boy told me he used his half-hour commute to and from school to relax, listen to a Walkman, and cool off. He thought if he had to go right from his intense after-school activities to homework, he would have a "major breakdown." His thirty-minute break put him into a better frame of mind. Although he was not an alcoholic, this boy described the Alcoholics Anonymous method of coping when he said, "I've been taking one day at a time."

Another boy told me he walked around until he got rid of his anger. Sometimes, he said, he goes home and "fixes stuff, like make a speaker. We have lots of stuff that we can't use and I try to fix it up." He has found that concentrating on repairing a speaker takes up his energy and focuses him away from his anger.

After his friend was shot, another boy told me he began to listen to others and "take in new ideas." Unfortunately, it took a trauma to open his mind up to other ways of being a man.

Many boys turn to sports, a traditional vehicle for the release of pent-up male energy. "It's a safe way to take out your aggression," said one boy I interviewed. "If you've had a rough day in school, you get out there in practice and kill the guy." He went on to say the football players were "tight," all good friends, and that they expected this roughness from one another.

The best way to relieve stress is by talking with a parent, a counselor, or a friend, but it is not always easy for a boy to open up. When I asked boys who in their family they felt most comfortable talking to, most of them responded immediately, "My mother." But when I asked them whom would they turn to if they had a serious problem, the question usually drew a long pause. Evidently, most boys don't think about sharing a problem at all. They have learned to "tough it out," ignore the problem, or take the frustration out in other ways.

Problem Solving

A son will learn best how to handle his stress from a mother who shares his concerns, shows a willingness to listen, provides a home free from daily tension, and talks about outlets for frustration. He also would benefit from learning a few problem-solving techniques. Bettie Youngs, in her book *Helping Your Teenager Deal with Stress*, mentions a four-step problem-solving process that can be effective.[26]

First, ask your son to describe the problem as specifically as possible (tough guy at school is making life miserable). Second, ask *him* to think of various ways to solve the problem (beat him up, get his friends to beat him up, avoid him, talk to him in a safe place, talk to a school counselor, switch classes, change schools). Then figure out what would happen if he chose each one. The more alternatives he thinks of, the better. If a solution sounds unrealistic, Youngs suggests guiding him back to "reality" by asking him again to focus on the problem. Third, after he discusses each solution and its possible consequences, have him decide which plan he will take. Fourth, after he acts on the problem, discuss with him how effective his solution was.

This four-step process can be applied to any problem: His girlfriend is pressuring to have sex; everyone gets drunk on weekends; his best friend talks about suicide; his grades decline; a teacher acts unfairly; he takes drugs; his girlfriend is pregnant; drug dealers are putting on pressure; the rival gang is closing in.

Stress management, conflict resolution, and problem solving are taught in some school and youth programs. The Carnegie Council on Adolescent Development has published a survey of such programs that can be adapted to a local situation.[27]

As I visited a large secondary school in an inner-city neighborhood, I overheard one boy say to another, "Fighting about it won't help." When I mentioned this to the principal, he told me that their conflict resolution program has worked so well that the students seldom have to use their new peer-counseling skills. He said the student peer counselors feel cheated. While they were learning how to defuse student confrontations, the teachers were showing the students how to avoid conflict. It worked. The administrators and teachers, in a community of housing projects and slum buildings, provided the students with an atmosphere of physical safety and emotional security. Their success was evident in the productive and enthusiastic learning that I saw in every class I visited.

Most mothers provide that safety and security in their homes, and their sons appreciate it. As one boy explained, "She's very understanding and cares a lot about me and my brother. She is always there for us—which is weird 'cause you never think about your mom doing that."

When sons learn that solving problems with their heads and hearts is more effective than with fists or weapons, they will have "proven" their manhood and prepared themselves for the twenty-first century. And mothers can help that process.

Memos for Moms

1. Appreciate your son's natural physicalness.
2. Teach him that fighting is not the way to defend himself.
3. Provide him with games and videos that encourage cooperation and problem solving rather than violence and winning at all costs.
4. Talk with him honestly about family pressures, including money problems.
5. Include him in the decision-making discussions about family problems.

6. Acknowledge his realistic fears of violence on the street and in the schools.

7. Don't take the stress between yourself and your spouse out on him. Give him the emotional security he needs and tell him it's okay to cry.

8. Monitor his television, video, and movie watching. Let him know you deplore violence toward anyone.

9. Be alert for any signs of violence turned against himself. Watch for talk of suicide or evidence of depression.

10. Remove all guns from the house.

11. Show him how to resolve conflict without violence. Use the four-part problem-solving process with him.

12. Remain firmly committed and accessible to him.

8

Living Up to His Potential

School and the Adolescent Boy

Mother's Beliefs • Turning Him into a Student
Study Skills
The Influence of Teachers and Schools
Mother-School Cooperation
Learning Disabilities • Attention-Deficit Disorder
Trouble Schools, Trouble Students, Good Solutions
Memos for Moms

One of the best kept secrets in Washington," researcher Theodora Ooms announced during a congressional briefing, "is that families are educators' most powerful ally."[1] This acknowledgment that families and schools must work together is welcome and makes sense to mothers who are faced daily with the challenging task of keeping adolescent boys motivated and in school.

Too many boys are "underachieving," performing below their natural abilities. Mothers, fathers, and teachers who place confidence in a son can supply the margin of difference between his succeeding, barely passing, or dropping out of school. Adolescents want to live up to caring adults' reasonable expectations, and if adults expect a boy to withdraw from school interests just because he has reached adolescence, they increase his chances of failure.

In some school districts, families blame schools for a son's academic apathy. And, in turn, teachers and administrators bemoan the failure of parents to set higher standards, turn off the television, supervise homework, or provide a safe, secure home. Boys often fall through the cracks, with everyone blaming and no one assuming responsibility for guiding them through middle and high school.

Adolescent boys are beset with competing energies. One minute they appear full of vitality and the next minute they seem weighed down with exhaustion. In any one classroom, a teacher may encounter boys with high energy and boys in a chronic stupor, boys who look 10 years old and boys who look 18, boys who want to learn and boys who hate school—not an easy teaching situation.

"I grew seven inches in seventh grade. I got into a lot of trouble," a boy told me. "I was a delinquent, a jerk. I got arrested for throwing a rock through a window. I failed four classes one quarter. It was a waste of time."

When I asked him how he recovered from seventh grade, he replied simply, "In eighth grade, I was five foot seven and stopped acting like an idiot." He also mentioned that he thought his parents should have been stricter, a surprising admission from a 17-year-old.

Early-adolescent boys not only differ from one another in size and energy, but in cognitive skills as well. Some think concretely and need hands-on experiences to understand the course work. They benefit from playacting in English class, measurement tasks in math, a miniature United Nations in social studies. Others, a minority even in eighth grade, think more abstractly and are capable of making an outline or understanding algebra. But most students flounder when the teacher talks and they are required to sit and listen. By the time boys reach tenth or eleventh grade, they are better equipped to tackle abstract discourse and math work. But it may be too late, they may have tuned out or dropped out.

At a time when early-adolescent boys need close attention paid to their entire development, they are taught by specialty teachers who see them for forty-five- to fifty-minute periods and who teach up to a hundred fifty different students a day. Counselors in some schools are assigned three hundred students. Just when adolescents need to participate in decisions that affect them, schools clamp down tighter to control their adolescent "urges." At a stage of life when their intellectual curiosity yearns for stimulation and they love to question, challenge, concoct their own theories, and defy traditional strategies, they are "tracked" into ability groupings and told to be quiet. All students should be exposed to the stimulating hands-on experiences of the top track, the animated discussions in the gifted students' classes, and the special field trips offered to bright students.

When a distraught boy in Massachusetts pulled out a gun in a crowded school, threatened his classmates, and then killed himself, no teacher could be found who knew him well enough to try to stop him. No one in the school realized he was so disturbed. The sheer size of the school made the important job of counseling students almost impossible.

Many schools are addressing the problem of their impersonal and unwieldy size. A high school I visited in the East Harlem section of New York City requires every teacher, staff person, and administrator to advise ten students. The advisers meet with their advisees between three and five hours a week, often have lunch together, and provide a personal warmth in a large school. The advisers are responsible for developing such a close relationship with their students that "they can teach them to use their minds well." When a boy doesn't show up for class, the adviser calls his mother and addresses her by name. It would be unlikely that a boy in that school would resort to gunfire to attract attention.

The well-regarded Carnegie report on early-adolescent education called for small schools, flexible schedules, an end to tracking, and a low student-teacher ratio.[2] Grades six through nine encompass one of most critical times in a boy or girl's academic life (second only to learning to read), and a successful middle-school or junior-high experience leads to better performance in high school. Although exciting programs are springing up throughout the country, early adolescents remain the stepchildren of American schools.

Parents can compensate for poor schools and teachers can counteract some aspects of a harried, troubled home life. A teacher's expectations or a parent's confidence can make a difference in a son's school attitude. But if a boy finds that his adolescence is not welcome at home and his learning style does not fit into the school's teaching style, his chances for success are lessened.

Mother's Beliefs

Schools cannot do the job by themselves. Teachers in overcrowded classrooms and deteriorating buildings with dwindling supplies and little staff assistance need all the help they can get from parents, but some mothers, assuming that adolescent boys possess a natural dislike of studying, remove themselves from involvement in their sons' school or academic life. Mothers who appreciate a son's desire to excel in basketball, guitar, or on the street often fail to associate his talents or ambitions with academic goals.

Yet a mother's confidence in her son's abilities and her willingness to help him with homework and appear at school functions can make the difference between staying in and dropping out. A "laidback" boy in a middle-class home sometimes thinks he doesn't need to work very hard to graduate, but he, too, will benefit from a mother's keen interest in his academic work and her dogged belief in the possibility of his academic awakening.

Besides possessing and expressing confidence in his ability to handle classwork and seek help if needed, a mother needs to respect her son as a unique and valued individual, and this will provide the groundwork for academic success. My children attended a Montessori school (a hands-on approach to education first developed with inner-city children) that influenced me profoundly. I observed an absolute respect, almost a reverence for children, whether they were 3 years old or 15 years old (the age range of the students). This respect did not manifest itself in a "Sit back, let children do what they want" attitude, but was an acknowledgment of the worth of each child, his unique developmental pattern, his individual learning style, and the value of his opinions. Adolescent sons—and all children—long for that type of respect.

A study from the University of Georgia confirmed the significance of parental respect: Rural black mothers who thought that an important goal for their children was to have self-respect became involved with their children's schooling and had children with high grade-point averages.[3] Clearly, mothers who value and respect their sons and daughters have children who internalize that respect and gain confidence in themselves.

Respect fosters a willingness to undertake academic risks, an "I can do it" attitude. A son tries harder when he knows his parents won't make fun of him if he fails. He realizes that even if he doesn't succeed, his mother will be proud of his efforts. Eventually, perhaps with additional help, he will understand the assignment or pass the test or develop an exciting project. Competence in anything does not happen without effort and, many times, is preceded by failures. Competence in itself elevates a boy's self-respect and engenders respect from others—a goal of all people.

I learned something else from the Montessori school that my children attended. The teachers were completely convinced that children—even boys—possess an innate desire to learn. We adults often set roadblocks on that ambition by making instruction tedious and repetitive. However, most children survive that boredom because their desire for knowledge is so intense. The assumption that sons want to learn may make a mother examine more closely the reasons why he doesn't learn. Is the material too difficult? Has he missed an important explanation? Is there a bully in the class who is tormenting him? Is the teacher indifferent? A mother doesn't just blame a son for failure, she tries to understand what is behind his lack of success.

When a boy reaches adolescence, his friends can sidetrack him from his academic pursuits. Sometimes these friends may seem to have an upper hand, but a strong mother knows she can and must intervene. She creates an expectation for her son by letting him know that she expects nothing less than attendance in school.

"There was a thing about my son not going to school," an inner-city mother said. "I told him there are certain things we talk about and certain things we don't talk about. And going to school is one thing that we don't discuss." Her son went and he graduated.

What parents think about adolescence often affects how they handle their sons. If a mother concludes that her son's brain will cease functioning from age 12 to 17, she may not notice her son's neglect of homework, his absence from class activities, or his lame excuses for unexplained absences. She expects the worst. After all, boys will be boys.

If, however, a mother believes that her son's brain has not stopped operating, but is stalled in neutral, she will patiently jump-start his intellect. Then she will seize the opportunity to reassert her confidence in his ability, ingenuity, and intelligence.

Mothers who presume that their sons will turn out fine seem to have sons who fulfill those expectations. But beliefs need reinforcement through action.

Turning Him into a Student

"It happens every year," one mother moaned. "I think he's doing fine and then the first report card comes home. I get incredibly mad at him and then it blows over." Many mothers can sympathize with her plight. Yelling at a son, however, is not an effective way to change his work habits or motivate him to do better.

One mother, at her wit's end, told her 15-year-old son that she would no longer monitor his homework. She had been reminding him about homework since he was in second grade and the scenario had not changed in eight years. So she told him she was tired of rescuing him and went in to talk to his guidance counselor. "Look," she said to the counselor, "I need permission to step back from this kid because I can't keep this up. If I spend the next four years rescuing him, what will he do in college? I told the counselor to give him all the detentions he deserves and I will support the school fully, but let me get out."

A mother's dilemma—when is monitoring a son not enough and when is it too much? When applied to schoolwork, the quandary increases because she realizes that his grade-point average will determine whether or not he goes to college. Should she let him vegetate until he is rudely awakened? Should she enlist the school to help change her son's attitude, as this mother did? Or should she persevere and ask every night whether his homework is done, if he has any tests tomorrow, when his finals are scheduled? Is there a better way to increase his motivation?

Research into adolescent behavior certainly emphasizes the positive effect of parent involvement on an adolescent's academic achievement, and mothers cannot give up prodding their sons.[4] But a boy does not always want his mother hovering over him, and if her immersion into his homework has not changed his attitude about studying, she must rethink her involvement. Is there a better way?

Some boys acknowledge that they need the structure of Mother's reminding them nightly about homework. A boy who lived in a housing project and was about to enter a fine technical high school appreciates his mother's monitoring: "My mother asks me if I did my homework every night. She's going to find out if I don't do it. She asked me when they give homework and I told her Monday through Thursday, so now she asks me on those nights. Sometimes she goes to school and checks and if they gave some, [and if I didn't do it], she grounds me." I asked him if he liked that and he answered, "No, not really, but if she didn't do it, it might mean she didn't care. It's good how she is doing it."

Other boys rebel and told me that if they are "bugged" about homework, they will just go into their room and stare into space. Still others feel enormous pressure from their mothers to do more and more homework, even though they are good students and complete their homework regularly.

"Even if I get an A in the class, my mother says you could have done better, should have handed in extra homework and gotten an A-plus," one boy said, exasperated at his mother's nagging. "There's no end to it. It makes you so mad. If I try hard and get good grades, I still get the same response. What's the difference? If I did nothing and got a C, they'd treat me the same way."

If a son is a good student and living up to his potential, a mother should trust that he knows what he is doing. Good students spend more time doing homework than poor students, and his grades will confirm that he is studying. Even a good student needs help at times, though, so a mother should let her son know that she is always available for questions or help. But if his report card is satisfactory, questioning him may be unnecessary. He has proven himself trustworthy and responsible and probably will ask her for assistance when he needs it.

I frequently read, at my sons' requests, their compositions or essays, asked clarifying questions, or commented on the punctuation, grammar, or spelling. They appreciated my involvement, but the work was their own and they knew that my expertise did not include advanced math or scientific experiments.

Good students talk to their parents about their studies and involved parents enjoy discussing everything with their sons. Which comes first? I think that the direction usually comes from the adult. A mother who converses with her son about world events, local politics, environmental issues, family chaos, television, and radio shows provides a basis for discussing what he is studying. A son then realizes that his mother takes interest in the world around her and he can take pride in adding to her knowledge. A mother does not have to nag her son to find out about schoolwork. Course work and reading lists of the nineties often differ from the academic requirements of the sixties and seventies, and parents can have fun comparing and contrasting the two. Moments like these offer sons the opportunity to describe their studies without the irritation that nagging produces.

Study Skills

Sometimes a boy just doesn't know how to get started on a homework assignment. He still is thinking in concrete terms and finds it daunting to tackle a assignment like "Explain the author's use of metaphors" or "Discuss Britain's role in the European economy." He needs to tackle an assignment in small chunks, not in large abstract pieces. Most teachers will not assign something beyond a student's capabilities, but if this does happen, encourage your son to ask questions. Teachers usually are ecstatic when a student shows interest in a subject and are more than willing to help him analyze the assignment.

If a teacher is not available or is unwilling to give a son extra time, a mother can suggest that they think an assignment through together. For instance: "Let's think about metaphors for a minute. Remember when you said that Grandpa is our anchor? An anchor is the perfect metaphor to show the stability that Grandpa brings to the family. Let's look at the assignment and see if the author makes the story more alive by using metaphors like the one you used." Or a mother could ask, "If Grandpa [or anyone a son knows] were a car, what kind of car would he be? Why do you think so?" This type of discussion could be fun and it gives a son practice in drafting his own metaphors. Not only is a mother paying attention to her son's work, she may be learning something about herself—and him.

Some boys don't know how to take notes or use resource rooms—a real handicap when they undertake research. Because no one has taught them note-taking, they don't know where to begin or may not even realize that they need that organizing skill. Libraries contain books about reading skills—finding the topic sentence, etc. Mothers and sons may have to search our these resources and learn research skills together. Mothers also should point out these gaps in skills to their sons' teachers. These skills must be taught; a child doesn't learn them by osmosis.

Try to make a boy's bedroom as comfortable for studying as it is for sleeping, music, and friends. I found that some boys like to visualize projects, so they arrange their rooms to reflect that. They buy notebooks in different colors for each class. They arrange papers on open shelves according to subject color so they are easily identified—no messy file cabinets. Pencils, pens, pencil sharpeners, and plenty of paper are within view. These boys use colored pens to write outlines (red for main topics, blue for subtopics, green for sub-subtopics). They hang up maps when they are studying other parts of the world. Every boy eventually discerns how he studies best and wants his mother to appreciate this uniqueness.

I, for instance, like to visualize an overall plan of something I'm working on and use very large sheets of paper so I can view the whole project (or chapter) at one time. I learned this technique ("mind mapping") when I was studying for comprehensive exams and signed up for a weekend course on "How to Learn with the Right Brain." Although I should have been cramming for exams that weekend, I chose to learn how to study better. Without the benefit of that course, I might still be organizing my notes for the exams.

Creating the right working environment also will help a son concentrate on schoolwork. If a son doesn't share a room with siblings, he should be allowed a free hand in the upgrade of his bedroom/entertainment center/study space. Mothers can insist on a few requirements like refusing to let him have his own television and making sure that he has a table or desk to work on. Then he can create his own design, his own area for schoolwork. Remember, school is his work during adolescence. Show him how to treat schoolwork like real work. If he does not have his own bedroom or prefers working in a family area, then a mother and son should figure out a corner of a dining room, living room, kitchen—

someplace where he can have a permanent spot for his school-books and a place where he can write and work. He may have to clear the work space every night, but all family members know that is his spot for schoolwork.

A boy who is familiar with his school or town library has an advantage. Many librarians are valuable sources of information for young minds and will help students tackle research projects. Also, if a boy comes from a large family, he may find a quiet space in the town library for study.

Some boys manage to do homework and listen to music at the same time. I could not study that way, but if a son's grades are acceptable and he insists that the music does not interfere with his concentration, there is no reason to pursue the issue. Each person has his or her own learning style. When I seriously read or write, I must isolate myself from unnecessary distractions. My sons do not.

Within reason, an adolescent boy should manage his own study time, especially as he progresses through high school. His mother's trust and belief in his capabilities and her willingness to help him strengthen his study skills will give him the incentive to devote as much time to schoolwork as he does to physical activities, socializing, or television.

The Carnegie Council reported that on a typical school day, seventh graders spend an average of 135 minutes watching television; ninth graders spend 173 minutes; eleventh graders spend 150 minutes. The same report showed that seventh graders read for schoolwork 57 minutes a day; ninth graders read 63 minutes, and eleventh graders read 69 minutes.[5] Television is winning and mothers must strive to elevate academics to the top of a son's priority list.

The Influence of Teachers and Schools

When I taught seventh and eighth grades for a year in an inner-city school, I developed a deep and lasting appreciation for middle-school teachers. Since then, I have observed many middle, junior-, and senior-high classes in poor and wealthy school districts, and I continually am impressed with teachers who work successfully with this age group.

Teachers who love their students and understand puberty's effect on their adolescent bodies and minds are the most effective and competent. They challenge their students because they know that adolescents thrive on dares, and they never lower their standards of achievement. They realize that all children want to live up to expectations (even under their bravado) and provide adolescents with every opportunity to succeed and become competent. They manage to accomplish this feat with a smile and a sense of humor.

Because 15 to 30 percent of American students drop out before finishing high school, many researchers are looking at junior high schools to identify what factors contribute to a student's success or failure. Most academic problems surface in junior high when a boy enters a more impersonal environment and is confused by class schedules and many teachers with different teaching techniques. Educators have suggested that a mismatch often takes place between adolescents and middle-school environments. Some schools do not acknowledge that early adolescents have educational needs different from those of younger students, and some teachers are convinced that students arrive from elementary school already beyond hope and can't be taught.

A University of Michigan study suggests that this observation of teacher abdication may be true. In this particular case, math teachers had a profound positive or negative effect on a student's motivation.[6] When students moved from high-supporting elementary school teachers to low-supporting junior-high teachers (teachers who did not think they could do much to help their students achieve), the adolescents ended their first year in junior high with lower expectations for themselves regarding their performance in math, and higher perceptions of the difficulty of math. The worse-affected were the low-achieving students, setting the stage for school failure.

When young people moved, however, from confident and capable elementary school teachers to equally capable junior-high math teachers who believed in the students' capacity to learn, math motivation remained high. It was not adolescence itself, but the math teachers who made the difference in motivation. This increase in motivation also occurred with students who did not have competent math teachers in elementary school but found them in junior high. Other studies have confirmed that teacher competence and encouragement are related to the value students place on their academic work.[7] The more support a student receives from a teacher, the more he wants to work.

Academic difficulties are high-stress factors with inner-city male students. School stress makes the boys' school success even more improbable, causing a Catch-22 situation. (Academic difficulties cause more stress and more stress causes more difficulties.) No wonder these boys drop out.

Middle-school expert James Garvin tells of visiting shopping mall arcades and observing early-adolescent boys' absorption and skill in playing the video machines.[8] In one mall, he tracked down the ten top winners (their names are recorded on the machines) and found that nine of the ten were boys and eight of them were "at risk" students. These boys were able to "read directions, to act quickly, make split-second judgements and anticipate future encounters," but could not or did not want to transfer those skills to a classroom. What a waste—an obvious mismatch with a passive classroom setting.

Adolescent boys care about their schoolwork, but they need opportunities to move around with interesting projects, to be heard and have an impact. The right educational philosophy combined with teachers keen on motivational techniques and knowledgeable about adolescent development will reduce the possibility of poor performance and loss of motivation. School leadership, made up of administration and local school boards, has to set the pace and use the suggestions of the Carnegie task force for a small student-teacher ratio, a classroom structure that encourages discussion, group work, and student problem solving, and an assumption that all students can achieve.

An outstanding and innovative inner-city educator described a respected colleague to me this way: "Every thug in the area knows him because all you had to do was call him up and tell him you have a kid with a problem and he'd say, 'Send him over.' The staff wanted the school to be the Bronx High School of Science [an award-winning school] and didn't particularly want these kids. And we said to them, 'You know what? Treat these kids like they *are* in the Bronx High School of Science and they will live up to that expectation.' Quite frankly, that's what happens because we believe very strongly that *how you treat people is how they will behave—it's not how they behave is how you treat them.* It is a very humanistic approach to how kids should be educated."

"When I went to a big school, I hated the teachers," a boy in an alternative school told me. "Here, I have real rapport with my teachers. I'm really close to them." His attitude and his grades reflected his feelings. Rapport is possible in a large school—with a lot of creative ideas and hard work.

Mother-School Cooperation

A successful home-school partnership relies on two-way communication between school and home. A mother wrote in a parent newsletter that she always thought that the teachers knew best and was surprised when her son's teacher called and asked her to participate in a process called "parent review." In this type of assessment, a mother or father presents a picture of the whole boy by telling the teacher about his hobbies, musical tastes, study habits, and family situation. Together they discuss how to improve a son's study skills—before he gets into trouble and his mother has to see his teacher.

Authoritative parents (parents who are highly demanding and highly responsive) are involved with their children's schools. In nine high schools in Wisconsin and California, children of authoritative parents performed better academically than students from nonauthoritative homes.[9] Not a surprising result (see Chapter 5), but this same study pointed to the importance of parental school involvement, even during high-school years. These parents knew what was happening in their sons' schools, attended functions, guided their sons in their choice of courses, and helped them with homework, if necessary.

Many mothers shy away from middle-school or high-school activities because they think their sons will be embarrassed if they show up. The younger sons may be, but mothers should ignore their sons' chagrin and go anyway. An older son will appreciate his mother's involvement. Since research shows a definite link between a mother's dedication and a son's school grades, mothers should grab opportunities for school involvement.

Some mothers expect too much from schools. One mother told me that she had asked her son's guidance counselor in a large high school to call her if he showed signs of slipping in his grades and was furious when his report card arrived. He had received a D in a class. A counselor in a big school struggles to keep track of at-risk students and is not notified of every decline in grades. A mother must keep track of her own son if she is concerned about his grades. She should be aware of the amount of time he spends studying and inquire about test schedules. To expect a counselor to know what is happening with one hundred to two hundred (or more) students is unreasonable. A direct inquiry to the teacher of a specific subject that troubles a son may be more productive. If a school adopts the adviser-advisee system I described earlier in this chapter, then a mother would realize when her son is not working. But until that happens she and her son—not his counselor—are responsible for knowing his academic progress.

Learning Disabilities

"Don't call them disabilities," one speaker on the learning disabled told me, "call them learning differences." Although adolescents exaggerate any flaws and don't want to be singled out as "disabled," some differences are bona fide disabilities and need to be recognized early. The earlier a son faces his disabilities, the quicker he can be taught to compensate for them and avoid potentially serious problems. Students with learning disabilities encounter increased difficulties when they reach adolescence and receive more demanding class and homework assignments.

"My son dropped out of school," a mother revealed. "He was placed in a special-education class and because of his macho image, he wouldn't go." He rebelled at the thought of attending a special class that would separate him from his friends and draw attention to his inadequacies. His macho image remained intact on the street.

Some schools maintain learning-disabled students in regular classrooms and provide special sessions in a designated "resource room." Although even this distinction may be embarrassing to some boys, they need that special tutoring. Boys should be reassured that requiring extra help does not mean they are dumb. Most learning-disabled children have average to above-average intelligence.

A mother should work with a counselor to obtain the best placement—in a classroom or a special-ed room. One mother told me she would not let her son be placed in a special class and insisted that he be mainstreamed. Last I heard he was hanging out in his suburban streets because the mainstream classes were incomprehensible.

The National Center for Learning Disabilities estimates that between 10 to 15 percent of the population has some form of learning disability (commonly referred to as LD).[10] Although people with slight disabilities (spelling problems, for instance) may never need special attention, more severe deficits often surface in middle or late elementary school grades. By the time a boy enters middle school, his learning disability usually has been diagnosed. If, however, he has charmed his way through elementary school, he will crash on reaching the more impersonal, abstract halls of middle school.

Research generally shows that most LD children are boys, a ratio of four boys to one girl. However, new studies are suggesting that the problem may be more widespread among girls than previously thought.[11] Because girls tend to adapt to a school's "Sit and remain quiet" standards, they rarely attract attention and therefore remain undiagnosed. Boys usually are sent to be tested when they act out their classroom frustrations.

A school that is motivated to help its LD students allows teachers to test knowledge in less traditional ways. Depending on the disability involved, a teacher may permit untimed tests, extended deadlines, and taped reports. Many LD students listen to books on tape, a surefire method of comprehending a reading assignment. Often they lack organizational skills and need constant reassurance, along with tutors and resource rooms, in order to succeed. Their learning difference has nothing to do with intellectual aptitude. Boys are happy to discover that Albert Einstein was learning disabled, as was Governor Nelson Rockefeller (and Tom Cruise).

If a mother suspects that her son's dismal school performance is due to a learning disability, she should talk to his counselor about having him tested. Many deficits fall under the LD umbrella and a son's specific problem can be helped with focused tutoring.

Some teachers recommend that parents and adolescents play board games that reward ordering sequences to develop his organizational skills. Since most homes do not have personal computers, a son should be urged to use the school's computers, especially word-processing and spell-check programs. Many computer educational games explain complex concepts with graphics rather than words. A son should use every tool possible to boost his self-confidence and improve his skills.

An LD adolescent can achieve a productive school experience if his teachers and parents remain actively involved in fitting his education to his aptitudes and skills.

Attention-Deficit Disorder

Another learning handicap that is related but very distinct from learning disabilities is Attention-Deficit Disorder (ADD). Because its symptoms read somewhat like normal adolescence, it is more difficult to diagnose. The criteria of hyperactivity, distractibility, and/or impulsivity must show at least eight of the following "disturbances" for a duration of at least six months: fidgeting, squirming in his seat, being easily distracted, giving answers to questions before they are completed, talking excessively, interrupting others, appearing not to listen, losing things, engaging in physically dangerous activities without considering the possible consequences, plus difficulty in remaining seated, waiting turn, following instructions, sustaining attention in tasks, shifting from one uncomplicated task to another, or playing quietly.[12]

This behavior, defined by the American Psychiatric Association, must be inappropriate for the boy's age and interfere with his daily functioning if it is to be diagnosed as Attention-Deficit Disorder. Because many of these "disturbances" in a mild form are normal for early adolescents as they try to coordinate their growing minds and bodies, mothers can be confused. The symptoms also could indicate drug use in some adolescents, so an accurate diagnosis is not easy.

The bottom line is to know a son and his patterns. If the type of behavior listed above has persisted since childhood, it is more likely to be attention-deficit. If it arises during adolescence, it may be absolutely normal temporary behavior or may indicate some drug use. The boy's entire temperament and usual disposition must be taken into account. If a mother suspects Attention-Deficit Disorder, she should seek professional help. But she should be aware, too, that there are no universally agreed-upon criteria for the diagnosis or treatment of Attention-Deficit Disorder. Some have claimed that medication, frequently used to treat ADD children, is helpful. But side effects do occur and parents must be wary before placing a child on long-term drug therapy.

Trouble Schools, Trouble Students, Good Solutions

Children of poverty study in dilapidated, dirty, undersupplied, and overcrowded facilities while wealthy children a few miles away receive the best education our country can offer, a reality powerfully described in Jonathan Kozol's book *Savage Inequalities*. The problem of unequal education in the land of equal opportunity diminishes the possibility of each generation's rising above the previous one and makes those who assert that Americans live in a child-oriented culture look ridiculous.

Every adolescent, each child, regardless of his parents' income, deserves the same high standard of education found in affluent communities. If this problem is not solved, our nation faces the grim reality of becoming a two-tier society of haves and have-nots, a characterization usually associated with developing nations. Although deplorable, the situation is solvable and innovative educators are addressing it.

The Coalition of Essential Schools, established at Brown University in 1984, grew out of the findings of "A Study of High School," a five-year research project headed by Theodore Sizer. The coalition works with 125 schools throughout the country, turning unsuccessful schools and students into productive schools and graduating students.[13]

Administrators and teachers in Public School District 4, located in the East Harlem section of New York City, have developed an innovative school-choice system that is studied by educators from Europe and the United States. When I visited the district with two of the originators of the plan, Sy Fliegel and Colman Genn, the results of their creative thinking were evident in the fervor of the students and the enthusiasm of the teachers.[14]

The innovations are based on a belief that the chances of academic success are increased when parents, with their children's input, can choose the school they want their son or daughter to attend. Each sixth-grade parent in the sixteen elementary schools in the district must select a junior high school. Through a combination of orientation sessions, school visits, and printed information, a parent and student involve themselves with a preferred school from the beginning. If a parent cannot participate in the choice process, a teacher works with the student to make the right decision. The district has found, however, that parents care where their children go to school and participate willingly.

One administrator advises mothers when they move into the district to find out what schools and classes the children of the Parents' Association president are attending, and then say, "I'd like my kids in those classes." He says that a parent would not go wrong following the PTA or PTO president's choices. Good advice to all parents in any district.

Each intermediate junior high in District 4 has a clear, distinct vision of its mission. Some have unique curricula, stressing language, math, music, or science, and may be one of three or four mini-schools in a large building. A junior-high mini-school may occupy one floor or two floors, but maintains its own identity, name, and director. Because of the small size, teachers are acquainted with most of the students and every administrator and teacher is required to advise a small group of students (around ten). They often visit the homes of their advisees and are familiar with their extended families. By connecting so closely with a school, these families and teachers build a sense of community that can only benefit the children.

When a school curriculum is inadequate or the teachers seem apathetic, parents will not choose the school and it will close. Since the last large junior high school in the district was changed over to a mini-school configuration in the early nineties, it is too early to tell the true success of the choice reformation. However, students from the schools that were first involved in the choice system are performing well. In one of the two alternative high schools in the district, forty-eight of the fifty graduating seniors continued their education and forty-six of them are presently freshmen in college—an impressive record in any school, and particularly noteworthy in an economically depressed neighborhood.

And the parents count. The director of one school said, "The parents in this school are eighty-five percent African-American and Latino, and we have about one hundred percent participation at meetings when the parents come in to talk to the teachers about their kids. I don't know parents who are not interested in their kids. I know parents who are overwhelmed. I know parents who are in homes that are tough—that have too much dope in them—but I don't know parents who aren't interested in their kids. They're not interested in going to big meetings. Poor people are too smart to go to many meetings, but they will go and talk about their kids. I know eleven kids in this school very, very well [he is their adviser]. Some of their families are very poor, as poor as you could imagine, but they'll come and talk to me because they know their kids."

Belief in children, belief in parents: No wonder this school is succeeding. Hopefully, parents and schools in every community will take responsibility for educating adolescents so boys no longer will underachieve in such disturbing numbers. Communities of parents and teachers who demand success and provide opportunities for adolescents to master skills compatible with their abilities will be rewarded with boys who live up to adults' high and reasonable expectations.

Memos for Moms

1. Remember that many junior high or middle schools do not match an adolescent's energy and abilities. Be understanding with a son's school frustrations.
2. Believe in his ability to succeed in school.
3. Respect his individual capabilities, his unique developmental pace and learning style. He may not be a genius, but he does have talents that can be developed by confident parents and teachers.
4. Understand that adolescents have a strong desire to learn, although they may conceal it behind a mask of bravado because they fear failure.
5. Insist that he attend school, no discussion. It is his job for his adolescent years.
6. Talk with him about current events. Show him you are interested in increasing your knowledge so he will be more inclined to talk with you about his social studies, English, math, or science classes.
7. Encourage him to confer with his teacher if the assignments are vague, too difficult, or if he has questions about the class.
8. Help him with organizational skills. Often adolescent boys don't know how to get started or complete a project.
9. Let him arrange his bedroom or family space so it

becomes an office for learning—a big desk or table and no television.

10. Escort him to the local library so you both become familiar with its resources.

11. Find out the best teachers in your school and ask to have your son placed in those teachers' classes. If you have a choice of schools, ask about the best school and select it for your son.

12. Participate in school events, especially ones that affect a son directly. Talk to his teachers so they know you care and are monitoring his work.

13. If your son's performance is consistently lower than his ability, ask the school to have him tested. His learning problems may be related to a learning disability.

14. Become active in education issues at the local and national level. Work to make every school in every neighborhood as excellent as the best school in the country.

9

"Get Them into Something"

After-School Activities

Why He Drops Out of Organized Activities
Athletics • Coaches • The Downside of Athletics
Extracurricular School Activities
Outside School
Working During the School Year
Summer Jobs • Memos for Moms

When I asked a 16-year-old how mothers could help their adolescent sons, he immediately responded, "Get them into something, physical or mental. Something they can think about. Because when they're bored, they get into trouble."

His plea came from the heart. He knew from experience that teenage boys benefit from "physical or mental" activities—they need challenge and stimulation. I think this boy expressed clearly and urgently the desirability of after-school involvement. Some boys I interviewed filled every afternoon with activities while others chose to hang out—waiting for action.

Mothers always have realized the value of exercise and commitment for boys. In after-school programs, their sons meet other boys with shared interests and they develop a sense of belonging. They learn more about themselves and who they are and experience the satisfaction that comes from learning new skills.[1] Leisure-time involvement in early adolescence also can spark a life interest. Many adults still enjoy activities they discovered in junior high or high school. Mothers who realize these benefits often dedicate themselves to keeping a son totally occupied so his adolescent energy will not lead to trouble. Homework and sleep are all he can manage as he arrives home exhausted every evening.

An upbeat and wise inner-city mother told me her 13-year-old son belongs to a community track team and comes home worn out every night, "too tired to think." He does his homework and goes to bed. She won't let him hang around the neighborhood because drug dealers recruit children "as young as ten to work for them." She and her son visited every community center and school in the area until they found the one that offered after-school activities that they both liked.

For many families, the after-school hours cause real concern. Adolescents gather in empty homes or on unsupervised streets, and parents rightfully worry about what is going on during those hours. As the numbers of unsupervised adolescents increase, so do the statistics on early sexual activity and early-adolescent involvement in drug and alcohol use.[2] Most schools release students by three o'clock, and their energy level (which seemed to be in a state of collapse during the last class) springs into high gear and they are ready for fun. Where's the action?

Mothers desperately want their sons to remain safe and healthy through their junior-high and high-school years, but they can't chaperone them during every nonschool hour. They would like a son to develop interests, talents, and lifetime skills during his leisure time. While he is looking for action, his mother is praying for safety. Hopefully, mother and son will coordinate their search and arrive at activities exciting enough for him and satisfactory for both.

Why He Drops Out of Organized Activities

Little boys often get very excited about participating in organized leisure activities. Their mothers sign them up for sporting programs, playground camps, and arts and crafts instruction, and they participate willingly. But in early adolescence, many drop out and refuse to cooperate with Mother's suggestions.

Boys in an Arizona study listed several reasons for not joining an after-school activity or for dropping out of one: Their parents wouldn't let them join; they had no way to get there; they didn't have good enough skills (sports); or they didn't like the leader of the activities.[3]

If a son balks at signing up for activities, a mother should try to find out the reasons. If he has taken a dislike to the leader, she can encourage him to talk to the leader about their differences or she may have to seek out organizations that have leaders who are more attuned to young males. If he worries about his skill level, she could persuade him to talk to the coach about joining another division. Or a mother can find a more suitable team with a coach who is willing to teach her son the skills he needs in order to feel part of the group.

Although a mother may have good reasons not to want her son to participate in extracurricular activities, I think she has to remind herself of the positive side of involvement, even if it is inconvenient for her to take him (perhaps carpools or public transportation can substitute). A young person involved in after-school activities is more likely to take greater interest in school-work. When a boy feels comfortable and wanted in one area, he is more willing to participate in another.

There are not many negatives, if any, to a son's participation in after-school activities. Perhaps he could become so overly com-mitted that his grades would slip, but that seldom is the case. Usually, activities stimulate his energy level and the renewed vigor spills over to his studies. Benefits override the negatives. His taking part in activities with caring adults can offer him nothing but advantages. While there are many after-school clubs, organi-zations, and volunteer groups that search for participants, I want to focus on a few that seem to attract the most boys.

Athletics

Because my sons loved athletics from the time they were very young, I witnessed the great benefit of physical exercise on their young minds and bodies. One son told me I should devote a complete chapter to athletics because they meant so much to him during junior and senior high school. Sports dominated their after-school life, and through them my sons made lifelong friends and learned what it meant to be connected to a group, to cooperate with one another, to coordinate game plans and team movements. Among them they played soccer, baseball, basketball, lacrosse, football, rugby, and tennis, as well as skied, swam, and rock-climbed, and I am convinced these physical outlets helped them concentrate in their studies. My husband and I introduced them to some of those activities and their friends enlisted them in others, but their elementary school coaches encouraged them to try everything. So they did.

"If I didn't have sports, I don't think I'd do as well in school," one high-school boy said. "I'd get more lazy. I think if I just came home from school, I'd just watch TV and keep postponing doing homework. Now I get home from soccer at five-thirty and get to bed by ten."

A sport has helped this boy get organized, and the exhilaration of pushing himself physically has carried over to the classroom. Many countries, acknowledging the interrelationship of mind and body, direct their youth in both physical and mental education. We may puzzle at pictures of large groups of Chinese students practicing synchronized movement early in the morning, but the Asian cultures recognize movement as an integral part of education.

Many adolescents in a typical American middle school or high school avoid physical education classes because the classes discourage rather than inspire boys to play sports. Classes that pit one boy against another in embarrassing tests and competitive games or force a slow-maturing boy to change clothes in a communal locker room may deter a child from learning physical skills. The average adolescent boy likes vigorous movement, but participation can be frightening if he will be compared, tested, and graded. Boys who think they will not fare well soon lose their desire to participate in any sport. Boys can relate agonizing stories of being made fun of, of not being picked for a team, of being undersized and embarrassed. No wonder many boys don't want to participate in sports when they reach puberty. They can be made to feel inadequate.

Parents can make the same mistakes as coaches. If parents push a son into sports before he is ready, they will set him up for failure. A boy must possess a certain amount of coordination before he can kick, catch, or throw a ball, maneuver on ice skates, or balance on a bike. And the weather can make a difference. Parents, for instance, who try to get their children on ice skates in subzero temperatures soon find out that their sons learn much quicker when the thermometer is up in the twenties.

Since each child develops uniquely, mothers and fathers should be patient and introduce games when a son can be successful. If he fails in an athletic activity and disappoints himself and his parents, he may be reluctant to try again. Success, even in small doses, is the best preparation for the next step in learning.

Physical education programs designed around an adolescent's need to feel good about himself are being introduced into many middle-school curricula. These newer-thinking phys ed instructors teach cooperative as well as competitive games, instruct the students in individual athletic skills as well as team sports, demonstrate the advantages of physical health and mental strength, and stress the noncompetitive benefits of exercise.

Fortunate students at San Rafael High School in California can choose from forty-two activities for physical education credit, many of them untraditional. Their life-skill sports include t'ai chi ch'uan, body conditioning, yoga, scuba diving, and rock climb-ing.[4] Many boys who claimed they did not like athletics have loved these alternative sports. All physical education classes are coed, so boys and girls are not stigmatized for choosing classes that used to considered only "male" or "female." Most nontraditional athletics demand concentration, risk-taking, and stress manage-ment (as in rock climbing), so the students are learning both practical and athletic skills at the same time.

The exhilarating feeling of accomplishing a physical feat or feeling at one with mind and body through exercise is beautifully described in a book by George Leonard, *The Ultimate Athlete*.

"The athlete that dwells in each of us is more than an abstract ideal," Leonard writes. "It is a living presence that can change the way we feel and live. . . . We can learn to experience our bodies as models of the environment, the world, the universe, as aids to the highest philosophical speculation. Athletics can return to their rightful place of honor in the arts and humanities."[5] Leonard, a traditional athlete in his youth, took up the Japanese defensive martial art called aikido as an adult and discovered an almost spiritual connection in performing the art. The ultimate athlete, Leonard says, experiences mental and spiritual uplifting from total commitment to the mastery of a physical sport.

Traditional athletes also can feel this same unity of mind and spirit as they race to a finish line, execute a beautiful pass, connect to a well-thrown curve ball, arch a basketball into a net, skate with abandon toward a goal, extend the arms for the last lap, or feel the beautiful rhythm of body, skis, and snow.

Many team sports offer solid overall development for an ado-lescent boy, combining action and camaraderie. Many parents agree that soccer seems to be the best sport for young athletes and it is increasing in popularity in the United States. Soccer, called football by Europeans, requires speed, skill, and coordination. "I enjoy the competition," a soccer player said, "the physicalness of it, staying in shape, and lots of practice."

High-school team sports like basketball, baseball, tennis, swimming, lacrosse, rugby, volleyball, gymnastics, and track provide all the necessary ingredients of camaraderie, skill, and commitment and are less malicious than football and hockey, two sports that more and more recently seem to be fostering aggression rather than skill. Because all varsity sports have a limited number of spaces, intramural programs should be supported by schools and parent groups. Then all boys could join a school or class team and savor the camaraderie and competition of good, clean athletics.

Many boys have found a challenge in bicycling, a sport available in any community. With the advent of helmets (an absolute for any rider) and better bikes, bicycling is now a relatively safe sport. A boy who races bikes told me that his daily training has kept him away from "drinking and smoking pot." Any mother would agree that exchanging pot and alcohol for bicycling is a great trade-off.

Running has been shown to improve one's overall physical and psychological health. All a boy needs is a good pair of shoes (a reflective vest if he runs at night) and he can practice anywhere— a most democratic sport. Track teams always seem to need long-distance runners, or a boy can just run by himself without a team and enjoy the sport.

Boys also should be encouraged to participate in and organize their own pickup games. "When I'm bored," one boy said, "I just call a bunch of guys and go outside and play sports." Passionate, intense basketball and handball games can be observed in empty spaces throughout towns and cities. Schools in some communities are keeping their gyms open after school for neighborhood basketball, and at least one school has introduced midnight basketball during the summer, keeping adolescents off the street and in the gym from ten at night until 2 A.M.

My discomfort with football as a sport for adolescents was somewhat mollified by Andrew Malcolm, a *New York Times* journalist who gave me an insight into his love of football when he wrote ecstatically about his high-school football career.

At the end of my first season we turned in our equipment and along with it went my enthusiasm for pretty much everything. . . . Without football there was no joy, no light. All was gray. Without football, there was no belonging to the other guys and the delightfully grueling routine of practices, the intense uncertainties of such legalized combat, and the emotional highs of the games. Those emotions, even the low ones, were addictive. So were the silent personal vows to do better next week. The chance to start over every few days, only one step higher, or maybe just a half-step, or maybe even slide backwards and have to struggle back up and feel that warm sense of accomplishment in doing just that. . . . To me football was life. How could there be any higher achievement? Certainly there could be nothing else that touched so many parts of my being.[6]

In spite of Malcolm's praises of football (which he played in spite of his small size), I personally don't think the pleasures of that contact sport are worth the risks. A mother's worst fears of a son's getting hurt could be realized on a football field. My sons played football in elementary and middle school and one continued playing in high school, but I still shudder when I watch boys playing football. A boy's body can be destroyed, not built up, during a high-school or college football career.

If a son (or mother or father) insists that he play football, he must use the best equipment available to protect his head, kidneys, and back. Parents must demand that the coach stress safety at all times, and that the league require safe football gear, warm-up drills, drinking water, and a trainer within reach. The boys must be trained to optimal condition so their spines, legs, and knees are protected from serious injury.

Both football and hockey exhibit the most sport violence because of the nature of the contact and the constant violation of the rules. Hockey used to be appreciated as a game of skill and coordination, but now the cameras focus on fights in the professional games and the fans react with enthusiasm. The beauty of skating with incredible speed and the deft controlling of a hockey puck is being overshadowed by fights and rule violations. And the violence is trickling down to the high-school hockey rink.

A boy who plays hockey defended his choice: "I think I chose a great sport. Hockey is the fastest game around. People like controlled violence like hockey. You know, they like to watch it." And he was providing the entertainment.

"Yeah," agreed another boy. "When you're mad you can let it all hang out in hockey." Yet another boy looked at hockey differently. "I look at it as a skill," he said, "and always play it as a sport. I don't take out my frustrations on someone on the ice. I don't think that is right." His sincerity and enthusiasm impressed me and I hope his attitude spreads to his teammates.

Boys can communicate quite eloquently about their sports lives. One boy described rugby, a game making its way into high-school sports in the Northeast: "I love it. I used to play other sports, but I didn't have as much fun. I love rugby. I love playing the game. I enjoy it. There's a physical part, but there's a gentlemen's quality to it. It's a great game. There's a handshake at the end and the players don't talk about it, not like other sports where someone will talk about taking someone out or hurting him. In rugby there's never a thought of hurting another player. They get hurt from the physical aspect, but it's not intentional." What wonderful enthusiasm from a 16-year-old who can use the word *love* so frequently and with such fervor.

I first watched rugby when my youngest son discovered the sport. He came off the field elated, beaming broadly, with blood running down his face. He felt the same excitement and thrill as the boy I interviewed. I thought the game was violent, but as he and his teammates became more skilled, I came to appreciate the harmony of a line of young men moving together down the field and the "gentlemanliness" of the sport. I admit that their compatibility was not my first impression of the game and initially agreed with the mother of the boy above who "is afraid he'll kill himself."

Every boy can find the athlete within him. He can feel a natural emotional high as well as physical exhaustion when he performs well or pushes himself in a daily practice. He doesn't have to participate in team sports to experience that high, but if he does choose a team, a good coach can become a major influence in his life.

Coaches

Good coaches are the key to organized adolescent athletics. Effective ones know how to motivate boys, teach teamwork, and inculcate a unifying team spirit. "I knew these men really cared," Andrew Malcolm writes about his high-school coaches, "that they saw secret things in me that I did not discern, that they knew the secrets of unlocking the full joys of football (or any sport) within me. If only I worked hard enough."[7]

Unfortunately, some unenlightened coaches still advocate a "kill the enemy" mentality, substituting vengeance for team spirit. I will never forget the community football coach who gave my 12-year-old son and his teammates pieces of the opponent's jersey to chew while they yelled out the opponent's name. This coach taught aggression, not skill. I don't want to imply that winning is not good, but I do believe that coaches of the young must emphasize skill and movement. If a game is well played by boys who love their coach, work hard, and are respected by him, they probably will win. If they don't win, they will know they played the best they could and the coach will be proud of them. A brute mentality does not have to become part of the game.

Many fathers devote their weekends to coaching their sons' teams. "I played ten different sports and my dad was coach for all of them," one boy reported. This boy believed strongly that everyone should play a sport. When I asked him what if a boy didn't like to play, he said, "I wouldn't force him to play, but I'd have him try out when he's younger. I think I'd make him play until middle school and after that the decision would be his."

A study from the University of Washington found that boys in a Little League baseball program (average age: 11) responded most positively to coaches who were reinforcing and encouraging and instructed them the most. The boys reacted negatively to coaches who did not encourage or instruct them.[8] This finding was especially true among children with low self-esteem. A coach who praises his charges, pats them on the back, gives reassurance after mistakes, and continually instructs them is a valued member of any community.

I watched with horror one day as the coach of a Little League team ranted and raved on the sidelines, yelling at his players as they tried their best. Halfway through the game this coach suffered a heart attack, and later he died in the hospital—a tragic ending to a children's afternoon. I would be surprised if he had instilled a love of baseball in any of his players.

Parents also need lessons when their sons or daughters are playing sports. Some push their children rather than encourage them, clocking them with stopwatches, yelling at them when they drop a ball, or becoming impatient when they are teaching them a skill.

Other mothers and fathers get so carried away by the spirit of a game that they join in wholeheartedly. My oldest son told me once that I embarrassed him by cheering too loudly at his high-school basketball game. From then on, I rooted for all my children with more restraint.

Mothers and sons can forge a common bond through sports. He can show her the intricacies of planning and executing teamwork, and she can enthusiastically endorse his absorption in athletics. Unfortunately, some sports have shifted from the mission of training young men for a productive adult life to providing an outlet for aggression.

The Downside of Athletics

"I enjoy going out and not having to hold back my aggressions. I just go and hit someone and I like to see him hurt. I don't know, it feels good for some reason." This statement from a hockey player, a senior in high school, can send chills through any mother. Hostile aggression is the downside of athletics.

A boy who takes out his frustrations by hurting someone on a playing field or ice rink is not releasing anger in a healthy way. And if a coach congratulates him after a fellow student is "taken out," the boy is learning that aggression and anger get rewarded. Being a nice guy doesn't earn credits from some coaches. "Nice guys finish last," said former Dodgers manager Leo Durocher. And some boys still pick up that message from their coaches.

The nightmare of many mothers is that this aggression will be carried over to adulthood and jeopardize a son's home life. Coaches and organized leagues must put an end to this intentional violence and institute regulations to ensure the safety of all players. Skill and energy, not aggression, are the traits that should be associated with athletics.

Myriam Miedzian, in her excellent book, *Boys Will Be Boys: Breaking the Link Between Masculinity and Violence*, suggests regulations that would move youth sports away from "current violence-oriented direction."[9]

All coaches should be trained in child development and physiology, Miedzian says. Certified trainers should be present at all times and not allow any injured player to participate. If a boy deliberately tries to "take out" another player, he should be removed from the game and his coach should be suspended if he encourages that behavior. Violent language should be prohibited, handshakes encouraged, and no monetary gifts allowed for a boy or his parents. Miedzian also recommends that parents be required to attend a meeting at which possible injuries and risks to their sons will be discussed and permission slips signed. As the boys reach older grades, they must maintain a C grade-point average in order to play, and they shouldn't be allowed to repeat a grade to enhance their physical size. High-school athletic events should not be televised because televising the games "intensifies the already fierce emphasis on competitiveness and introduces all the problems of college sports at a high school level."[10] These excellent recommendations would curtail the dangers of adolescent athletics.

Another growing concern of mothers is the use of drugs among top athletes. Boys I interviewed spoke openly about drug and alcohol use by athletes, habits that previously would not have been tolerated by coaches. A coach who kicks a boy off a team for drinking or drug taking should be commended. One action like that could halt the use of drugs by other team members. Boys need to know that a well-trained body does not need drugs to enhance its performance. A drug-induced athlete may attain a high but will eventually crash, his brain along with his body.

Besides the usual suspects (pot, cocaine, alcohol), steroids are increasingly finding their way into the young athlete's locker. The majority of steroid users are between the ages of 16 and 24. High-school athletes buy them on the black market to increase their muscle mass, in megadoses up to one thousand times higher than a regular prescription dose. "The user begins to think he's omnipotent and becomes very egocentric," explained one hospital official. "He becomes very selfish and into himself and he suffers a complete altered body state where his body and personality have changed so much that he's not the person he used to be."[11]

Such a boy was pointed out to me by a high-school teacher who said he was sure the student suffered from "roids rage," the term coined to describe the uncontrollable anger caused by steroids. When a boy takes these drugs, his weight and aggression increase and so do his injuries. Because steroids impair his immune system, injuries and infections take longer to heal. A number of other signs can clue coaches and parents into an athlete's use of steroids. Besides rage, his time perception is impaired and he is constantly late, misses practices and meals, stays up late, and sleeps at inappropriate times. He exhibits diminished motivation, as well as lack of hustle or performance on the playing field, and his hygiene and appearance deteriorate. His respiratory tract becomes inflamed, causing recurrent colds, flus, and a constantly runny nose. He suffers frequent injuries that do not heal normally, and his mood swings are extreme. Boys also can experience infertility, low sperm count, impotence, testicular shrinkage, baldness, high-pitched voice, and enlarged breasts. In addition, there are even more serious health risks that could lead to strokes or coronary disease. The steroid habit is very difficult to stop and the effects are sometimes irreversible.

Coaches must let players know that steroids absolutely will not be tolerated. Doctors and parents should expect that boys will be dismissed from a team if they take steroids, even under the guise of vitamins. Steroids are not vitamins, they are dangerous drugs.

Drugs are not the only temptation for young athletes. Sex can also be a problem, for many boys think their exalted status as athletes entitles them to it. Athletes recently have been involved in a number of sexual assault cases, which I will discuss in more detail in Chapter 10.[12] Parents and coaches must unequivocally tell players that they have to respect girls, even if the girls have pursued them. Any rumors should be immediately investigated and the boys kicked off the team if evidence links them with sex and violence. The California athletes who kept score of their sexual partners used sports terminology to describe their conquests (many, perhaps most of which were forced). These boys were defended by their fathers and greeted as heroes by other students when they returned to their high-school campus—a sad commentary on high-school athletics.

Sports should be returned to its rightful place in the development of young men, to strengthen their minds, spirits, and bodies. As one boy told me, "It's just as important as school itself. I need to play."

Extracurricular School Activities

A study of adult men and women found that "those who had actively participated in their schools' extracurricular activities fulfilled their primary adult roles successfully and were generally mature."[13] On that basis alone, mothers have reason to encourage their sons to pursue after-school interests—both in school and outside of school.

Adolescents can aspire to change the world, and school clubs can provide outlets for their missionary zeal. Tapping into the idealism of adolescents can be a rewarding and taxing venture for parents. A son who joins an environmental group may decide that his mother needs reforming, that she must recycle, not use dangerous chemicals in cleaning, watch her shopping habits, and donate to his chosen causes. Our family car frequently sported bumper stickers advocating our children's philosophies. We usually agreed with the messages (I particularly liked the LOVE YOUR MOTHER bumper sticker, despite the fact that it referred to Mother Earth, not to me), and if we didn't agree, we received strong counsel about the significance of their crusade.

Many school clubs support worthwhile projects and prepare young people for adult involvement. Students often plan their own agendas, raise money, and learn to articulate the needs of their group. Some clubs are organized around a common thread, a shared interest in a game like chess, for example, or a lively concern with Third World hunger. Some schools encourage students to form their own clubs. A student first must find fellow students with similar interests and then persuade a teacher to sponsor the organization. When a good match between students and sponsor occurs, both benefit.

An example of lively student-teacher affiliation occurred in the inner city of New York when a teacher sponsored and coached such an exciting chess club that the students were invited to play in Russia. At first the Russian players were taken back by the unorthodox "street-smart" chess moves of the American players, but as the matches continued, each side grew to appreciate the other's strategies. The teacher had managed to inspire his students, make it "cool" to play chess, and attract funding for the trip, an experience neither side will ever forget.

Music and drama departments probably offer the most after-school activities (after the athletic department). I'm sure many a band director cherishes the pictures of President Clinton playing a saxophone, a winning combination of leadership and music. If a son shows any interest in a musical instrument, mothers usually are grateful—even if they don't understand the music itself. The camaraderie fostered in a musical group, be it an orchestra, band, string quartet, or rock group, is enviable to nonplayers. Certainly, adolescents and adults marvel when a friend can sit down at a piano, pick up a guitar (or sax), and add a special ingredient to an evening.

A group of mothers I interviewed complained about their ninth-grade sons' absolute devotion to their fledgling rock group, which had grown out of the school band. The mothers had to drive them to one another's houses for practice, the noise level was unbelievable, and they worried that the music was distracting their sons from academics. But when I asked them what else they would like to see their sons doing, they admitted they were very happy that the boys at least were occupied after school.

At the same time, though, I sensed these mothers feared their sons would abandon all for the sake of music. Most boys want to create music with friends for only a short period of time—during their high-school years—and mothers don't have to worry. If he thinks he is talented enough to pursue music full-time after graduation or during college, he should elicit opinions from talented musicians in his own area of music. Their honest assessments may confirm his talents and help him establish a career path, or help him decide to concentrate on his studies and play music as a hobby.

Drama also provides wonderful creative outlets for adolescent sons. Boys who participate in school plays have such a good time and often form strong bonds with their peers onstage. A boy who is shy can come alive behind the footlights. Even if he doesn't want to act, he can help with theater management, lighting, set design, publicity, ticketing, ushering, and the many other jobs needed to prepare a production for opening night. Backstage can offer just as much fun as center stage.

Outside School

After-school activities don't have to be confined to organizations sponsored by schools. Peterson's Guides has published a handbook, *150 Ways Teens Can Make a Difference*, an excellent guide to volunteer work, offering step-by-step instructions to adolescents who would like to make a difference in their communities. The manual lists sixteen categories with a hundred fifty organizations that welcome adolescent volunteers.[14]

A boy who took a leadership role in a community teen center told me he learned a valuable lesson from that experience—that it is not easy to run things. "You don't know the effort until you do it yourself." He said he liked the people he met and now appreciates the real meaning of skillful administration.

The Boy Scouts continue to offer leadership training to boys. An organization called ScoutReach is dedicated to offering a "traditional Scouting program to nontraditional Scouts." Boys who come from neighborhoods usually not associated with scouting are meeting with specially trained leaders who present them with alternatives to hanging out on street corners. Even though tying a knot or setting up a campsite may seem like strange crafts to teach an inner-city boy, this exposure to life outside his immediate neighborhood helps him develop self-confidence and coping skills.[15]

Camping, hiking, and canoe trips sponsored by youth groups also teach students outdoor skills that they can enjoy the rest of their lives. These outdoor activities don't have to be initiated by organizations, however. Parents willing to suffer a few bruised ankles or sleep on hard ground can qualify as good companions. Fathers and mothers who canoe or hike with their sons (or daughters) can establish a deep bond as they share the beauty of a sunset or the challenge of hiking up a steep path. My sons and daughters always liked that special time with their father, and I respected their time alone with him.

One boy told me about his approaching Eagle Scout status, the highest ranking in Boy Scouts. His grandfather had been an Eagle Scout, but his father, he said, "had dropped out, but he likes the idea I'm becoming one. He tried camping once but didn't like it." Like many active boys, this boy enjoyed many activities but liked driving off-road with his father most of all—a special time.

Parents also can look to churches and synagogues for year-round youth activities for adolescents. Some of the most successful of these groups participate in fieldwork, offering services to soup kitchens, construction help for poor families, or distribution of food or clothes to the needy. One group of suburban high-school students makes regular trips to New York's Central Park to distribute blankets and clothes to the homeless.

A mother and son may have to do a little research to come up with the after-school activity or project he likes, but, hopefully, the results will be worth the effort.

Working During the School Year

The issue of a son's working during the school year is so complex that serious researchers now are addressing it. Whereas boys and girls used to work primarily to supplement the family income, now they tend to quickly spend their wages on consumer items for themselves.[16] And the jobs they hold usually are low-wage, not directly offering career opportunities. Many boys I spoke with were working and saving to buy a car, not exactly a small-ticket item. They liked having money in their pockets and a feeling of independence. But is working after school helping their adolescent development or grade-point average?

The answer seems to be "Not necessarily." The number of hours, type of work, and parental standards determine the outcome. A study that looked at the relationship between adolescent development and the part-time employment of four thousand adolescents did not extol the positive side of working after school. "Compared with their classmates who do not work or who work only a few hours each week, students who work longer hours report diminished engagement in schooling, lowered school performance, increased psychological distress and somatic [physical] complaints, higher rates of drug and alcohol use, higher rates of delinquency, and greater autonomy from parental control. The deleterious correlates of employment increase as a direct function of the number of hours worked each week."[17]

No mother would want that outcome for a son or daughter, but many adolescents are badgering their mothers for permission to work. If a son insists on working, mothers must set a few guidelines. First, he can work a maximum of ten to fifteen hours a week. That amount of work time may have a beneficial effect, according to some research, especially if he is working in a job that calls for some input from him or is training him for an after-graduation job. Second, the agreement should be that if his grades drop and he is not fulfilling his main obligation of schoolwork, he has to quit the job.

Some teachers and counselors see an improvement in a student's classwork if they are employed in a job that is training them for future work. A boy working part-time for an electrician or a boy who likes computers and works part-time repairing them may choose these fields as careers. Vocational development is an admirable goal for schools and students. When a school emphasizes a work-study program and actively seeks companies that will take on students as apprentices for pay, the students do benefit. But most jobs are in the fast-food or retail industry, and most adolescents are working for pocket money, not to build careers.

If a son works less than fifteen hours a week (ten hours seems to be the "breaking point") and his grades are not affected, still other considerations must be taken into account. The environment of the workplace and the influence of his fellow workers can affect his overall sense of well-being. If his boss puts undue stress on him, if he is exposed to harsh working conditions, or if his workmates make fun of him or ridicule any ambitions he may have, the work experience may turn him off to work in general.

Or a boy may discover he never wants to work at a certain job again, if he has the choice. My son worked as a busboy during one semester to pay for the damage he inflicted on the family car. He quit as soon as the cost was covered and was determined not to work in a similar situation the following summer.

All these issues should be discussed with a son and the pluses and minuses of a job fully explored. In some communities, those with shopping malls in particular, teenage workers can find ample opportunities for employment. But will the costs outweigh the benefits? Families must come to their own decisions after consulting with their son's school adviser and, again, bearing in mind that ten to fifteen hours should be the maximum number of hours allowed for work.

Summer Jobs

Summer employment does not interfere with a son's primary responsibility of school, and he will benefit from being occupied during the long summer days. His summer work, ideally, should provide an opportunity to learn new skills, but these jobs are not readily available. Just the process of applying for a summer job, filling out applications, and facing the possibility of being rejected is a learning experience. Many employment opportunities exist but have to be sought out. Persistence, constant telephoning, and consulting with friends may be necessary before a job is located.

Boys often form their own summer businesses: painting, lawn maintenance, tutoring, driving children, or starting a day camp for children of working mothers. If a family does not need the income, volunteer organizations offer opportunities to serve others in the community. Summertime should not be a time of complete relaxation. Adolescent boys need activity.

"Get them into something," the admonition of one boy I interviewed, was good advice. Mothers can encourage their sons' interests and talents in many ways, but the quest requires cooperation, with both of them discussing his hopes and ideas and matching them with the school and community's resources. The efforts of mother and son will pay off with the added assurance of a son's safe passage through adolescence.

Memos for Moms

1. Realize the educational, psychological, and physical benefits of after-school activities.
2. Help your son find an activity he likes and help him arrange transportation if he does not drive.
3. Work with him to accommodate his fears of joining organized activities. Discuss the reasons he will not join.
4. Encourage his participation in some physical activity or sport that will offer challenge and develop his skills. He will benefit from physical exercise.
5. Help your son discover the athlete within by researching with him a physical activity he will enjoy. Many

great athletic opportunities exist beyond the school playing field.

6. Insist on all safety measures if a son plays in a risky contact sport like football or hockey.

7. Be aware of drug and alcohol use by high-school athletes. Know the signs of steroid use.

8. Remind sons that all males have an obligation to respect girls and women, that being a high-school athlete does not excuse them from responsible behavior.

9. Obtain lists of extracurricular school clubs and organizations so a son can decide which one appeals to him.

10. Find out what the community volunteer organizations offer for adolescent boys.

11. Help out when needed in his after-school activities.

12. Do not let him work at a paid job more than ten to fifteen hours a week during the school year.

13. Insist that he find a job or volunteer position during the summer months.

10

"I Only Have Sex with Virgins"

Sex and the Adolescent Boy

Sex in the Nineties • The Pressures
Girlfriends • Sex Without Feelings
What Parents Can Do • Topics to Discuss
The Hope • Memos for Moms

Be careful," was all a father could say when he finally talked with his 17-year-old son about the dangers of AIDS (Acquired Immune Deficiency Syndrome). "Don't worry, Dad," his son replied, "I only have sex with virgins." His father laughed heartily as he related his son's "clever" strategy to me. I did not share in his amusement.

His son, a senior in a prestigious prep school, sounded very much like an inner-city boy I interviewed, who told me, "I was going with a girl and she was a virgin so I didn't use a condom." If these two boys are typical of the American adolescent, and they are, parents urgently need to teach sons common sense, sexual responsibility, and the virtues of commitment and abstinence. And it won't be easy.

A double standard for boys and girls has existed for years, with mothers and fathers tolerating a son's sexual activity far more than a daughter's. A woman grinned as she told me, "My son has a notch in his lapel for every girl he's had." A mother would not smile about a daughter's behaving in a similar way. She would be heartbroken, concerned about her daughter's physical and psychological health, and seek advice.

However, with the advent of AIDS, the resurgence of other sexually transmitted diseases (STDs), the increase in date rape, and efforts of some states to hold boys responsible for pregnancy, parents are rethinking their relaxed attitude toward a son's sexual activity. Teenagers have never wanted to talk with their parents about sex, and most parents are reluctant to even mention sex to their children. I remember rehearsing different ways I would broach the subject to my sons, but I seldom accomplished my mission in the way I had envisioned. They could sense a discussion (or lecture) in the making and quickly distracted me or told me that they knew everything (which they didn't).

Today, in spite of the increasing rates of early teenage sexual intercourse, most parents still cannot bring themselves to speak directly to their sons. "My husband says he'll just learn, not to worry about it," one mother told me. Only one mother in a group of ten women who gathered to talk about adolescent boys had discussed sex with a son. Some had attempted to initiate conversations but quickly turned aside when their overtures were rejected.

"I tried, but he said he didn't want to talk about it," asserted one mother. "They learn in school," said another with a tone of relief. "It never occurred to me to talk to him," said a third. "I keep thinking that he's the boy and my husband's the man and they should talk to each other, but that doesn't work 'cause my husband's not comfortable." Then she laughed. "If it's football, yes, but if it's sex?"

Some women I interviewed were startled when I suggested that they, as well as their husbands, teach their sons about sex and become their sex educators. Ideally, both fathers and mothers would talk with their sons (not at one planned time, but continuously), discuss values, and teach the importance of respecting all women and girls. But in many homes fathers are unavailable or too uncomfortable to deal with sexual matters and must be convinced of the importance of their voices. If a father refuses, a mother must speak out herself or leave her son's instruction to friends, the street, and the media. Waiting for Dad to enter the picture may take too long and prove too costly.

Sex in the Nineties

Many parents mistakenly think that media attention to sexually transmitted diseases (for instance, the rapid escalation of AIDS) will change a son's behavior. Yet boys are initiating sex at earlier and earlier ages. Statistics vary as far as the exact percentages, but all reports agree that the steady increase in early sex has not abated. One national survey showed that by age 15, 16 percent of white males and 48 percent of black males have had intercourse. These numbers steadily climb, and by age 19, 76 percent of white males and 96 percent of black males will have had sex.[1]

Because the explosion of AIDS has been so frightening (63 percent rise in AIDS cases in the first two months of 1993 compared with the same period in 1992) and Magic Johnson's revelation of his HIV-positive status so distressing, mothers mistakenly believe their sons automatically will be less sexually active.[2] Yet as the percentage of adolescents who are engaging in sex rises, so do the numbers of boys exposed to the HIV virus. Between 25,000 and 35,000 high-school and college students tested positive for the HIV virus that causes this deadly disease. Moreover, these thousands of young people may represent only a small percentage of those who are carriers of the virus, since most students have not been tested.[3]

A mother's concern about her son's health and safety extends beyond AIDS to all sexually transmitted diseases. Herpes simplex persists as the most pervasive STD in the United States, with a half-million new cases showing up every year, endangering its victims' overall health. There is no known cure. The genital wart virus is rising in "epidemic" proportions among adolescents, and while it can go undetected in a boy, it is easily transmitted to his partner. If his female partner is under the age of 18, she is even more vulnerable to the virus that can cause precancerous lesions in her cervix. Chlamydia also is rising and can cause infertility.

The Centers for Disease Control warn that adolescents are putting themselves at greater risk for STDs and AIDS because of the increase in multiple sexual partners.

In spite of these facts, many sexually active boys are not protecting themselves or their partners during intercourse. Only 58 percent of adolescent boys, ages 15 to 19, reported using condoms alone or with other methods the last time they had sexual intercourse.[4] Although condoms do reduce the risk of pregnancy and STDs, the belief that they give the green light for "safe sex" is not grounded in reality, and boys have been deceived into believing contraception solves all problems. "Safer sex" is more accurate, given the fact that contraceptives can and do fail. The only risk-free sex is no sex, yet boys seldom think in terms of abstinence or postponement.

Many adolescent boys are fathers. In 1990, 68 percent of teen births were to unmarried mothers. Adolescent boys must take responsibility for nearly a third of those statistics. Not all of the births are to adolescent fathers, many of the fathers are older, but adolescents account for a substantial number (32.2 percent of the fathers whose age was reported on the birth certificate, but only 58 percent reported fathers' ages).[5]

A mother can be shocked into an action-alert when she reads about the multiple sexual partners reported by adolescent boys—an increasing trend in the nineties. In a study that examined males only, sexually active boys (ages 17 to 19) reported having an average of six sexual partners since their first intercourse.[6] For some boys this number is too low. Police in Lakewood, California, a suburban white middle-class community, uncovered a gang of boys who collected points for each girl they "did." One father defended the gang, saying they only were following the lead of "Wilt Chamberlain, who came out in his book and said he had twenty thousand women." One of the accused boys told reporters that he had learned all about sex in school, but no one had taught him how to "behave."[7]

A boy I interviewed recounted his brother's experience when

he went to college in California: "He said the girls out there start young, like thirteen. So if you think about it, when they're eighteen or nineteen they've had lots of partners and you have to be careful. He said that he had a girlfriend and he told her that he would not have sex with her until she had a test and he had one, too."

No wonder mothers can get discouraged about their sons' physical, psychological, and moral safety. A more common trend in high schools is "serial monogamy." Boys and girls pair off for a length of time, break up, and then pair off with another boy or girl. Even though the number of girls adds up, a boy does not consider himself promiscuous (as he would have in the past), but faithful— to the girl of the month, semester, or year. Although STDs spread quickly in such a multiple-partner atmosphere, this message does not seem to come across to adolescent boys or girls.

The statistics are frightening to parents and adults who work with youth. They can feel overwhelmed because in spite of their love and concern for a boy or girl, one sexual encounter can endanger the adolescent's health and many encounters with different partners escalate the odds. Yet when I asked a boy whom he talked with about sex, he gave a typical answer: "My friends, really. We have sex ed, but that's watching movies called *Are You Normal?* It's not really parents, either. You never really get told, it just sort of develops. You just sort of start thinking about it."

And when boys "just start thinking about it," wise mothers, attuned to the sexual trends of the nineties, will pick up on this and articulate their sexual and marital values.

The Pressures

American culture promotes youthful sexual intercourse. If adults want to guide the next generation safely into adulthood, that cultural message must be reversed and the sexual pressures reduced. Many influences are fostering this norm for early sexual involvement, including home influences.

Not only are few parents discussing values with their children, but many boys are led to believe that there is something wrong with them if they are not having sex. Even fathers can give the impression that sex is commonplace and normal for adolescent boys.

Some single fathers share sexual stories with their sons. "My dad talks to me about his sex life, not mine," one boy confided. "When he was single he used to talk to us more about it. He had girlfriends in their early twenties and he was in his forties. But now he is married and can't talk about it that much. Now that he's married, it's not a very exciting sex life, I'm sure."

One mother told me that her son's second-grade teacher called to tell her that she had better start talking about sex to her son. The teacher said her son was learning about sex from the second-grade boys who watched the Playboy Channel with their fathers. Parents have to remember that the nineties are not the sixties and the era of free love and permissiveness has ended. A father who cares about his son will advise caution, restraint, commitment, and values.

Fathers are not the only ones who think "boys will be boys." The mother who boasted about her son's notches in his lapel was giving a clear message to her son that it was okay for him to have sex. Some mothers I interviewed presumed that their sons would have sex during high school and seemed oblivious to the consequences. When no one tells a boy he shouldn't have sex, he interprets their silence as approval.

A boy's use of drugs and alcohol also can sway him to initiate sex at too young an age. A study of adults found that a high percentage of those who reported use of marijuana, alcohol, and/or cigarettes before the age of 16 also reported sexual experience before that time.[8] Being drunk or high fosters the adolescent's sense of invulnerability and dulls his natural vigilance so that he will do things that he might avoid in his sober moments.

Other factors in a boy's life can contribute to sexual risk-taking. Boys from intact two-parent homes were found to be less sexually active and older at the time of their first intercourse than boys from single-parent homes.[9] Because boys of single parents often receive less supervision, they can find more opportunities for sexual experiences. But single mothers who parent authoritatively with confidence in themselves and communicate constantly with their sons about sexual values can raise sons who are sexually astute.

Single mothers and single fathers who are dating confront an added dilemma. A divorced mother told me her two sons were furious when her male friend moved in under the pretense of just being a "friend." She still had not reconciled with her sons when I interviewed her. An adolescent boy who is sexually charged can be disturbed and angry at the invasion of his home by a lover. Mothers should be aware and sensitive to their sons' keen sexual antennae and keep their male friends away from the intimacy of a home bedroom. If an adolescent son assumes he can have sex because his single parent does, he should be reminded that adults possess mature minds and bodies and he does not. Sex is for grown-ups.

Music videos also contribute to early-adolescent intrigue with sexual experience. Mothers who watch music videos or listen to rock music with their sons are familiar with the message of sexual promiscuity and violence. Because I am not a regular viewer, I decided to watch a music channel (MTV) for a few afternoons and evenings to grasp the appeal to adolescents.

Much of the choreography, camera work, and settings was fascinating, displaying the vitality and talents of performers and directors. Although groups have legitimately complained about rock lyrics, I could not comprehend a lot of them (especially rap) and was relieved to read in a music review that most lyrics are not intended to be understood—that's part of the rock mystique. And I now appreciate how captivating and addictive music video can be.

At the same time, however, I felt sympathy with children who are constantly exposed to MTV—the sexual innuendos, the gripping, pulsating beats, and the male conqueror who thrusts his pelvis and grabs his crotch. Adolescents who constantly watch these videos (and many are in middle school) can think themselves inadequate in their own sexuality (who could be so tititlating, provocative, and sexy at all times?). They also are led to believe that being sexually seductive and abusive to women brings adulation. Through constant exposure, boys become immune to vulgarity and are more likely to imitate the performers (as researchers on violence in television found). Some videos provoke sexual images throughout and these are the ones that are most disturbing; others beautifully and subtly call attention to social problems; still others forcefully voice anger with city streets and police authority.

In a review of a concert by the rock star Prince, critic Jon Pareles wrote that he had gone "back to the bedroom" after attempting songs that had social relevance. "He has a cornucopia of songs that bump and grind," Jon Pareles writes, "sounds that whisper erotic endearments and songs that command listeners to party. . . . Unfortunately, he feels the need to talk tough and put down women."[10]

The word "unfortunately" does not convey the anger of many mothers (including myself) at the flagrant and offensive exploitation of women as sexual property in many music videos. This debasement must be recognized by sons and denounced by parents. A boy's knowledge of a girl comes from what he observes, and if he constantly sees females being put down and degraded, he begins to believe that they like that sort of treatment. If mothers enjoy MTV themselves, they must watch critically, thinking constantly about its effect on children and adolescents. A few mothers I interviewed refused to introduce cable television (that carries MTV) into their homes when their children were young. They were wise. Sex is for adults.

A Carnegie report on the influence of music in early adolescence concluded that when adolescents are exposed to music videos, their attitudes often change in the direction of what they have seen, read, or heard.[11] The music video industry, because of its appeal to adolescents, could make a strong positive impact in the lives of young people. Until that time, parents who know music's powerful effect on their children should make every effort to counteract its influence.

Television sitcoms that highlight teenage sex also set the "norm" for adolescent sexuality. Within a short period of time, teenage characters on "Roseanne," "Beverly Hills 90210," "True Colors," "Facts of Life," and "Growing Pains" lost their virginity. Even a TV critic for the *New York Times* felt compelled to comment on this sudden rise in teen sex on television: "There is a question of whether the social realities are being merely reflected or actually created by television," writes John J. O'Connor. "Peer pressure, the oft-heard explanation for the behavior of young people, is not concocted out of thin air. Certain airwaves are undoubtedly a contributing factor. . . . *A child is inevitably following through on the messages coming incessantly through the television into his own home* [emphasis mine] . . . and children are taking their cues from the multi-million-dollar image factories plucking recklessly at their daily lives."[12]

Experts in adolescent development agree. "The influence of the mass media in the sexual socialization of teenagers is of singular importance," writes Herant Katchadourian, professor of psychiatry and behavioral sciences at Stanford University.[13] When Doogie Howser, the popular adolescent prodigy TV doctor, lamented that "being a virgin is driving me crazy," he gave the message that giving in was better than remaining strong.

The Carnegie Report on Adolescent Development quotes *TV Guide*'s statistics that American television viewers are exposed annually to 9,230 scenes of suggested sexual intercourse or innuendo, and fully 94 percent of the sex on soap operas involves people not married to each other.[14] Furthermore, those scenes show no one appearing concerned about contraceptives, disease, or pregnancy. Although some programs are becoming more "responsible" (Doogie grabbed his condoms before heading out the door and Roseanne took her daughter to the doctor), the "Do it" message clearly says, "Get acquainted through sex." Not the right message for adolescents.

Mothers and fathers can regain control of the television, watch mutually agreed-upon shows with their young adolescents, and discuss the values they see depicted on the screen—some exemplary values and others not so commendable. Many teen shows portray adolescents who care for one another, listen when their friends are suffering through parental or school problems, and are true friends. These examples deserve praise and recognition. When the characters make mistakes or deliberately violate another, a mother may ask, for instance, "What do you think would have happened if they waited?" and discuss the situation with her son. The conversation could give mothers a chance to see how a son is making decisions. Talking about media characters, rather than himself, may allow him to relax and talk more openly about how he thinks boys or girls his age should act.

A teenager's friends can influence the decision to postpone—or not postpone—sexual intercourse. In a study of eighth graders in inner-city Atlanta, only 40 percent of the students thought their friends would disapprove if they had sex.[15] In the same survey, 73 percent of the students thought their parents would be very upset if they had sex. In this case, the friends' opinions were making headway, so Henry W. Grady Memorial Hospital initiated a peer-based program focused on helping students resist peer and social pressures to have sex. The five-session program for eighth graders, led by a boy and a girl from the eleventh or twelfth grade, was added to the already-existing sex education course. Students watch videotapes and slides showing examples of media and peer pressure, practice ways of responding to those pressures, and learn how to say "no" without hurting anyone's feelings. Initial program evaluations indicate success in helping students postpone sexual involvement

Girlfriends

A son needs friends, not sexual alliances, when he is developing his own style, imagination, ideas, dreams, and hopes. A boy wants girlfriends as well as male friends to go out with and have fun with, but seldom does a boy want to get emotionally involved with a girl. And yet if he has sex with her, she rightly will expect him to stick with her. "I don't have a girlfriend," a boy told me, "because my friends do and all they do is fight with their girlfriends."

An adolescent girl naturally becomes attached to her boyfriend, and if they have had intercourse, she feels a special closeness to him and will often make demands on his time that he is not willing to fulfill—and so may her parents. I was surprised when some mothers told me about the possessiveness of their sons' girlfriends' mothers. These mothers enveloped the boyfriends, acting almost like mothers-in-law. Rather than throwing a boy out of the house for having sex with her daughter, the mother was rewarding him by providing the beds and the unsupervised time. Some mothers of sons were mad, as was this mother of a 15-year-old boy.

"He came to me and wanted my approval [to have sex]," she said, "but I stuck to my guns. I thought it would be too much responsibility for someone his age. Then his girlfriend's mother took my son and her daughter to the gynecologist. This mother is making her fifteen-year-old daughter available for sex and will do whatever it takes to make the relationship work. I caught them having sex in my house and that made me crazy. I threw her in the car and took her home and by the time I got home eight minutes later, her mother had left a threatening message on my machine that I better not break them up. She should have been a little concerned about the propriety."

Two other women nodded in agreement and told stories of mothers' supplying boyfriends with beds and comfort. One woman said the girlfriend's mother told the young couple about her own sexual experiences, including "faking orgasms." Some mothers of sons also are "enablers" and don't react when a girl walks out of a son's bedroom on a Sunday morning. Other families separate a boy's room from the rest of the house, providing him with a bachelor-type pad and giving him the message that he can do what he wants in that space.

Adolescents often want the privileges of adults before they are ready, but adults who act like adolescents and conspire with their children to arrange sexual encounters are not doing their sons—or daughters—a favor.

I think these accommodating women are not the average mothers. Most mothers of daughters (and I have interviewed many) do not add to their daughters' pressure, but shield them from it. But a boy should be warned that if he gets sexually involved with a girl, he may be absorbed by her family, and chances are that is not what he bargained for when he wanted sex with his girlfriend.

Some mothers are not upset but grateful to a son's girlfriend, especially if she persuades him to study more and shares in his interests and activities. A girlfriend can be a good influence in his young life, offering stability and friendship. One mother told me how heartbroken she was when her son broke up with his girlfriend. This mother had included the girlfriend in their family festivities, had grown to love her like a daughter, and missed her when they broke up. Sometimes it is hard to stand back and not promote a particular girlfriend, but mothers must maintain their distance. Overinvolvement in a son's romance will not help him make mature decisions, and sometimes a mother pushing a romance can mean the kiss of death. My sons accused me at one time of not liking their girlfriends because I did not pay "enough" attention to them. I liked the girls my sons brought to the house, but I knew they would have many girlfriends in their adolescent years and I didn't want to take sides. The choice was not mine. In spite of the girls a mother may recommend (like her best friend's daughter), a son will choose his own girlfriend and a mother can just hope that the girlfriend will be his good friend.

Keeping an adolescent romance on a nonsexual basis is difficult today for young people who love each other and are bombarded daily with messages to have intercourse, but two adolescents who share the same values and are willing to express their love through kissing and hugging and not having intercourse are able to develop their own individuality and aspirations to the fullest. "I know one other guy in my class who is going to wait," a boy told me. He talked about his girlfriend and how much fun they have together and how they both know they will not have sex until they are married (and probably not to each other). "I believe my wife is out there somewhere," another boy said, "and if I am having sex now, I'm cheating on her." I admire these boys for taking a stand that is difficult to maintain in our sex-driven society.

The clear and urgent message of mothers and fathers should be abstinence and postponement. An adolescent boy should postpone sexual intercourse until he is ready to love, respect, and communicate with his partner, an ability rarely present during adolescence. Some sons will follow their own or their religion's strong values and wait till marriage, certainly the only guaranteed way of avoiding fatherhood or disease. Others will choose to wait for a serious adult relationship before they commit themselves sexually. However, all sons should know that waiting—even if it seems too long—is far better than acting too early.

Sex Without Feelings

Some boys believe that the way to achieve status is through sexual conquests. The Lakewood, California, football players whom I mentioned previously showed no remorse for tallying "points" for each girl they seduced or forced to have sex with them. The father

of one proclaimed on television that it was the girls' fault. His son
had not provoked the attacks, he said, but girls always telephoned
his son, liked him, and were willing participants. That type of
defense stings at the heart of women who know that a boy is
responsible for his own sexual behavior and in sexual assault cases
is most certainly the provocateur. I don't recall a girl ever being
accused of rape.

The well-reported gang rape in New Jersey of a mentally
retarded girl by popular high-school athletes shocks even more
when the defense charges that the girl instigated and wanted the
abuse, that the boys were not responsible for violently penetrating
her with a baseball bat.

Young athletes are increasingly involved with sexual assaults
on women.[16] Some girls have told me they refuse to date football
players. Mothers have a special obligation to sensitize their sons to
the importance of respecting girls and women at all times. Being
an athlete does not exonerate violent or stud behavior. Young
athletes often hold places of distinction in a high-school community, and teachers and coaches must constantly remind them of
their place as role models. Because many students look up to the
athletes, their behavior deserves to be scrutinized. Unfortunately,
in some schools they have taken advantage of their exalted position and used girls to enhance their macho reputations. The male
who ignores or disregards the rights of women does not belong on
the playing field. Coaches must enforce this principle, and
mothers and fathers must stand firm in upholding it.

Sex and love have become separated in the lives of many
young people, not only macho athletes. Said one boy, "I have a
friend who has slept with six or seven girls, and I asked him if he
liked any of them and he said, 'No, I slept with them because they
want to.' That's so strange to me. They think sex is so material. I
think sex is feelings. A boy or girl who sleeps with everyone is a
prostitute."

The boy I interviewed was not a prude, but a very likable,
popular boy who was concerned about his friend and his values.

When a boy has sex without love, he is providing a stud service and is not helping himself or his young partner. If he is the one with the difficult task of saying "no," because the girl is pushing him, then he has to develop strategies to avoid intimacy with the girl ("I like you, that's why I don't want to have sex. There are too many dangers"). He, not his partner, is responsible for his behavior and its consequences. Some girls will want to "make love" and he will be flattered, but he does not have to cooperate. He can be his own man and make his own decisions.

When love is divorced from sexual involvement, brutality and domination can enter easily. When a boy desires "points" in a society that disassociates love and marriage, forcing himself upon a girl (who may like him) seems acceptable to him. Later, it comes as a shock when she lets him know that sex was not what she wanted or expected. Boys have to be taught that because a girl likes him, even loves him, does not mean she wants to have intercourse. Some boys cannot understand how girls can be affectionate and loving without sex.

Years ago, psychiatrist C. G. Jung wrote, "I must regard it as a misfortune that nowadays the sexual question is spoken of as something distinct from love. Sexuality dished out as sexuality is brutish; but sexuality as an expression of love is hallowed."[17]

Mothers and fathers can begin early in their sons' adolescence to teach that sex is hallowed, that it means love, commitment, and respect, not violence or stud service. The decision and responsibility belong to each individual. His partner cannot coerce him and he cannot coerce her. A "no" means no, and even if a girl first has consented, she can change her mind—and so can he. And a girl will admire a boy who says he respects her and wants to wait till he is older.

What Parents Can Do

Although sex education programs exist in many schools, most stress sexual knowledge rather than sexual behavior. "Sex ed programs don't stop people from having sex," one boy told me. "All they do is tell you about disease and symptoms." And statistics bear this out. Knowledge alone does not change adolescent behavior or attitudes. They need to be told what is the right behavior. They don't learn that from the current cultural message, and it is difficult to get the message in a classroom.

Schools already are overloaded and cannot be expected to handle the emotional aspects of a boy and girl in love, or counteract the divisive societal message "Get acquainted through sex." Since parents are the primary carriers of values to the next generation, they must become the sex educators of their children.

Ellen Hopkins, a contributing editor to *Rolling Stone* magazine, wrote in the *New York Times* that abstinence "need not be the province of right-wing crazies. . . . I once thought I'd tell my young son that anything goes—so long as he used condoms," she remembers. "Now I'm not so sure. Not only do I want my son to live. I don't want him to miss out on longing—longing for what he isn't yet ready to have."[18] She now realizes the physical harm and the psychological loss endured by many sexually active adolescents and calls on parents to wake up to the new reality.

When I asked a high-school senior what advice he would give mothers, he said, "I think they should be strict. My parents should have been stricter. I'm going to be strict, especially with my daughters, 'cause I know how the boys are. They're not going to hang out with just anybody. Boys are pretty bad."

Boys want guidelines, and when mothers and fathers do discuss sex, they should talk naturally about morals and values and good judgment. How a mother approaches the subject often reflects her feelings about sexuality. Does she value sexual intercourse as something "hallowed" or as just another bodily function? Perhaps she rejects the whole concept of sexuality. If a mother cherishes and respects her own sexuality, she automatically conveys, by her words and actions, those feelings to her son. She is happy that she is a woman, admires other women, and appreciates the men in her life (especially his father—even if they are divorced). He will realize that sexuality is part of a person, not a separate appendage to be used as an outlet or a service.

As discussed in Chapter 6, a mother who speaks directly is appreciated. "I was in second grade and I asked her how you get babies and she didn't beat around the bush," a junior in high school told me. "I know some kids who never find out from their parents. She told me exactly what happens, gave me a book, and I told a lot of my friends."

Explaining "the birds and the bees" to a second grader is far less complicated than discussing sexual conduct with a sixth to twelfth grader, especially if he has a girlfriend. Getting the message across before he begins an active social life is critical. After his first sexual encounter, he may have a harder time reversing himself or he may think that unprotected sex is the way to go.

"I like hearing my dad talk about sex and stuff," said one of the few boys who talked with his father. And the message he received was "There are too many young fathers. It's not that cool 'cause when you grow up, you don't want to stay with that girl and you got to pay child support, to buy clothes and stuff. If you don't use protection, it happens."

Another boy said his mother found some of his older brother's condoms and decided to talk to him. "She told me she didn't want me to have sex with anyone without protection 'cause it could ruin my life. Every weekend she asks me if I have condoms. It's just an extra precaution."

"My mother just jokes about it," said one boy, describing another common way parents deal with sex issues. "She'll come into my room and see a condom on my dresser and ask if it's one of hers, and I'll tell her no and she just laughs and walks away."

Yet most of the boys responded to my question in the following way: "Nobody talked to me. Just my brother now and then. I don't think parents teach too much. It's a hard subject for them. I think they're scared, they think you're too young. You know, parent kind of things. I went away this summer, so my dad said something like, 'Be protected.' "

A mother who speaks directly and openly about sexual conduct can convey her values. A mother who avoids the subject or only jokes about it neglects passing on values and misses the chance to influence her son's decisions, not only about whether or not to have sex, but how to protect himself if he does, no matter how young or inexperienced he and his partner are.

One mother told me that she had a long talk with her 16-year-old son about condoms. Later that week her husband brought some business friends home and during dinner her son had laughingly told these men about their condom conversation. She felt like crawling under the table, but a guest said to her son, "I don't know one sixteen-year-old boy who can cope with the emotions of a sixteen-year-old girl. Stay away from it." This was, she said, the most powerful comment and greatest gift. Her son listened. Men who talk abstinence with boys have an impact mothers can't always deliver.

Topics to Discuss

When talking about sexual intercourse with a son, four areas should be discussed. Assuming he has had the basic birds-and-bees talk, a mother first should concentrate on the value of sexual abstinence and postponement, stressing that sex is for adults; then shift to the pressures he will confront to have sex (including his peers and girlfriends) and the best ways to respond to these pressures; then stress the consequences of unprotected sex; lastly, emphasize the necessity of using condoms and a spermicide if or when he does decide to have sex, regardless of what his partner says she is using.

Regarding the first point, boys need to know that their parents value abstinence and promote postponement, that it's all right not to have sex. Marion Howard, in her book *How to Help Your Teenager Postpone Sexual Involvement*, suggests some good arguments for abstinence and postponement: fear of disease, fear of fatherhood, religious belief, not wanting to hurt parents, respect for a girlfriend, not feeling a need to have intercourse, not wanting to risk interference with future plans, not being old enough, not being ready to make a commitment.[19] Any one of these offers grounds for abstinence or postponement, and all of them make sense. Boys who are reminded of these by their parents may eventually make them part of their own reasoning process.

The longer a son waits, the more mature he will be. His ability to make a commitment and establish a deep bond with his partner will increase. To desire a monogamous relationship with a woman he loves, without the fear of disease and unwanted pregnancies, is a laudable and obtainable goal. If a son decides he will wait until marriage, he must search out, primarily through religious organizations, other young men and women who share his belief.

Second, mothers and fathers can talk about the subtle and not-so-subtle pressures to have sex, from culture, from friends, from girlfriends. Together they can discuss movies, videos, rock releases, rap songs, and advertisements, asking what message the young person has received. These discussions can be lots of fun and parents can obtain a glimpse into the adolescent mind.

Parents also would do well to examine their own messages—are they unconsciously or consciously expecting their sons to have sex? Adolescents assume that their parents will disapprove of their sexual involvement. When parents make it easy for them or blithely accept their sexual activity without attempting to dissuade them from it, their sons will think their resignation is permission. Parents are expected to set guidelines, not condone adult sexual behavior in adolescents. Sex is for grown-ups and adolescents know that is how it is supposed to be.

Third, parents must talk about the consequences of adolescent sex. All boys realize that a girl can become pregnant, but some have the mistaken notion that virgins don't get pregnant. Mothers can easily correct that misinformation. However, they also need to talk about the other physical consequences, STDs and AIDS. A pediatrician or gynecologist can supply charts of STDs, along with their symptoms and long-term effects, to aid in the discussion. One middle-school teacher make a lasting impression by showing his student a picture of a genital wart on a penis. As I mentioned above, the Centers for Disease Control attribute the increase in STDs among teenagers to multiple partners. An STD can spread very quickly when the infected person has sex frequently and with different partners, and the symptoms often are not recognized by adolescents.

It may be harder to articulate to a son the psychological disadvantages of adolescent sexual activity. Boys can feel hurt, rejected, inadequate, and become distracted. They need time to develop confidence in themselves before they can make a commitment to a relationship. Boys who flit in and out of sexual relationships are diluting their energy, turning from the goal of addressing these important questions, "Who am I?" and "Where am I going?"

Fourth, along with any discussion of sexual values and intercourse, a parent must emphasize that a son protect himself and his partner if he does engage in sex. Parents can tell a son about the best methods of contraception, always emphasizing that nothing works 100 percent, except not having sex. The research is showing that a sexually active male will have the best protection from fatherhood and STDs by using two methods of contraception, a good-quality condom with a highly efficient spermicide.[20] A mother certainly doesn't have to show him how to use a condom and spermicide, but she can tell him not to be embarrassed to ask his doctor how to do it. Safety is more important than embarrassment. However, both methods must be used every time if they're to be effective, and he has to make sure the condom doesn't leak—not an easy task for an adolescent.

The Hope

After wading through the statistics about adolescent male sexual activity, mothers can become discouraged. The fun of parenting a son may be overshadowed by his risk-taking and her fears that he will not survive adolescence without lifelong repercussions. However, a strong, confident mother helps him overcome the odds and emerge safely from adolescence.

A mother who has set a good foundation for a son's development, openly discussed sexual values, and placed confidence in his ability to handle difficult situations must now trust his judgment. Most adolescent boys have common sense and want to live up to their parents' expectations. A son needs a mother's reassurance and trust that he will turn out all right.

Memos for Moms

1. Take an active role in discussing sex with your son. Don't wait for someone else to do the job.
2. Be aware of the rising number of sexually active boys, the alarming increase in births, and the rapid escalation of sexually transmitted diseases (STDs), including AIDS, in adolescents.
3. Talk to your son about the dangers of many sexual partners.
4. Examine your own sexual values. Are you giving a

message that boys are expected to have sex during high school?

5. Be aware that early alcohol and drug use can lead to early sex.

6. Use common sense and caution in your own social life, if you are a dating single mother.

7. Discuss with your son the sexual messages he sees and hears in music, on music videos, and on television sitcoms.

8. Talk to him about the pressures he will receive from his peers and girlfriends to have sex. Develop and practice some lines to deflect the pressure.

9. Avoid becoming overly involved with or promoting a particular girlfriend.

10. Remind him that girls rightfully expect sexual involvement to include emotional commitment and he is not ready for that.

11. Encourage him to abstain from sex and to postpone sexual involvement. Stress that sex is for committed adults.

12. Always discuss love and commitment when discussing sex, so he associates the two.

13. Be knowledgeable and tell him about the best type of male contraception (condoms plus spermicide), emphasize correct use, and let him know there is no "safe sex."

14. Don't get discouraged about adolescent sexuality. Let him know that you believe in him and trust his good judgment.

11

"Kids Do What They Want"

Alcohol and Drugs

How Widespread? • What's So Different?
What's Wrong with Alcohol? • Other Drugs
Cigarettes and Smokeless Tobacco
Parents • Friends • Personality
What to Do if He Has a Problem
Additional Reading or Contacts
Memos for Moms

When Mayor Richard Daley of Chicago stood before a crowded news conference, reporters did not interrogate him about urban problems. Instead, they barraged him with questions about charges brought against his 16-year-old son, who had hosted an unsupervised party at the Daley summer home. A boy had been seriously injured, a windshield shattered, a shotgun waved threateningly as the party got out of control, and police were called in. Daley's highly publicized and tearful account of his son's unauthorized partying and drinking met with a sympathetic response from parents in the press corps who faced similar situations every weekend. Police departments in any American municipality are familiar with this adolescent "party" routine.

Most of the time, parents "disappear and the kids do what they want," said a boy describing his neighborhood scene to me. Mayor Daley, however, had left instructions for his son to stay at a friend's home, but his son could not resist the prospect of buddies, alcohol, and an empty house. Word spread quickly among local teenagers and the situation turned unruly, more than a 16-year-old could handle.

Not all drinking parties are held in unsupervised homes against parents' wishes. "This weekend," a junior told me, "all you had to do was bring five dollars and you could have all the beer you wanted. The kegs were right in the entry. The parents were home." Some parents permit drinking and pot smoking in their homes, rationalizing their actions by claiming they do not let the teenagers leave in an inebriated condition, therefore they are responsible parents. Or they take the car keys away so inebriated teenagers cannot leave (if the guests are old enough to drive). Certain homes in communities are dubbed "party houses," where boys know they can drink as much as they like and spend the night when they get drunk. By the time an adolescent arrives home the next day, sobriety has reemerged, so his own parents remain unaware of his condition the night before.

Although many boys reveal conflicting feelings about drinking, they accept its presence. "Drinking is really bad now," one boy told me. "It's not like alcoholism because no one does it every day. Only on weekends do people get trashed. You get away from parents and teachers and get rowdy and drinking makes you have a better time." Although this junior realizes the drinking scene is out of control, he is naïve to think it's "not like alcoholism" for all his friends.

"When I was in seventh and eighth grade in a really small school," another boy said, "the kids had to go off someplace like in the alleys if they wanted liquor, but the next fall it was weird to see how everyone had reacted to ninth grade. A lot were drinking and doing drugs. Some were really messed up. They had lost it in their new high-school groups."

The combination of alcohol and pot is not uncommon with adolescents. When I asked boys about drugs other than alcohol, pot was mentioned all the time as familiar and available. "It's pot, mostly pot," said one boy. Another told a similar tale: "Sometimes I see LSD and mushrooms, but I would say it's mostly pot."

Other adolescent boys face an even more dangerous prospect when they "lose it." In their neighborhoods, getting involved with illegal substances is flirting with death or jail. Once you take that first step, it is difficult to back away from the source. "I don't let anyone influence me to do drugs," a boy from a housing project told me. "I make my own decision on things and say to my little brothers that if they get involved in drugs, it's going to be their life, using or selling drugs, so you take a chance of dying or going to jail. They believe me 'cause they know I don't use drugs."

This boy and many boys I interviewed have withstood the drug culture in their neighborhoods, but the monetary rewards amassed from dealing are tempting to others. "Some, like in middle school, are selling drugs to buy clothes, like Timberland boots," another boy explained to me. "They have to have these. They have all these new hairstyles. They have girlfriends and money in their pockets. Everyone wants to be tough these days in middle school or in the street."

Are these boys from different neighborhoods telling me about isolated cases of adolescent drugs, or is drug and alcohol abuse reaching across most segments of adolescent life?

How Widespread?

Adolescent boys have always liked to experiment and challenge the odds. I remember breathing a sigh of relief when I would hear the back door open and realize my teenage sons were home safely for the night. Any slight change in their routine or mannerisms, the way they walked or spoke, put me on alert. Sometimes I just wanted to make sure they were safe. Other times, if I suspected they were partying, I wanted to check out their condition so I could talk to them about it in the morning. My best sleep in those years came after they arrived home and went to bed.

This scenario is reenacted nightly in countless homes as parents remain on edge while their children make the rounds of houses, apartments, or bars that serve underage drinkers. Other adolescents take even greater risks by hanging out on street corners tempting others to buy their drugs or running drugs for dealers.

Not all students are spending their weekends looking for drinking or drug opportunities, but a disturbingly large percentage is. A national survey of high-school students reported that nearly 90 percent of boys have used alcohol (all types), 62.2 percent are current drinkers, while some 43.5 percent have binged recently by having five drinks in a row. Marijuana showed the next highest drug usage, with 35.9 percent of high-school boys reporting they have smoked marijuana and almost 17 percent reporting continued use.[1]

Surveys of high-school students are conservative estimates. Dropouts, institutionalized adolescents, college students, and middle-school children are excluded from most surveys and, according to the Children's Defense Fund, drug use among some of those populations is higher than in the general population.[2]

A survey released by the Parents Resource Institute on Drug Education (PRIDE) in 1992 reported that the use of all ten categories of drugs (cigarettes, beer, wine coolers, liquor, marijuana, cocaine, depressants, stimulants, hallucinogens, and inhalants) has increased in grades *six through eight*.[3]

I don't think these statistics come as any surprise to mothers who are familiar with middle- and high-school students. Statistics are cold and impersonal, but when a son staggers home or becomes disturbingly unmotivated about school or activities, numbers quickly become reality.

What's So Different?

Are drinking and drug-taking a natural part of growing up or are parents now facing a new threat to the safety of their children? I think it is both. Some adolescents, especially boys, have always tried to get away with what they could and enjoyed the sport of not getting caught. But now middle-school and early-high-school children are being presented with the same enticements that their parents faced in their late teens.

Parents, for instance, who smoked pot in college now find their 13-year-olds being offered marijuana that contains 470 percent more tetrahydrocannabinol (THC) than it did in 1974.[4] Because marijuana is fat-soluble, traces of one joint linger for as long as a month in the brain cells. And if a boy smokes frequently, the accumulated THC affects his motivation and he can quickly acquire the "laid-back" attitude of the addicted flower children of the sixties. A boy who can't "get his act together" and who can't put action behind his plans should be looked at closely. He may not be going through an adolescent stage; he may be doing pot. Adolescents who know the "potheads" and "burnouts" among their classmates reveal their own youthful immaturity when they talk about them.

"A lot of rich kids are burnouts [from pot] because they get the money from their parents," a boy confided. "You can't really judge who's a burner. There are some that are smoking pot more than others. I hang out with friends who smoke it a lot. Truthfully, I don't smoke it that much, but a lot of smart kids do. I don't think it really affects your knowledge." But his friend jumped into the conversation and said, "It slows you down, but I don't think it makes you stupid. It can't take your brain away. But if you're already stupid and you started smoking it, then you're in trouble." "Yeah," laughed the first boy. "We know some people who smoke pot who have 440 SATs [scholastic aptitude tests] combined."

Another high-school senior told me that parents shouldn't be concerned about pot, they should be more worried about cocaine because you can "die on that." When I asked about pot's being a gateway to harder drugs, he replied, "I don't know about that. You really can't get addicted to pot. I don't think it's a gateway drug 'cause a lot of kids can handle pot." After a pause he added, "My two friends haven't moved into hard-core drugs, but they smoke pot every day and *it's totally ruined their lives*." I asked him if he was worried about his friends (who were star athletes) and he responded, "Yeah, I told my good friend, 'Calm down, you're getting overboard with it and it's controlling your life.' Another friend and I noticed it and we said, 'We don't like you that much anymore 'cause you're never thinking about us. All you can think about is getting fried again and we think you should cut it out.' "

This boy, also an athlete, summed up precisely what happens to a boy who gets addicted to marijuana. All he thinks about is getting "fried." For a while he can keep up his grades and his sports, but eventually the pot will catch up and he will search out people who also are hooked or selling, abandon his old friends, and his life will change.

The boy I interviewed reflected the incredible naïveté of adolescents. He said he did not believe marijuana was a problem drug and you couldn't get addicted to it, yet he had two friends who were addicted and I suspect that his concern about them revealed an anxiety about himself. He was a restless young man who was irritated at everything—his parents, teachers, and friends. Yet he would not consider talking to anyone about his or his friends' problems. Because I was an impartial, unknown interviewer, he was willing to open up for a short time, but when I asked him if he would go to a school counselor, he said, "We'd have too much to lose as athletes if we went to counselors."

Another boy described his parents' attitude toward pot: "My parents were both sixties children, so they're tolerant. They know I use pot. Of course, they'd prefer that I wouldn't use it, but they know that I probably am, and as long as it doesn't interfere with what I'm trying to do and I'm using it at appropriate times and in appropriate amounts, it's not that big a deal."

Many parents who grew up in the sixties and seventies share these parents' viewpoint about marijuana. They used pot as a symbol of protest against war and the establishment, and for peace and justice. They were part of a national movement that inspired young (and many older) people to advocate for an idealist society and equality for all. They rejected their parents' traditional values and substituted their own. For many of these protestors, sharing a weed (smoking pot) represented this new attitude. Some parents, unfortunately, are still stuck in this mentality and are now faced with young adolescent children who need guidance. These parents need to reassess their attitude about drugs and realize the serious consequences of pot-smoking on developing brains and bodies.

Marijuana quickly enters the brain and remains in the fat surrounding each brain cell. It impairs short-term memory, affecting, for instance, the usefulness of cramming for a test. It slows down the nerve impulses between the brain cells so the ability to evaluate situations and react to them is impaired. It affects the motivational impulses of the brain, producing apathy and lethargy.

Most boys do not realize that pot alters their reproductive systems as well as their brains by decreasing the sperm count and testosterone level. It also can cause chromosome damage. In addition, marijuana depresses the immune system, increasing adolescent susceptibility to sexually transmitted diseases, particularly herpes simplex and AIDS. Parents must remind themselves of these effects and tell their sons that pot stays in the system longer than water-soluble drugs (that's why withdrawal symptoms are more gradual than with other drugs); they must also tell them what the pot does to their systems, and inform them that the current strains are far more powerful (again, 470 percent stronger) than earlier strains.[5]

"It's hard for people to believe, but a lot of kids I know started smoking pot in ninth grade," one boy told me. "A lot are still in that phase and smoke weed every weekend and get wasted every weekend. Some of them just can't cope with life." And the more they smoke pot, the less they will be able to "cope with life."

Many parents want to deny the presence of marijuana. One mother told me she has discovered pot twice, hidden among her eighth-grade son's possessions, yet she still believes him when he tells her that he is holding it for someone else, that he does not use it.

Far better for parents *not* to "tolerate" the use of marijuana and to teach their children that it is an addictive substance and a "gateway" drug. With its widespread availability, pot is easy to obtain (ask any boy). Drug dealers often introduce a young person (even in middle school) to drugs through marijuana and then move them up the scale when they become dependent on their supplier. (A high-school student who uses marijuana is about one hundred times more likely to use cocaine than a non–marijuana user.[6]) If parents do not let a boy know that they are *firmly* against his smoking pot, he stands a chance of becoming a person incapable of standing on his own or making good decisions.

What's Wrong with Alcohol?

Nothing is "wrong" with alcohol that is consumed in moderation by adults, but adolescents are not adults and drinking alcohol under the age of 21 is illegal in the United States. In my opinion the government made a mistake in advancing the drinking age to 21. I think it should have remained at 18 or 19 (the age when a young person graduates from high school). The percentage of adolescents who drink has not lessened and the number of middle-school children who do drink has increased (30 percent had their first drink between the ages of 9 and 12, and 54 percent between 13 and 15).[7] The decrease in deaths from drunk driving cannot be attributed to the 21-year-old drinking law, but to the excellent campaigns against drinking and driving waged by organizations like Mothers Against Drunk Driving (MADD) and Students Against Drunk Driving (SADD), and to the crackdown on drunk drivers by police officials.

I think most boys who have graduated from high school and are in college or working are mature enough to enjoy a drink with friends and old enough to moderate their consumption, especially when they have to pay for their own drinks. I think we are encouraging duplicity by not allowing 19- to 21-year-olds to drink. They do drink and often the goal is to consume quickly as much as they can. If the young adult population had to pay retail prices and heavy taxes for drinks at public bars with a publike friendly, responsible atmosphere, they would drink less. An 18- or 19-year-old is considered an adult in the United States and should be treated like one. Young adolescents think that the age 21 is almost beyond their lifetime. They can visualize the end of high school, equate it with adulthood, and may be more willing to wait. However, until the law is changed, parents must respect the 21-year-law and so should their children and the local bars and liquor stores.

Middle-school and high-school students are not young adults and are more vulnerable to alcohol impairment, becoming addicted more quickly than adults, especially if they are combining alcohol and marijuana. Many young adolescents, presented with seemingly endless supplies of alcohol, do not drink with moderation but with intent.

"The object is to see how much you can drink and how much you can get screwed up," said a junior, "so when you wake up in the morning it's who has the biggest headache. Who has had the most is the big thing." Some of the older boys I interviewed saw the folly of such behavior and commented on the increasingly young age of drinkers.

"When I was in eighth grade, the drinking began," said a senior. "But now it starts in sixth and seventh grade. The freshman class this year, all they do every weekend is go out and get drunk. It used to be the tenth and eleventh graders and we'd have to sneak it. Now parents are involved."

Michael Schick, director of Hazelton's Pioneer House, a chemical-dependency treatment center in Minnesota, says, "As a society I'm not sure we want to admit the problem [of teenage drinking]. We think teenage drinkers are sowing their wild oats or experimenting, or we say 'I did it when I was young and I'm OK.' But 85 percent of the kids we get in here have been drinking four or more times a week, and they started drinking at an average age of twelve and a half. I don't think we're facing the fact there are some kids who just can't say no."[8]

Because parents usually are not on guard to the possibility of a 12- to 15-year-old's drinking, they may ignore the signs. Certainly, a youngster getting sick to his stomach is a sure sign, and that unpleasant experience can keep him away from alcohol. "Last year I went to a party," said a boy, "and I drank a lot. Later that night I threw up and I don't want to have that feeling again, so I don't drink. Some of my friends are really bad. I don't know if it's going to mess up their lives."

Unfortunately, when alcohol is combined with pot smoking, a strange phenomenon occurs. Marijuana inhibits vomiting, so the natural tendency for the body to purge the toxins is suppressed. Because the body is not detoxified, adolescents are becoming alcoholics quicker and more are dying from alcohol overdose because the body is not expelling the poison. Doctors used to estimate that it took fifteen to twenty years after the first drink for a person to be called an alcoholic, but now they are seeing many teenagers who are alcoholics within three or four years of their first drink. The combination of alcohol and marijuana is extremely toxifying and can be lethal.

Alcohol is acknowledged as a major problem in most schools and educational efforts now extend down to elementary level, but public acceptance of teenage drinking has hindered efforts to steer children away from alcohol. Some parents are relieved that their children are "only" drinking, not doing drugs. And in a strange way, that notion is comforting. Generations of parents have faced teenage drinking episodes, so they tend to be less anxious about alcohol than they are about drug taking and drug dealing.

As relieved as they may be that their children are not doing drugs, parents are mistaken to believe that adolescent drinking is harmless. It is not harmless and youthful addiction is climbing dramatically. The youth market presents a lucrative opportunity for companies. Malt liquor in forty-ounce bottles has replaced beer as the alcohol of choice of young adolescents in some neighborhoods. Called "liquid crack" because of its high potency (it contains as much alcohol as five five-ounce glasses of wine or five 1.5-ounce glasses of mixed drinks), malt liquor has been heavily promoted to inner-city youths. "What they [liquor companies] do is diabolical," said an inner-city minister, deploring the rise of malt liquor consumption in his community. "They know exactly what they're doing."[9]

Parents have to fight not only advertising but an adolescent's attraction to instant action and experimentation. Thankfully, studies point out that parents can make a difference in deterring a boy from drinking. According to a study from the Research Institute on Addictions, when a son receives emotional closeness and support from his family, he consumes less alcohol and has fewer delinquent problems.[10]

An adolescent boy is confident of parental support when his parents acknowledge his new sense of self, include him in decisions about his life, *and* monitor his behavior. A strong mother grants a son "psychological autonomy" as she discusses issues with him in an adultlike manner and is not surprised when he voices contrary opinions. However, his autonomy is tempered because he realizes Mother still exerts "behavioral control."[11] The winning combination of highly demanding and highly responsive parenting that I described in Chapter 5 works particularly well when mothers are faced with the current social pressure on their sons to drink more and at younger ages.

Even if mothers are under emotional stress themselves because of economic hardship or marital problems, they can continue to parent their sons and monitor their behavior. A mother's stress will be lessened when she has confidence in her parenting skills.

Mothers and fathers who supply alcohol to their sons and their sons' friends are intruding into the lives of adolescents, denying them their youth (let them figure out their own ways of getting into trouble), and giving their sons the impression that parents will always be there to supply their needs and fulfill their desires, even if those desires are illegal.

Parents must make it as difficult as possible for underage adolescents to obtain illegal substances (alcohol, cigarettes, and drugs). When an adolescent is drinking or smoking pot, parents should make it tough for him, not collaborate with him.

Other Drugs

Crack cocaine is making large inroads into the urban adolescent population. Cheaper than pure cocaine, crack gives an instant high and becomes addictive after a relatively small number of uses. Because both drugs strike the central nervous system, sudden death may occur from cardiac arrest or respiratory failure.[12]

Some boys in cities and suburbs openly fear crack and cocaine because they associate its use with death. What they fail to see, however, is that gateway drugs could introduce the user to more lethal drugs. A study that examined adolescents undergoing treatment for addiction reported that 40 percent of these patients had used *more than one drug during the week before admission and a large percentage used cocaine and marijuana.* "With few exceptions," *cocaine users also smoked marijuana at least once a week.* Daily cigarette smoking was also high among the marijuana and cocaine users. The researchers noted that in order to obtain maximum effects from marijuana and crack cocaine, the user must inhale, a skill developed from smoking cigarettes. Therefore, "he may be more likely to move on to other drugs that involve this behavior."[13]

Sometimes parents are astounded when they learn how many substances can be abused. Inhalants, for instance, are used by some young adolescents to obtain highs. Common chemicals such as solvents, aerosols, model airplane glue, and nail polish remover can cause death by depressing the central nervous system. A middle-school boy in my area died in the school playground while he was inhaling a stimulant that was intensified by a bag placed over his head.

Hallucinogens, like LSD, angel dust, and mushrooms, are also gaining in adolescent use. Even though the numbers of users of these drugs remain small, parents should be aware that some adolescents search out many kind of drugs to alter their minds. Some will experiment with different drugs indiscriminately, so parents must be alert and aware of all possible dangers.

Heroin is an opiate that is not only addictive but increases the likelihood of the spread of the HIV virus through the use of dirty and shared needles. Experts fear a new heroin epidemic because of new, more potent strains being shipped from Southeast Asia coupled with a decrease in heroin prices. Adolescents are always a target market when drugs make a resurgence.[14]

Cigarettes and Smokeless Tobacco

Just as the statistics on adult smokers of cigarettes decline, a surprising number (66 percent) of high-school seniors have smoked cigarettes, and children as young as age 11 are using cigarettes.[15] Since cigarette companies are facing a dwindling demand from American adults, they have refocused their marketing strategies on the adolescent and dropped their prices. Cartoonlike characters appeal to "cool" personalities and promise the good life with each puff. Adolescents who like to appear in control are tempted by this allure, often sent to them through direct mail. If smoking is all it takes to gain status, why not try it?

Again, some parents are not too concerned if their sons smoke because they are grateful they are smoking cigarettes rather than marijuana. But that attitude is shortsighted and, as the report cited above points out, cigarette smoking may prepare an adolescent for other drugs that are inhaled.

"I've been trying to kill myself for some time now," writes a recent Ivy League graduate, "but if it hadn't been for a routine dental checkup I might never have known it." This young man has been "dipping" smokeless tobacco since he tried a friend's and soon dipped three to four times a week as a "substitute for alcohol." Before he knew it, he was addicted, his mouth "in shambles." Now he can't sit still and concentrate for more than fifteen minutes at a time because "my mind wanders as my body thirsts for that instant nicotine high." This young man, a Phi Beta Kappa graduate, has not been able to kick the habit even though his dentist told him he was developing mouth cancer.[16] High-school as well as college students are attracted to smokeless tobacco. Almost 22 percent of high-school students have dipped to enhance their masculine image, unaware that this also is an addictive substance and can lead to cancer.

Because many books detail the signs of alcohol and drug addiction and warn parents what to look for (see "Additional Reading or Contacts," page 252–3), I am going to focus more on the personal and family characteristics of boys who are at risk for drug and alcohol abuse and those who are less at risk.

Parents

Mothers and fathers who are responsive and adequately supervise their sons do *not* place them at risk for alcohol and drug problems. Numerous studies have documented that parents who care about their sons and respond to their sons' intellectual and emotional needs have children who are less likely to take actions that would seriously contradict their parents' standards.[17] These mothers (and fathers) praise their sons when they do something well;

frequently hug, kiss, or pat them on the back; do things together that they both enjoy; and are available and willing to give counsel and good advice—even if the father is not living in the home. "Levels of high support by mother and father are associated with the lowest levels of regular drinking, illicit drug use, deviance, and school misconduct."[18]

Coupled with strong support is the equally important factor of monitoring a son's behavior. When the adolescents perceive that they have rules governing their behavior, they act more responsibly. Many parents themselves can look back at their adolescent years and remember the rules that were laid down. However, in order to have effective rules, adolescent boys need to participate in the discussions and the negotiations. Confident parents do a lot of explaining about why high-school students should not drink or take drugs. These parents are curious about their sons' feelings about drinking and drugs and together they problem-solve, searching for alternatives to joining the smashed or burned mentality every weekend.

A group of parents questioned by researchers from Catholic University about adolescent problems were more concerned about a son's alcohol consumption than about other matters, for instance a possible drop in his grades.[19] When these parents were asked what they would do if a son came home after having too much to drink, they responded that they would seek counseling, forbid him to use alcohol, punish him, call up other parents, monitor his behavior more closely, or try to keep him away from places that served alcohol.

If a mother and father care about their son and monitor his behavior, they certainly will not be supplying him and his friends with alcohol. They would be actively supporting teen activities that engage the boys' energy, curiosity, and intelligence without endangering their brain and their health. When parents capitulate to teenage requests for alcohol, they should be held responsible by the community of caring adults.

Unfortunately, parents in many neighborhoods cannot leave

their homes unsupervised, even for a night. Many teenagers are dependable but peers often seek out homes without " 'rents." A responsible adolescent who is baby-sitting for his younger siblings probably will not turn the house into a party scene for the night. But adolescents left alone are more of a worry. Neighbors should be alerted and told that the house is off-limits and given the phone number where parents can be reached. Some wise parents call their home phone once in a while when they are gone and some have interrupted parties in their "empty" homes. Police in some towns will cruise past a home if parents have requested their cooperation.

Mothers can be responsive and monitor a son's behavior, but still, he may break the rules because he is an adolescent. That is why it is important for a mother to know the signs of alcohol use and the smell of pot, and be awake when he comes home. Mothers who know their sons well can spot a difference in their attitude, physical demeanor, and behavior. And sons know parents can detect their use.

"One of the biggest problems we have is the complacency of parents," said former Surgeon General Antonia Novello, when commenting on adolescent substance abuse.[20] And I am afraid that many parents are becoming more tolerant of their adolescent sons' use of alcohol and drugs.

Single mothers of boys face even tougher odds in monitoring their sons' substance use. Studies continually show that adolescent males from single-parent homes are more likely to experiment with substances than boys from intact homes.[21] Some studies indicate that boys from white, middle-class, single-parent homes may be at particular risk. In summarizing the studies, one researcher found that "effects of father-absence appear to relate to delinquent behaviors mainly in white middle-class males."[22]

These reports do not suggest that mothers in intact families can let up on their vigilance and concern for their sons. All mothers, regardless of their married state, must guide their sons, show them compassion and understanding as they face the city and suburban streets, discuss with them ways of avoiding involvement, and monitor their activities. Mothers must always keep in mind that adolescents will experiment, but they must *not* have Mother's permission to do so.

Friends

Many mothers agonize over their sons' hanging out with the "wrong" crowd and being drawn into their alcohol or drug habits. When friends drink or take drugs, they want everyone to join in the "fun," yet many boys are able to withstand that pressure and their wishes are respected. When I asked one boy how he avoided the drug dealers in his neighborhood, he replied, "They say, 'What, you scared?' and I tell them I'm not scared, but I'm not getting caught and going to jail and they back off."

Another boy, whose father is an alcoholic, told me he is planning never to drink and his friends are fine with his decision. "Nobody has ever asked me why I'm not drinking," he said. "There's a small percentage that go to parties and don't drink and there hasn't been a problem."

These two boys have strong motivation not to drink or take drugs, but other boys have less desire to stay away from it and friends may more easily persuade them to indulge. However, most boys do not want their friends to go overboard and are concerned when drinking leads to more serious problems. They may participate in a social scene, but they get concerned about friends or acquaintances who are getting burned. Best friends can help turn a young person around.

If a mother suspects that her son's friends definitely are influencing him the wrong way, then she has to take a strong stand. However, criticizing friends has never worked. If she has fairly good evidence that his friends are heavy drinkers or drug takers or dealers, she has to talk to her son about the effects of these friends upon *his* behavior and safety. A son has to learn from his mother that his safety is paramount, rather than that his friends are no good. If she condemns his friends, he will only rise to their defense.

Profiles of drug and alcohol abusers in the seventh and eighth grades suggest that they spend a lot of time in drug/alcohol-related activities with friends, even at this young age. Nonusers in a study tended to be highly involved in extracurricular activities and to spend more time with family.[23]

"Our son is in a party crowd," a mother of a 17-year-old told me. "He is really drinking and we were making excuses for him, rescuing him. We have finally reached a point where we told him he had to decide to follow our rules or leave the house." This mother wisely sought out professional help and met with parents of her son's friends. They all agreed to let one another know if one of their sons was sleeping at another one's house.

This get-tough strategy worked for this family. Her son did stay away, spending some time at a friend's and some time at a relative's. Now he is living at home, accepting his parents' limits and rules, and preparing to go to college. However, this turnaround did not happen without tears and trauma. "He's a boy who needs limits," says his mother now, "and my husband and I didn't realize that at the time. He has many friends, is very sociable, warm, and sensitive, but covers it up. We have all learned a lesson the hard way."

Many families learn the hard way, but the decision to be firm yet loving to a son, in spite of his friends or habits, pays off. Being emotionally distant will not help him. He wants his parents to remain close and try to understand, but they must remain strong in their goal to see him drug- and alcohol-free if they are going to help him.

One mother of a particularly taxing son gave me good advice to pass on to mothers: "Listen to them. Let them say what they want, even if you don't agree. Give them your views, too. Don't judge their friends because they have long hair or their clothes ripped off or whatever. Ask yourself, 'Are the friends there when he needs to cry on someone's shoulder?' "

Personality

Some boys seem more disposed to taking risks than others, and that disposition extends to the social scene. However, risk-taking itself is positive if he develops confidence to take risks in the academic, sports, or extracurricular arena. A personality trait may be positive or negative. But when his risk-taking extends to illegal practices or self-destruction through excessive drinking or drugs, then mothers must beware.

A boy who is impulsive also may be more susceptible to alcohol and drug abuse. His inability to delay gratification often leads to a craving for an instant high, wild friends, fast driving, and action without forethought. But whether that boy becomes a substance abuser depends on other factors, including his parents' parenting style, his school, neighborhood, any history of drug abuse in the family, whether a sibling does drugs, and how much he is monitored by his family.[24]

Boys who are heavy drug users tend to view themselves as the only authority in their lives and discount parental authority. This situation does not happen automatically. It arises slowly when the adolescent thinks, "No one cares what I do, so why should I be responsible to anyone? I'm my own man." He becomes one of the many adolescents who feel accountable to no one. The deeper a young user falls into the web of drugs, the less responsibility he will assume for his behavior. Parents must be in the picture long before he reaches the stage of heavy drug use. Some boys have to weigh their own family history of alcohol or drug abuse and think long and hard before drinking. The decision must be theirs, not their friends', and certainly should come after they finish high school. Some families bribe adolescents into waiting until they are

21 by offering monetary rewards. A few adolescent psychologists agree that anything that works to postpone drinking, particularly with more vulnerable boys, should be encouraged. This is a family decision, but a family that has a history of alcohol or drug abuse should talk very frankly with a son, warning him about the family trait of alcohol intolerance.

Getting sons involved in many activities that challenge their minds and bodies will help them set goals and give them good reasons to postpone or moderate their involvement in the drinking, drug-taking party scene.

But above all, a boy who knows his mother and father will listen to him, counsel him, and monitor his behavior has no need to prove himself through alcohol or drugs. The time for parents to intervene is when their sons are young, by supervising their parties, enforcing drinking rules, meeting with other parents, attending school functions, and being knowledgeable about the local social scene. Once a son has an alcohol or drug problem, intervention is more difficult but still very necessary.

What to Do if He Has a Problem

Some drug therapists estimate that it takes parents two to three years to detect their children's drug use. Drug paraphernalia shops sell booklets about how to conceal drugs, and some mothers never suspect that a son's unusual behavior is drug-related. Mothers of boys who have gone over the edge into constant heavy drinking or drug taking must seek professional help. The school or local health association is the first line of inquiry. They can guide a parent to a professional who can advise on a more personal level. Each family has different circumstances and family pressures and each son possesses an individual personality. One son may shape up quickly if his parents, out of love, take action and not let him into the house until he cooperates. Another boy may welcome the chance to leave home and never return or get deeper into trouble, a possibility most parents would like to avoid.

A mother whose son is not heavily into drinking or drugs must still be alert and aware of his condition. If she has talked with a son about the local alcohol and drug scene, received his input, agreed on his behavior, and he continually breaks his mother's trust, she must enforce the consequence that they have discussed. Whether he is grounded, the car is taken away, or he is given added responsibilities to keep him busy and out of trouble is up to each family. But he must know that his behavior will not be tolerated. This process of discussion, trust, being vigilant and aware of his breaking trust, paying the consequences and reestablishing trust may be played out over and over during his high-school years. That is the job of parenting, never giving up on him and always expecting the best from him. He may disappoint a mother time and time again, but trust and love eventually win out as he matures into a fine young man.

Additional Reading or Contacts

Ken Barun. *When Saying No Isn't Enough: How to Keep the Children You Love off Drugs*. New York: New American Library, 1988. A personal story and still a reliable reference book with complete descriptions of symptoms of drug and alcohol use, drug paraphernalia, and effects on adolescents. Offers good advice about how to prevent use, how to detect use, and how to proceed if a child is an abuser.

Mathea Falco. *Making of a Drug-Free America: Programs That Work*. New York: Times Books, 1992. Well-reviewed discussion of successful community and school preventative and rehabilitative programs.

Sheila Fuller and Leigh Rudd. *The No-Nonsense Parents' Guide*, 1992. Parents' Pipeline, Inc., P.O. Box 11037, Greenwich,

CT 06831. A short well-documented review of drugs and their effects on adolescents. Focuses on Connecticut laws and agencies but may be adapted to other states. Call 1-203-352-4704 for information.

PRIDE, whose main office is in Atlanta, has programs in eight hundred cities to help parents prevent adolescent alcohol and drug use. Contact them at 1-404-577-4500 or write to PRIDE, 50 Hurt Plaza, Suite 210, Atlanta, GA 30303.

Memos for Moms

1. Understand that the alcohol scene in middle school and high school has not abated.
2. Realize that experimenting in every category of drugs has increased in grades six through eight.
3. Be aware that marijuana contains 470 percent more THC than in the sixties and can cause long-term damage to young adolescents.
4. Look for signs of lack of motivation and lethargy that indicate marijuana use. Adolescents can get addicted.
5. Do not tolerate adolescent use of alcohol or drugs. Let him know that you understand their availability and the pressure on him to use. Help him develop skills and words to counteract the pressure.
6. Include him in discussions about alcohol and drugs. Listen to his concerns, but remain firm and committed.
7. Be knowledgeable about all drugs and be alert to any change in his disposition or behavior.
8. Remember that cigarettes and smokeless tobacco lead to cancer.
9. Give a son strong emotional support and monitor his behavior.
10. Respect his friends and let them know they are wel-

come in your home but they cannot drink or take drugs in your home.

11. Challenge his desire to take risks in more productive ways.

12. Remember that the sons of highly demanding and highly responsive mothers are less likely to become involved in alcohol and drug abuse.

13. Love him, challenge him, trust him, monitor him, and don't give up. If he has broken your trust, reestablish trust after he has paid the consequences of breaking trust. Keep repeating the process.

12

"Is My Son Gay?"

A Mother's Fears

Is Mother the Cause? • Is It Father's Absence?
Can an Older Man Make Him Gay?
Was He Born That Way? • Being a "Sissy"
Being Different • In Adolescence
Can He Be Changed? • Religion's Influence
Teaching Boys to Be Tolerant of Gays
One Story • If a Son Is Gay
Additional Reading • Memos for Moms

A woman asked me why I didn't mention homosexuality when I wrote "*Don't Stop Loving Me*," my book addressed to mothers of adolescent girls. When I interviewed mothers for that book, they did not seem to think of the possibility of a daughter's being gay. And the daughters themselves did not express concern about becoming lesbians or of understanding lesbian friends.

Perhaps the subject of homosexuality did not arise because most mothers are delighted when a daughter enjoys competition and stands up to the boys. No one wonders about a girl who prefers dressing in jeans rather than dresses. And an adolescent girl knows she will not be labeled gay if she likes to play boys' games. The boys relax with her and are attracted to her both as a friend and as a possible girlfriend. Being an athlete or interested in boys' activities is not associated in either the girl's or mother's mind with being lesbian.

Yet the same acceptance of "cross-gender" behavior does not apply to little boys. When they prefer girls' toys or activities, or when they like to dress in Mother's clothes, they are looked at suspiciously. And some parents turn to therapists for advice.

"He acts like a sissy," a mother of an eight-year-old told Richard Green, a researcher from the University of California who was studying the development of homosexuality. "He doesn't play with boys. He's afraid of boys, because he's afraid to play boys' games. He used to like to dress in girls' clothing. He would still like to, only we have absolutely put our foot down. And he talks like a girl, sometimes walks like a girl, acts like a girl."[1]

Mothers—and fathers—don't know how to react when a young son ignores trucks, tries on dresses instead of baseball caps, and avoids rough-and-tumble games. Mother's first reaction may be amusement and an appreciation that he wants to imitate her. She may be flattered by his devotion and think he is cute, almost pretty enough to be a girl.

The fleeting thought of her son's being gay is outweighed by her feeling that he may become a more sensitive man, one who is willing to listen to her feelings or the feelings of other women.

But when he is a young adult and tells his mother he is gay, her heart sinks. She wonders if she did this to him. Did her tolerance of his behavior encourage his homosexuality? What could she have done differently? Why didn't his father take more of an interest in him?

Why or when a son becomes gay still incites debate. Not all sons who avoid boys' activities or dress in Mother's clothes are gay, and the issue of homosexuality is confusing and complex to mothers. Attributing blame or assuming blame for a son's becoming homosexual is not helpful. A gay son and his parents need understanding, not condemnation.

"I remind parents that you are not God," advises Father Lee Walker, an Episcopal priest at Christ Church in Greenwich, Connecticut. "You do not determine certain things about your child. You didn't do anything right or wrong that made your child a male or female. You didn't do anything right or wrong that made your child black or white. The only thing that matters with a gay son is where we go from here."

Each theory about homosexuality challenges the other and this lack of concrete answers can cause parents of young sons unnecessary anxiety. Mothers and fathers fret about what toys and dress-up clothes to give their boys. They worry if their teenage son doesn't like sports or appears uninterested in girlfriends. They wonder if a gay teacher will win him over or if his gay uncle's genes will show up in him. They will remain bewildered because no theory has been indisputably proved. *Mothers should raise sons with love, affection, and common sense and not feel guilty if a son turns out homosexual.* A mother may find it difficult not to feel guilty for a son's sexual orientation because women in our culture have been assigned complete responsibility for their child's life. However, shame and remorse do not help a young man struggling to find his way.

All parents want their sons to be accepted and liked by others. Knowing that a gay son may be derided and detested because of his sexual preference can cause pain and heartache. When Father Walker disclosed to his parents that he was gay, his father, after a few days of absorbing the information, said to him, "I've always wanted the best for both my sons. I'm not saying it's better or worse to be gay, I'm just saying it's a lot easier in the United States to grow up straight than gay and I wish you had the easy way." All parents can share this father's feeling; we want our sons to be happy and have an "easy" life. But we as parents cannot always call the shots.

The hormonal, biological, and family roots of homosexuality are discussed continually by researchers and psychologists. Family histories are taken and psychoanalyzed. The effect of behavior on the brain and the brain on behavior is scrutinized. Yet no one can give a definitive answer to a mother's question. Why are some men gay and others not gay? By "gay" I mean a person who has a constant sexual preference for a person of the same sex, a man or boy whose sexual fantasies are of other men. The life stories of gay men may have many common threads, but one solitary factor does not dominate their upbringing.

Is Mother the Cause?

Because the issue of homosexuality is complex and because a boy's sexual orientation is crucial to his overall psychological health and self-acceptance, I want to examine some of the most commonly held (and controversial) theories of why boys become homosexuals and suggest ways that parents of gay sons can help themselves and their sons accept the reality of their lives.

The classic view of gay development, originating with Freud, is a mother-bashing theory.[2] Mother made her son gay. A mother, the theory says, can create such an intense bond with her son that he identifies with her totally, to the exclusion of his father, and cannot detach from her.

When this same little boy becomes a young man, Freudian therapists argue, he cannot love other women because he has not separated psychologically from his mother. He is not his own person, but an extension of his mother. Only when he breaks away from his mother can he become heterosexual.

Parents of gays and many researchers question that argument. Yes, a gay man may have a very close relationship with his mother, and many do. But many heterosexual men also have strong attachments to their mothers. One young man explained, "A lot of people make assumptions about gays being close to their mothers. I was the youngest by five years. I was closer to my mother than my father, but I don't think closer than most children, although some people think I am extra close."

For most sons, an overprotective mother is a pain, an interference with his adolescent adventuresome spirit, and he tunes her out. It is unlikely that she can turn a straight son into a gay son. The same family can produce both gay and straight children and we don't know why.

Is It Father's Absence?

Some research has examined a father's involvement or lack of involvement with his son to explain homosexuality. Richard Green's study found that fathers of gay sons spent less time with their sons than did fathers of more typically masculine sons.[3] This was not true of all the families Green followed for fifteen years and should not be taken as an absolute cause of homosexuality, but the association was strong enough to be mentioned.

And in a well-known study on sexual preference by Alan Bell and other researchers, homosexual men generally reported negative relationships with their fathers. Bell concluded: "Poor relationships with fathers seemed more important than whatever relationships they may have had with their mothers."[4]

Does a father distance himself from his son because his son is less masculine and makes him uncomfortable? Or, conversely, does a father's lack of interest in his son make the boy more interested in femininelike activities? There is some evidence that a father backs away when his son prefers playing house to racing cars. He then devotes more time to his daughter or his more masculine son. When a father openly prefers a sibling, the little boy has only his mother to turn to for companionship and understanding. This situation removes the father psychologically and physically and leaves the child in a quandary, wondering what he did to make his father avoid him.

Thankfully, these studies are emphasizing that both mothers and fathers are responsible for raising a child and that a child brings his own disposition to the family circle. Giving a mother or father the omnipotence of completely molding a child is irrational. Not only does a son have his own genetic makeup, he usually has siblings, grandparents, aunts, uncles, playmates, priests, rabbis, or ministers in his life. All these people are trying to influence him—usually away from homosexuality and not toward a gay life.

Can an Older Man Make Him Gay?

Some people think that a man is gay because when he was young, he was seduced by an older boy or man. This fear, along with headlines about teachers corrupting students, can produce parental nightmares. Yes, occasionally a teacher becomes sexually involved with a male student and is indicted by a horrified community.[5] But this type of incident is a rare occurrence and should not cause excess worry. A good teacher wants to nurture a young man's mind, not violate him, and both gay and straight men can be excellent teachers.

But can an older man turn a boy into a homosexual? Homosexuality is not contagious and most adolescent homosexual experimentation is between peers. A boy who thinks he is gay may seek out older men and those episodes may confirm his homosexuality. But adolescent experiences alone do not make a homosexual. When Alan Bell interviewed homosexuals about the origins of their sexual orientation, he found that his sample of gay men were not seduced into their lifestyle.[6]

Still, boys should be warned about men who may entice them into sexual activities just as mothers warn their daughters about men who may take advantage of them. Most homosexuals, like heterosexuals, are trustworthy people, but some, like some heterosexuals, are rapists. To think that a son may never be attracted to an older boy or man is foolish. Boys can be enticed with small rewards and adolescents can be tempted through their built-in fascination with sexual experimentation. If an adolescent is lured by a man, especially someone he has trusted, he will be confused and may need psychological guidance.

However, most child abusers are heterosexual men and their victims are girls. A gay usually is attracted to other gays, and chances are he will not make a pass at a straight adolescent. But a son should know that if a gay boy or man makes an unwelcome advance, all he has to say is what a boy I interviewed firmly said to an offender: "I'm not interested. Get out of here." The odds are the aggressor will back off. Or a boy can say to the person the same thing I tell girls to say to unwelcome advances: "I will report you."

Was He Born That Way?

An emerging theory holds that a homosexual man's biology, his inborn physical body, something in his hormonal structure is different than in heterosexual men. This theory would suggest that no matter what influences impact on a boy's life, if he is meant to be gay, he will be gay. Some gay men who write about their childhood seem to corroborate this theory, as they believed they were different from a very early age.[7]

By age nine, Mark Thompson writes, he suspected that he was gay, because he was enthralled by male magazines and turned on by the men's locker room at his swimming pool. Another writes, "Having been called a fag for so many years by my peers, it came as no surprise to me that I should be sexually attracted to men. I always knew I was different from the other boys."[8]

Parents realize that all children are unique from birth, born with their own dispositions and biological makeup. The idea that a child is born with homosexual tendencies can make sense to some parents.

"What will be will be," the mother of a 15-year-old actor told me. "If my son turns out gay, there will be many people who will blame it on show business. And I know now that will not be the case. It was going to be that anyway, no matter what he did."

Simon LeVay, a neurobiologist at the Salk Institute for Biological Studies, examined the brains of nineteen homosexual males who had died of AIDS and discovered that a cluster of cells in the forefront of the hypothalamus, the section of the brain that controls sexual activity, was considerably smaller in these homosexuals than in heterosexuals.[9]

Why was this minute part of the hypothalamus smaller in the homosexual men? We don't know and we don't know if this finding is universal. The effect of AIDS was ruled out through later research, but *when* the hypothalamus in these men became this size has not been determined. Did homosexual activity stimulate the brain in such a way that this cluster became smaller or did the smaller cluster in the hypothalamus generate the homosexual desire? Intriguing questions, but at this stage we do not know the answers.

In a related type of discovery, Laura S. Allen and Roger A. Gorski of the University of California at Los Angeles found that in the bodies they examined, the cord of nerve fibers that allows the two halves of the brain to communicate with each other was larger in the brains of homosexual men than it was in either heterosexual men or women.[10] Does that cord, the anterior commissure, have anything to do with sexual orientation? It is too early to tell, but researchers are excited about the finding.

Still other scientists suspect a genetic link to homosexuality. Michael Bailey of Northwestern University and Richard Pillard of Boston University interviewed sets of brothers looking for patterns of sibling homosexuality. They found that 52 percent of the fifty-six sets of identical twins they interviewed were both gay and 22 percent of the fifty-four fraternal twins were both gay.[11]

Yet if genetics alone determines homosexuality, all the sets of identical twins would have the same disposition to homosexuality. Simply having a certain gene does not necessarily make a person gay, researcher Len Heston from the University of Washington commented in looking at Bailey and Pillard's work. For one, he said, the gene must be activated, and whether it is activated or not is just chance.

Recently, Dean H. Hammer and his colleagues at the National Cancer Institute reported that the X chromosome, passed down from the mother, may influence homosexuality. The gay brothers they studied had a particular region of the X chromosome in common and some history of homosexuality in their mothers' families. This finding, as with most research in homosexuality, has made newspaper headlines while at the same time creating controversy and discussion about its merit among leading researchers.[12]

Even though most gay men can trace their sexual attraction to other males back to their youth, not all social scientists believe that biology alone determines what we become as adults. Our genes or our brain structure incline us to certain ways of behaving, but at some point other influences help to shape our lives.

"I'm more convinced now than ever that genetics plays a big part in it," one gay man told me. "But I don't think that is the only thing. It's a combination of environment and heredity and a lot of other factors. Even the anti-gay forces seem to be accepting that it is set long before the child has any awareness of his sexual orientation."

Still another gay man commented to me, "It's a nature-nurture thing. A boy has a genetic predisposition, and if you are brought up in an environment that pushes you in that direction, you will go that way."

Commenting on the biological/genetic research, John Money of Johns Hopkins University said, "The real question is, When did it [sexual orientation] get there? Was it prenatal, neonatal, during childhood, puberty? That we do not know."[13]

Some characteristics of homosexuals' childhoods are similar enough that I want to discuss them more thoroughly. When many gay men discuss their childhood, they describe an irresistible desire to play like girls.[14] They may not always act on these urges, but they are present. A substantial minority of gays do not remember themselves as "sissies," but research and recollections by gays confirm that consistent feminine behavior during childhood may be an indication of homosexuality. A mother of a gay son, however, objected to a characterization of her son as being girl-like as a child. She said she could not distinguish her gay son's behavior from the behavior of her straight son.

Being a "Sissy"

In two different studies investigating homosexuality, both Richard Green and Alan P. Bell found that many gays recall play activities similar to those described by the parents at the beginning of this chapter.[15] Gender nonconformity at an early age—a boy's preference for girls' games, clothes, and girls as friends—is strongly linked to homosexual men. The researchers, however, warn that gender nonconformity was by no means universal and does not inevitably signal future homosexuality. When boys occasionally dress up like mommy, play with girls, and participate in girls' games, they certainly are not at high risk for homosexuality. They are having fun and parents should not be concerned. The researchers were studying boys who showed a consistent preference for girls' activities.

"I thought it [cross-dressing] was cute. It's just one of the normal things kids do, and I probably didn't think too much of it," a mother of a homosexual man told Richard Green when he asked her about her son's early boyhood.[16]

Green selected two sets of boys to examine whether playing like girls was related to homosexuality. First he contacted parents with sons ages 4 to 12 who were concerned enough about their sons' "feminine" (his term) behavior to seek therapy.[17] These sixty boys preferred playing with dolls, disliked rough-and-tumble games, and dressed in their mothers' clothes frequently.

Green then found sixty boys whose families matched the "feminine" boys in age, number and ages of siblings, marital status of the mother, religion, race, and educational level of the parents. In other words, all was equal except the boys had not been referred to therapists because of "feminine" behavior.

Green interviewed and tested these boys and their parents over a fifteen-year period. Two-thirds of the boys remained in the study until young adulthood. Of the "feminine"-behaving boys, 75 percent called themselves homosexuals or bisexuals as young adults. In the group of boys who preferred masculine activities (rough-and-tumble, transportation toys, blocks, games with balls, boys as friends), not one identified himself as homosexual and only one young man called himself bisexual fifteen years later.

Green reports that in the "feminine" families the mothers often were amused by their young sons' feminine behavior and sent unclear signals to the little boys about acting like a girl, at least for the first few years. As a mother recollected about her son at age six: "He got to the stage where he loved to dress and undress and I went to a rummage sale looking for dress-up clothes. So here was a box of clothes; but there was nothing interesting for men and I really didn't think too much of it. He liked jewelry, too."[18]

His father commented, "I haven't been much concerned with it until fairly recently. Initially he would wear his mother's clothing and still mostly it's hers. He was interested in color, so we tried to get him interested in colorful clothing that would fit into a man's role, but we really haven't done this enough. He will wear high heels, walk around in the house in high heels."[19]

Their son later identified himself as gay. The statistics in this study are impressive, but mothers reading them must keep in mind that 25 percent of the boys who were taken to therapy for their cross-gender behavior did not describe themselves as gay when they were interviewed as adults.

Some boys in this study did not receive clear signals about culturally appropriate gender behavior—an essential ingredient in their formation as men. In all societies, adults teach boys how men behave in their society.[20] A boy learns from his mother what he is not, that he is not a woman. He learns from his father that he is a man. He also should be able to observe that caring and nurturing are human qualities admired in all people, male or female. He does not have to pretend to be his mother to display these "feminine" qualities. However, I want to emphasize again that many boys occasionally pretend to be their mothers and at times prefer playing with girls, but these are not the boys the researchers are discussing.

Bell and his associates found in their study that this same pattern of cross-gender behavior was the only strong predictor of adult homosexuality. After warning that *this behavior does not always indicate homosexuality*, the researchers say, "Nonetheless, according to our findings, a child's display of gender nonconformity greatly increases the likelihood of that child's becoming homosexual regardless of his or her family background and regardless of how much the child identifies with either parent."[21]

Being Different

Most boys know at an early age that they will grow up to be like their fathers, not their mothers. They learn this by dressing like a boy, and by playing with other boys and boys' toys. This does not mean that boys don't ever play house or with dolls. In a perfect world, a boy would have a father who helped take care of the children and the house, so he could see that men are capable of nurturing. Then when he played house, he would happily take the role of a father, knowing that fathers are homemakers also. The boys in the studies mentioned above took the role of the mother when they played. They also preferred being with girls and did not like being with boys. They preferred everything about girls.

Not all gays recall their childhoods as being any different from other boys'. One man told me that he has examined his childhood movies looking for signs that he was different from his friends, but he could not find any. He doesn't know if that was because he was raised in Texas, where a gay suddenly could disappear from town and where he was terrified of being identified as gay. He wonders what he would be like if he had been raised on a desert island. He does remember, however, being corrected for acting silly like a girl at times and being given a Betty Crocker baking and cooking set when he was in fourth or fifth grade. Although he did not participate in "traditional male competitive sports," he liked swimming, hiking, boating, and playing with building blocks and Erector sets.

But he remembers, as do many gays, when he first heard the word *homosexual*. "The first time I heard a word for it, I was in fourth grade," he said. "I heard the gym coach talk about pansies and queers, and when I asked him what that meant, he said 'homosexual' and I asked what that meant. And he told me to look it up in the dictionary. That led me to other words, and for the next couple of months I would sneak downtown to Dallas on the bus and read things in the library." He now says he knew he was gay when he was in fourth grade.

Another gay man told me, "I remember when I first heard the word *gay*. I asked my mother what that meant and she hemmed and hawed and said in a very disgusted way that it's a man who falls in love with another man. I never knew there were normal men who felt that way. It wasn't until I could identify with a normal person who was gay that I could acknowledge it in myself." This young man is 26, and his mother still does not know he is gay. He said she suspects it but told his brother that when she thinks about it she puts it "out of her mind."

A few boys seem to enjoy the fact that they are different from other teenage boys. I interviewed a 14-year-old boy who was the youngest of a family of boys without a father in the house. A "mama's boy" by his own description, he supplied his mother with companionship and good entertainment. He told me that his favorite activity was sitting with his mother after dinner and "talking, talking, talking." They exchanged gossip, taste in clothes, and recipes. He had acquired all the characteristics and endearing charm of the daughter his mother never had. He was a singer but also wanted to be a cosmetologist because he enjoyed making people look good. I was impressed with his self-confidence, his seemingly complete acceptance of himself, his sense of humor, and his frank acknowledgment that he had no male friends his age. His best friend was a girl, but now he admitted sadly that she didn't like talking with him as much as before when they were younger.

Other men I interviewed remembered clearly not being with the "in" groups in school. "I never felt part of the crowd. I accepted these feelings as being a social outcast," said one man.

"I was teased a lot in school," said another. When I asked him why, he replied, "I was no good at sports, couldn't catch a ball. The gym teacher in fourth or fifth grade would put me on the team for a joke. Even he would tease me. Other boys were teased if they weren't athletic, but I took the brunt of it."

Other boys desperately try to cover up any feelings of homosexuality and develop "hypervigilance." "Rather than admit homosexual thoughts," one gay man explained, "these boys want to make sure other people don't have these thoughts and persecute others for gay behavior. You're proving to yourself that you are not gay."

No wonder the self-image of gays suffers during adolescence and the suicide rate is estimated to be three times higher for gay than straight adolescents. The world is turning against them and they don't understand why. "I can't understand why people object so much," a young man told me. "I'm normal. I'm a normal person."

In Adolescence

Homosexuality is barely mentioned in books about adolescence.[22] In the acclaimed book *At the Threshold: The Developing Adolescent*, commissioned by the Carnegie Foundation and edited by S. Shirley Feldman and Glen R. Elliott, only three paragraphs out of 641 pages mention homosexuality.[23] The following paragraph from *At the Threshold* substantiates my belief that parents and educators should be more aware of adolescent homosexuality activities so they can guide their children.

> Just as some children engage in sex play with members of their own sex, it is not unusual for adolescents to have homosexual contacts with peers, and sometimes with adults or children. Typically such encounters are of an exploratory and transient nature; they do not, as such, lead to a homosexual orientation in adulthood, although most adult homosexuals usually trace their sexual orientation back to adolescence.[24]

Some, maybe many, boys experience homosexual feelings during adolescence. They may develop a crush on a coach or become attached to an older boy or a friend. This may or may not mean that he is homosexual. Even if he acts on those feelings, he may not be gay. The famous 1948 Kinsey report stated that 37 percent of male adults had engaged, after puberty, in a same-sex experience leading to orgasm. Yet in the same Kinsey report, only 4 to 10 percent reported that they still were attracted, in varying degrees, to other men.[25] These figures are now disputed as being too high. One 1993 study found that 2 percent of its sample of men (ages 20 to 39) had some same-gender sexual activity during the last ten years and only 1 percent reported being exclusively homosexual during that same period. Another recent national study (men ages 16 to 50) found that 4 percent of those polled had engaged in homosexual behavior in the last five years.[26] Many experts now suggest that 2 to 4 percent of the male population may be gay.

Whatever the statistics, the intense hormonal surge in adolescence arouses boys' curiosity about all kinds of sex. Thinking about sex and ways to perform sex can draw some boys into experimentation with one another. These explorations can take place in a "clubhouse" they have built or in dark alleys where they gather, but they are transitory and usually have no lasting impact on a boy's sexuality.[27]

For most boys these episodes with other boys fade away, but for other boys they become the main expression of sexuality. A heterosexual boy may be aroused by such activities, but his fantasies are about girls and his desire is to make love with a woman, not a man. Men do not hold sexual fascination for him. He is intrigued by girls, heterosexually oriented erotic magazines, and women's bodies.

For gay adolescents, their sexual fantasies are about men. "I had your typical homosexual encounters at ten or thirteen," said one gay man. "I suppose I enjoyed them more than the other boys. My dreams were about men and my sexual fantasies were of men. Some boys may recognize it but suppress it. I really didn't give it much thought until I was older."

Most gay men begin to suspect they are homosexual during their high-school years.[28] They struggle to appear straight, but deep down they know they are attracted to other boys, not girls. "The big reason for not coming out in adolescence is the fear of rejection," one gay man said. "Kids are thrown out of the house by their fathers."

Another man told me, "I did not know during adolescence. I had some feelings for men when I was young, but I thought I would grow out of it, that it was a phase, but I haven't grown out of it yet. At the end of my freshman year in college I came to realize and accept that I was gay." In high school, he only told his best friend, a girl, of his suspicions.

Can He Be Changed?

Most therapists think it is impossible to change someone's sexual orientation. Laurence Steinberg, a leading expert in adolescence, writes: "Attempts to change an individual's sexual orientation exact a heavy psychological price. Suspicion, lectures, and pleas will only add to adolescent anxieties, whatever his or her sexual inclinations."[29]

For a boy who knows he is gay, the purpose of therapy is not to change his sexual orientation, but to help reduce his stress and anxiety. The suicide rate for gays has been estimated as three hundred times the national level, and adolescents are the most vulnerable to this loss of self-esteem and depression.

Yet some therapists disagree that sexual orientation is set early in life. Moses and M. Egle Laufer, Freudian analysts at the British Psycho-Analytic Society, believe that sexual orientation becomes fixed by the end of adolescence. If an adolescent agrees to treatment, the Laufers think the analyst must *not* remain neutral about homosexuality. Remaining neutral by not trying to steer the boy away from homosexuality "may also be experienced by the adolescent as yet another confirmation that sexual abnormality is the only right he has."[30]

There may be some boys who waver between homosexuality and heterosexuality and these boys need counseling.[31] When I asked a couple of gay men about adolescents or young men who may be "waverers," one replied, "Yes, I think waverers have a tough time and are the most confused. I have some friends who say they do like women and would like to get married and have a family, but they are afraid they will still like men."

But another man disagreed. He thought boys wavered because there was so much pressure on them to be straight. "I find boys only waver when people are giving them very heavy messages about right or wrong, better or worse, black or white. The waverer is a child who knows full well what he feels and is terrified of coming up with that answer [that he is gay]."

I believe there are adolescent boys who are legitimately confused about their sexual orientation—not from family pressure alone, but from inner uncertainty, and from society's new openness with all sexual concerns. Many boys—and girls—are experiencing a sexual awakening, often due to what they see in the media, before they are ready for it, and they are not old enough to make good decisions. A therapist who will listen patiently while a boy sorts through his turmoil, self-doubts, and often self-hatred is sorely needed. By the end of adolescence a boy should be able to fully accept his male gender and then acknowledge his sexual orientation as gay or straight.

Religion's Influence

In a book discussing the lack of sexual moral standards in our children, Dr. Ruth Westheimer, who receives calls from teenagers on her radio show, abhors the fact that no one is talking to children about their sexual behavior, including homosexuality.[32] Dr. Ruth interviewed clergy from many religions about what sexual standards they are teaching young people. Then she asked many young adults where they acquired their sexual values. It became evident that the clergy and young people were not talking to each other.

Young gays are looking for role models, for "normal" gays whom they can respect. Some clergy can offer them that role model themselves or lead them to gay men who are respected and would volunteer to guide and mentor a young gay safely through adolescence. Father Lee Walker commented that we all would be better off if we didn't spend a lot of time thinking about people's sex lives. "What we need to think about," he said, "is what kind of person walks out of the bedroom into the world. Does the relationship make him a good person?"

Father Walker himself did not reveal his homosexuality to a boy who was seeking help. The boy subsequently committed suicide after telling his parents he was gay (against the priest's advice) and receiving their hostile reaction. This priest decided then, "My job is not worth a teenager's life, and from here on, the minimum I'm going to do is tell anyone who asks me that I am gay and what I'm working for is how I can get someplace where I can be public." This Episcopal priest found a parish in Greenwich, Connecticut, where he could serve as himself, a real person. He recommended a book, *Coming Out Within* by Craig O'Neil and Kathleen Ritter, that he says helps gays with their spiritual problems.

No matter what a parent's or adviser's religious orientation, they should try to understand and help a gay adolescent. A young man told me, "I was raised with the feeling that homosexuality was so wrong. Negative messages are everywhere. I have come to realize that God could not be that way, and I am learning to accept my homosexuality as a gift."

However, parents and advisers also should warn gay adolescents of the habit of some men to "cruise" bars, looking for quick, uncommitted sex. This practice is dangerous, both physically and psychologically, for gay *and* straight men. The AIDS epidemic reminds us daily of the value of monogamous sex. Parents of gay as well as straight sons must keep reminding their sons that the era of promiscuity is over.

Teaching Boys to Be Tolerant of Gays

Our society has ignored and therefore encouraged homophobia, the fear and hatred of homosexuals.[33] And adolescent boys often are the worst offenders. Their language is peppered with brutal and offensive anti-gay slang. They make fun of gays, often verbally abusing them or physically assaulting them. A young 21-year-old in a quiet neighborhood in New York City was pulled from his car and beaten with a baseball bat because he "looked" gay. He made the mistake of having long hair, wearing an earring, and driving with another young man. Gay-bashing can happen to any young male who may not fit into a teenager's image of "straight."

Gay-bashing must be vehemently discouraged. And parents

can set the example and demand that gays be respected. Mothers and fathers can point out to their adolescent sons that they don't have to be threatened by gays. A gay man is not challenging the rights of straight men and will not seduce him. A gay prefers the company of other gays. If a son doesn't feel comfortable with gays, he does not have to hang out with them, but he may not harass them.

One Story

The development of homosexuality can be described best by a gay himself. Only he can recount his first recognition that he was different from other boys. Only he can describe his sexual attraction to other boys or men. Only he can feel his comfort with girls as friends and his discomfort with them as lovers.

Autobiographies of gay men relate their pain through adolescence and their desperate attempts to appear heterosexual so they would not be tormented by their peers. In an explosive, haunting memoir, Paul Monette relates the depth of his agony and despair because he could not tell anyone he was gay.[34]

He describes the self-control he used to conceal his true identity from his family and peers through middle school, high school, and college. His self-hatred pours from the pages as he desperately pleaded as a youth to be changed into a man whom others would love. But what he wanted and finally admitted wanting was to find a man who would love him as he was, a highly erotic, sensual man who loved other men. Ten years following his college graduation, Monette "came out" after finding a man to love and who loved him in return.

Yet he had known since he was a child that he was different as he "clumped up and down on the hardwood floors in my mother's heels, prancing even, right in front of the grownups. And I had a thing for paper dolls. I remember the tail end of a flareup between my parents, over the issue of my inappropriate fascinations. No word like 'sissy' yet, and the only subtext I picked up was the pleasure of being fretted over."[35]

Other men may not write as passionately about their lives, but when they do acknowledge their homosexuality they express a relief, a freedom. "The wonderful thing about homosexuality," one man told me, "is that we can explore a wide range of feelings and celebrate the feminine side of ourselves. It's a kind of freedom to say I can wear all kinds of colors. I can enjoy ballet music and verbalize. Sure, there are heterosexual men that can do that also, but it is harder for them to accept the feminine side of themselves. The more liberated men can do that."

If a Son Is Gay

I am impressed with how resilient and understanding many parents are of their sons' homosexual orientation. A man who was "traditional" to the core told me at my husband's college reunion that his son was gay and had recently died of AIDS. His son had returned to his parents' home during the final year of his life, and since his death his parents have become active in gay support groups. A decade ago, this man would not have mentioned his son during a college reunion.

This open acknowledgment of a relative's homosexuality has lifted a burden from families. A mother who told me she cried for a year after her son told her he was gay now advocates for the understanding of gay children. I don't know a family who would choose a gay life for their son. It is not what a mother has dreamed of for her beloved child and it can be a father's nightmare. But a mother's heart will be broken twice if, in addition to knowing a son is gay, she rejects him. Acceptance, respect, and love are what he desires from his parents, as do all children. A mother doesn't have to feel comfortable at a gay bar, love all her son's friends, or openly embrace his lifestyle in order to accept him. She may eventually reach that point and her son would love her complete approval, but for now the important step is to embrace him as her son and reassure him of her love and commitment.

When I asked gay men how parents could discuss homosexuality with an adolescent son whom they suspected was gay, they acknowledged that it was a difficult subject to bring up. They said that adolescents don't want to talk about sex in the first place and that asking a son directly if he was gay would be a serious mistake. One man said, "I don't think parents should confront a boy. He would do one of two things. He would either be greatly relieved or he would totally freak out, thinking that his behavior really showed his homosexuality, and he would go further into the closet."

Some men suggested that creating a home that is open and welcoming to all people, regardless of their race, religion, or sexual orientation, would provide a son with a "general atmosphere of openness and trust" in which he could feel free to discuss all issues with his parents, including his own sexuality. Most men I interviewed did not come out to their parents until they were in their late twenties, when they were ready. They believed a son should make the initial move.

Often a boy's siblings realize a brother is gay, even before his parents are aware. When a son has told both parents and siblings, they should openly discuss their worries, anxieties, resentment, or acceptance. Some siblings may fear they will be branded as gay or be avoided by friends because a brother is gay. They have to be reassured that each member of the family is an individual with his or her own sexual orientation. Parents can, by their example of respect and love for their gay son, assure each child that he or she is unique and lovable.

"The central message to parents," said one gay man, "is that this child is the same child you took home from the hospital. It is reprehensible for parents to divorce themselves from a child because he is homosexual. I know examples of outright hatred. Being a human being should mean being respected."

Father Walker advised, "There are things that can't be controlled, and I find a lot of time with parents they need to understand that their child can be happy, productive, and well adjusted as a gay person, and the best way they can do this is to help them grow and understand the life that has been given to them. Often I run into parents who really love their gay children and really want to support them, but often the motivating factor is they want grandchildren. They don't want the neighbors to know. They don't want to tell the guys at the office and often you have to say to the parents, 'Whose welfare are you concerned with?' "

A young man told a reporter he was "horrified" when he recognized his own homosexuality and that his parents were stunned. "I'll never forget what it felt like," he said. "Alone. Heterosexuals don't understand the price we pay for being in the closet. Now I look at all my friends. I look at how I'm closer to my family. What a wonderful thing it is to come out."[36]

In the present atmosphere of homophobia, parents and friends of gays have found strength from one another. An organization called Parents and Friends of Lesbians and Gays (Parents-FLAG) is located in Washington (see p. 280 for address). They will direct a parent to an existing support group or help parents begin a group in their area. They can support parents in loving and accepting their gay son.

Additional Reading

Now That You Know: What Every Parent Should Know About Homosexuality, by Betty Fairchild and Nancy Hayward. Updated version. New York: A Harvest/HBJ Book, 1989.

When Someone You Know Is Gay, by Susan and Daniel Cohen. New York: M. Evans and Co., 1989.

Parents Matter: Parents' Relationship with Lesbian Daughters and

Gay Sons, by Ann Muller. Tallahassee, Fla.: The Naiad Press, Inc. 1987.

Beyond Acceptance: Parents of Lesbians and Gays Talk About Their Experiences, by Carolyn W. Griffin, Marian J. Wirth, and Arthur G. Wirth. New York: St. Martin's Press, 1988.

Memos for Moms

1. Love your son for who he is. Do not try to mold him into the child you wanted.
2. Encourage and appreciate his masculinity.
3. Urge his father to discover activities they can enjoy together.
4. Don't worry if he doesn't like competitive sports—that does not mean he is gay. He can engage in many other activities that are just as "masculine" as sports.
5. Be sympathetic about a boy's struggle with his sexuality. Many adolescent boys are confused about their sexuality, and few people talk to boys about their natural preoccupation with sex.
6. Remain open to discussions about gays, always respecting gays as persons—even if you don't understand them yourself. Teach him to respect the rights of gays and not to harass them.
7. Provide a home atmosphere that shows respect for all persons.
8. Urge him to remain monogamous in his sexual relationships and always to practice "safer" sex.
9. If you suspect he is gay, do not confront him. You may be mistaken or drive him further into the closet. Wait until he is ready to tell you.
10. If your son tells you he is gay, be grateful that he told

you and contact a support group. The address and phone number for the national office of Parents and Friends of Lesbians and Gays (Parents-FLAG) is P.O. Box 27605, Washington, DC, 20038, 1-202-638-4200. To locate the Parents-FLAG chapter nearest you, call 1-800-4-FAMILY.

11. Love and respect your son.

13

"Soon You'll Be Wanting Us to Wear Bras"

The Dilemma of Being Sensitive and Strong

Remaining True to Himself

When I was attempting to engage my oldest son in a discussion about the merits of being sensitive and in touch with his emotions, he looked at me quizzically, then laughed as he said, "Soon you'll be wanting us to wear bras." I didn't reply to his comment that afternoon, but I have thought of our conversation frequently. Was he right? Did I want him to act like a woman? Was I trying to change him into something he was not? Was he again distancing himself, not willing to talk about feelings? Or was he kidding me, knowing that for years I had been trying to get his brothers and him to talk about their feelings?

He certainly was right on one score. If I wanted him to get in touch with his emotions, telling him to talk about them was not the right approach. As I have learned in researching adolescent boys and adult men, demanding an emotional revelation makes them withdraw, not open up. Although boys and men like direct communications, interrogating a male about feelings is about as effective as asking him to turn off the television when a game is going into overtime. He refuses to cooperate.

So here is the dilemma. Can a mother raise a son who presents a tough outer shell but still maintains inner contact with his fears, loves, joys, sadness? Can he be both strong and sensitive? Or will adolescence permanently obscure his emotions so he always puts up a front of invulnerability, an impenetrable mask, a "Don't fool with me" attitude?

That macho stance may have served him well during his teen years, but it can lead to the loss of love, friendship, and relationships in adult life. Dropping this mask of indifference is difficult when a boy is used to camouflage and subterfuge. How can he openly say, "I love you and need you," when he has spent his early years trying to prove he is independent and doesn't need anyone?

I have stressed throughout this discussion of mothers and adolescent sons the importance *not* of independence but of interdependence and trust, the cornerstones of stable relationships. A son can learn these basic virtues from his mother. He will see that depending on others (interdependence) is a quality of all human life, not a threat to his manhood. He will watch his mother reach out to others for support and observe that others, including himself, depend on her. She is teaching him interdependence.

Through a mother's trust in her son, her belief in his competence and his ability to get through difficult situations, she endows him with self-esteem, a confidence in himself. This self-confidence enables him to be with peers without the fear of being absorbed or losing his uniqueness. And he will not have to worry about being in control, the plague of adolescent males. His mother's trust has made him comfortable with himself and he knows who he is.

This is a mother's challenge, to free her son so he can manifest his outer strength of character and his inner sensitivity. Her wish for her son is that he combine his positive masculine traits with a nurturing spirit, an inner life, a soul that makes all life worth living.

But this ideal combination of strong and sensitive may not be apparent while he is an adolescent. A boy may think he has to prove his strength before he can appreciate his own and others' feelings; mothers must be patient and not give up. By drawing his attention to the feelings of others, she encourages him to look beneath the surface, to see the real person. A boy raised in this manner will not bully his way through the world of women, school, and work, but will cherish his own worth and that of the men, women, and children in his life.

Most boys possess this sensitivity, but are hesitant to reveal it. Only in a secure situation without fear of ridicule can they admit to their fears or joys, or even recognize them as emotions. Survival through middle school, high school, divorce, and loss of friends or family members builds a thick shield. He thinks that breaking it down may mean losing everything, that it's better to remain tough.

Remaining True to Himself

Strong mothers of strong sons celebrate the maleness in their sons and honor the traditional masculine qualities that have provided protection and sustenance for generations of families. Mothers can admire and nurture these virtues of responsibility and commitment to duty, for they are good traditional traits that need to be encouraged. Boys also should be made aware of the more extensive male roles defined by our evolving society.

In analyzing masculinity's current state of disrepute, Harvard University's Ronald Levant argues that the positive values of traditional masculinity should be honored, not rejected in favor of a vague "new male" concept. He also sees a definite need to teach men the relational skills that many women possess and many men are lacking.[1] By enhancing the basic masculine core with a deepened awareness of the vast richness of emotional life, a man will find a new harmony between himself and others.

Levant eloquently lists the positive attributes of masculinity:

A man's willingness to set aside his own needs for the sake of his family; his ability to withstand hardship and pain to protect others; his tendency to take care of people and solve their problems as if they were his own; his way of expressing love by doing things for others; his loyalty, dedication, and commitment; his stick-to-it-iveness and will to hang in until the situation is corrected; and his ability to solve problems, think logically, rely on himself, take risks, stay calm in the face of danger, and assert himself.[2]

We need to appreciate these traits, Levant says, and I agree with him, so men can "regain some of the lost esteem and pride associated with being a man."

Daughters, wives, and mothers do not want to return to the era of domineering men and wimpy women, and Levant does not advocate this. The qualities listed above, typically assigned to men, can be honored in all people. And so can inner relational, traditionally feminine, traits.

When I observe the solidarity between many women—friends, sisters, mothers and daughters—I often attribute it to their ability to connect with one another on an emotional level. Women are willing to share their emotions and talk about personal issues. I have sat with mothers and daughters on national television shows in which they have aired their differences in front of millions of viewers, yet as they walked away from the cameras, they talked amicably about the reactions of their family and friends back home, a happening most men do not understand.

Males often argue on more impersonal levels. When politicians harangue one another about philosophies and policy issues before the cameras and then play tennis with one another in the privacy of friends, women are perplexed. Conflicting opinions may intimidate women while conflicting emotions may terrify men.

Because they were taught through childhood that big boys don't show emotions and certainly don't cry, men often cannot sense when to weep or mourn or explode with happiness. They cannot give the feeling a name. In working with men like these, Levant uses a "psychoeducational" approach to help teach them to get in touch with their emotions. Together they develop a vocabulary of emotions (hurt, sadness, disappointment, rejection, abandonment, fear, warmth, affection, closeness, and appreciation). When men (and boys) do not recognize an emotion, they experience what Levant calls a "buzz," a tightness in the throat, constriction in the chest, clenching of the gut, "antsy" feeling in the legs, constriction in the face, difficulty concentrating, and gritting of teeth.

Men react to the buzz in four characteristic ways, according to Levant. "Distraction, which serves as a circuit breaker allowing men to disengage from the buzz; the Rubber Band Syndrome, in which the buzz builds and builds until it erupts in an explosion of anger; the Tin Man approach, which requires locking the buzz up tighter than a drum so that the man no longer feels anything; or the Mixed Messenger, in which the buzz oozes out through the man's nonverbal behavior."[3]

Women often wonder what brings on these buzz syndromes and men can't explain. The men in Levant's group, however, learn how to recognize the buzz as the first stage of reacting to an annoyance (antsyness and teeth grinding usually follow, ending with a full-blown eruption). By accepting the buzz's presence, they can name what is bothering them, then act upon it or put it aside. They are discovering themselves.

The ability to acknowledge and express emotions constructively is a skill mothers would like to impart to their sons, but even mothers themselves are uncomfortable at times with a son's feelings. She may have been raised by an unemotional father, the strong and silent type, and may not understand the worth of acknowledging his feelings of rejection as well as triumph. Despite her desire to emphasize the positive only, a boy needs his mother to help him understand all aspects of his inner life.

Sons also desperately want a closeness with their fathers, even though they may mask it out of necessity. "Sometimes my friends come over and ask where my dad is," one boy told me. "Sometimes I tell them he's out 'cause I don't want to face the truth that he's left, and sometimes I'll say they got divorced. It's changed my life, but I really try not to think about it much anymore. I just try to live my own life."

To live his life with the pain of father-loss can be an almost unbearable burden for a boy. He often cloaks it behind bravado and indifference. A mother cannot replace a boy's father, but she can help him recognize his feelings of grief and show him how to rely on traits that will connect him to other people, not withdraw into himself and deny his hurt.

As boys leave adolescence behind, they often uncover new depths of self-understanding, sometimes astounding not only themselves but their parents.

The year our oldest son graduated from college, he wrote to my husband and me, "The older I get, I find that the feminine side of me—compassion, emotions, outward expression—becomes more meaningful among friends. Relationships are rewarding because you get to know someone and that requires an openness, something maleness or 'machismo' tends to ignore. Many men are afraid to let the feminine side of them develop, but I think there must be a balance. I guess persons with a kind of balance of masculinity and femininity have a relationship that can always grow through understanding and love." I treasured his letter.

That balance, a mother's hope for her son, may not come until a son realizes that emotional pain can be as real as physical pain and emotional joy can be as real as physical pleasure. "I learned," my son later told me, "that emotions can hurt, that I was vulnerable."

Perhaps awareness and acceptance of one's vulnerability are the first step to maturity, compassion, and commitment. This consciousness can break through a young man's facade of insensitivity, dismantle his armor of defense, and release his inner life. Then he will be able to acknowledge to his wife—and children— "I love you, need you, and will stick with you, no matter what."

Then a mother knows she has raised a strong and sensitive son.

Notes

1. "Welcome to the Club"

1. Christiane Olivier. *Jocasta's Children: The Imprint of Mother*. New York: Routledge, 1989, p. 39.
2. Kasper Kiepenheuer. *Crossing the Bridge: A Jungian Approach to Adolescence*. Peru, Ill.: Open Court Publishing, 1990, p. 123.
3. Beverly I. Fagot and Richard Hagan. "Observation of Parent Reactions to Sex-Stereotyped Behaviors: Age and Sex Effects." In *Child Development* 62:617–28, 1991.
4. Judith G. Smetana. "Toddlers' Social Interactions in the Context of Moral and Conventional Transgressions in the Home." In *Developmental Psychology* 25(4).
5. C. Zahn-Waxler, M. Radke-Yarrow, and R. A. King. "Child-rearing and Children's Pro-social Initiatives Toward Victims of Distress." In *Child Development* 50, 1979.
6. Jeanne Brooks-Gunn and Wendy Schempp Matthews. *He and She: How Children Develop Their Sex-Role Identity*. Englewood Cliffs, N.J.: Prentice-Hall Press, 1978. This now-classic study relies in part on the work of Eleanor Maccoby and Carol Jacklin.
7. Fagot and Hagan, *op. cit.*

8. Eleanor Maccoby. "Gender and Relationships: A Developmental Account." In *American Psychologist* 45(4).

9. *Ibid.*, p. 516.

10. *Ibid.*, p. 516.

11. Lynn S. Liben and Margaret L. Signorella. "Gender-Schematic Processing in Children: The Role of Initial Interpretations of Stimuli." In *Developmental Psychology* 29(1), 1993.

12. Rita J. Casey. "Children's Emotional Experience: Relations Among Expression, Self-Report, and Understanding." In *Developmental Psychology* 29(1), 1993.

2. "Crazed with Madness"

1. Garrison Keillor. "About Guys" in *The New York Times*, December 27, 1992, p. 11.

2. C. J. Jung in *Aspects of the Masculine*. Princeton, N.J.: Princeton University Press, 1989, p. 52.

3. S. Shirley Feldman and Glen R. Elliott. *At the Threshold: The Developing Adolescent*. Cambridge, Mass.: Harvard University Press, 1990, p. 50.

4. J. M. Tanner has been studying his field of human growth since 1962. In his new updated book, *Fetus into Man* (Cambridge, Mass.: Harvard University Press, 1990), he offers a brief yet complete biology course on the fundamentals of human growth. His work is used in most studies of puberty and is the basis of the present discussion.

5. Roberts L. Paikoff and Jeanne Brooks-Gunn. "Physiological Processes: What Role Do They Play During the Transition to Adolescence?" In *From Childhood to Adolescence: A Transitional Period?*, ed. Raymond Montemayor, Gerald R. Adams, and Thomas P. Gullotta. Newbury, Calif.: Sage Publications, 1990. Also, a good discussion can be found in Richard M. Lerner and Terryl T. Foch, eds., *Biological-Psychosocial Interac-*

tions in Early Adolescence (Hillsdale, N.J.: Lawrence Erlbaum Associates, 1987).

6. Edward A. Smith. "A Biosocial Model of Adolescent Sexual Behavior." In *Biology of Adolescent Behavior and Development*, ed. Gerald R. Adams, Raymond Montemayor, and Thomas P. Gullotta. 1989.

7. Robert Bly. *Iron John*. Reading, Mass.: Addison-Wesley, 1990. On pages 45, 46, and 47 Bly describes the meaning of hair in an adolescent boy's adventure with his mentor, Iron John.

8. Alan Gaddas and Jeanne Brooks-Gunn. "The Male Experience of Pubertal Change." In *Journal of Youth and Adolescence* 14(1):61–69, 1985.

9. Bertrand Russell. From the *Autobiography of Bertrand Russell* and quoted in *The Man in Me: Versions of the Male Experience*, ed. Ross Firestone. New York: HarperPerennial, 1992.

10. James C. Dobson. *Preparing for Adolescence: Straight Talk to Teens and Parents*. Ventura, Calif.: Regal Books, 1980, p. 87. Dr. Dobson is not advocating masturbation, but demonstrates a compassionate understanding of masturbation as an outlet for sexual energy.

11. Richard Y. Handy. *Male Sexuality and the Challenge of Healing Impotence*. Buffalo, N.Y.: Promethus Books, 1988, p. 102. An autobiographical account of Handy's battle with prostate cancer with recollections of his young-adolescent sexuality.

12. Douglas H. Heath. *Fulfilling Lives: Paths to Maturity and Success*. San Francisco: Jossey-Bass Publishers, 1991.

13. Sanford M. Dornbusch, Ruth T. Gross, Paula Duke Duncan, and Philip L. Ritter. "Stanford Studies of Adolescence Using National Health Examination Survey." In *Biological-Psycholosocial Interactions in Early Adolescence*, ed. Richard M. Lerner and Terryl T. Foch. Hillsdale, N.J.: Lawrence Erlbaum Associates, 1987, p. 195.

14. David Gilmore. *Manhood in the Making: Cultural Concepts of*

Masculinity. New Haven, Conn.: Yale University Press, 1990, p. 88.

15. Nancy L. Galambos, David M. Almeida, and Anne C. Petersen. "Masculinity, Femininity, and Sex Role Attitudes in Early Adolescence: Exploring Gender Intensification." In *Child Development* 61, 1990, pp. 1905–14.

16. Richard M. Lerner, Jacqueline V. Lerner, Laura E. Hess, Jacqueline Schwav, Jasna Jovanovic, Rachna Talwar, and Joseph S. Kucher. "Physical Attractiveness and Psychosocial Functioning among Early Adolescents." In *The Journal of Early Adolescence* 11(3), August 1991.

3. Struggling for Identity

1. Andrew Collins. "Parent-Child Relationships in the Transition to Adolescence: Continuity and Change in Interaction, Affect, and Cognition." In *From Childhood to Adolescence: A Transitional Period?*, ed. Raymond Montemayor, Gerald R. Adams, and Thomas P. Gullotta. Newbury, Calif.: Sage Publications, 1990. A good review of the many studies that have noted the increase in conflict between parents and adolescents during puberty.

2. Laurence Steinberg. "Pubertal Maturation and Parent-Adolescent Distance: An Evolutionary Perspective." In *Biology of Adolescent Behavior and Development*, ed. Gerald R. Adams, Raymond Montemayor, and Thomas P. Gullotta. Newbury, Calif.: Sage Publications, 1989, p. 75.

3. Aletha Huston and Mildred Alvarez. "The Socialization Context of Gender Role Development in Early Adolescence." In *From Childhood to Adolescence*, *op. cit.* Huston and Alvarez are referring to an earlier work on power in the family by Steinberg and Hill (1978). Huston and Alvarez found in their research that maternal employment often increases a mother's power because of her role in providing family income.

4. Willard Gaylin. *The Male Ego*. New York: Viking Press, 1992, p. 30. A discussion of the "much misunderstood" male ego by a psychiatrist and cofounder of the Hastings Center.

5. Robert Bly. *Iron John*. Reading, Mass.: Addison-Wesley Publishing, 1990, p. 94.

6. Andrew H. Malcolm. *The Huddle: Fathers, Sons, and Football*. New York: Simon and Schuster, 1992, p. 23.

7. Guy Corneau. *Absent Fathers, Lost Sons: The Search for Masculine Identity*. Boston: Shambhala, 1991, p. 13.

8. Erik H. Erikson. *Identity, Youth and Crisis*. New York: W. W. Norton, 1968. Erikson's work has formed the basis of much of the analytic research on adolescent development.

9. Carol Gilligan and Lyn Mikel Brown. *Meeting at the Crossroads: Women's Psychology and Girls' Development*. Cambridge, Mass.: Harvard University Press, 1992. Other works written or edited by Carol Gilligan include *Making Connections* (Troy, N.Y.: Emma Willard School, 1989), *Mapping the Moral Domain* (Harvard University Press, 1988), and *In a Different Voice* (Harvard University Press, 1982).

10. Mark J. Benson, Paula B. Harris, and Cosby S. Rogers. "Identity Consequences of Attachment to Mothers and Fathers Among Late Adolescents." In *Journal of Research on Adolescence* 2(3), 1992.

11. Susan Harter and Ann Monsour. "Developmental Analysis of Conflict Caused by Opposing Attributes in the Adolescent Self-Portrait." In *Developmental Psychology* 28(2):259, 1992.

12. Gaylin, *op. cit.*, p. 50.

13. David Gilmore. *Manhood in the Making*. New Haven, Conn.: Yale University Press, 1990. Gilmore observed that men have to be "made" in many societies.

14. David Elkind. *All Grown Up and No Place to Go: Teenagers in Crisis*. New York: Addison-Wesley Publishing, 1984. Elkind coined the phrase "personal fable" to describe an adolescent's efforts to build a story of security. His concepts of adolescent thinking form the research basis in much academic literature.

4. "Should I Tell Him I Love Him?"

1. Russell Baker. *Growing Up*. New York: New American Library, 1982, pp. 8 and 10.
2. Nancy J. Chodorow. *Feminism and Psychoanalytic Theory*. New Haven, Conn.: Yale University Press, 1989, p. 73.
3. Jonathan Rutherford. *Men's Silences: Predicaments in Masculinity*. London: Routledge, 1992.
4. *Ibid.*, p. 20.
5. Carol Klein. *Mothers and Sons*. Boston: Houghton Mifflin, 1984, p. 73.
6. Jack Kornfield. "Parenting as a Spiritual Practice." In *Fathers, Sons, and Daughters*, ed. Charles Scull. Los Angeles: Jeremy P. Tarcher Inc. 1992, p. 38.
7. Robert E. Salt. "Affectionate Touch Between Fathers and Preadolescent Sons." In *Journal of Marriage and the Family*, August 1991.
8. Chodorow, *op. cit.*, p. 59.
9. Harry Guntrip. *Personality Structure and Human Interaction*. Madison, Conn.: International Universities Press, 1961. The quotation here was cited in Nancy Chodorow's *Feminism and Psychoanalytic Theory*, p. 62.
10. Andrew H. Malcolm. *Someday: The Story of a Mother and Her Son*. New York: Alfred A. Knopf, 1991.
11. Gail B. Werrbach, Harold D. Grotevant, and Catherine R. Cooper. "Patterns of Family Interaction and Adolescent Sex Role Concepts." In *Journal of Youth and Adolescence* 21(5):620, 1992.
12. Oscar Wilde. *The Importance of Being Earnest*, quoted in the "Mothers and Sons" chapter in *Mothers: A Celebration in Prose, Poetry, and Photographs of Mothers and Motherhood*, ed. Alexandre Towle. New York: Simon and Schuster, 1988, p. 43.
13. Judith Wallerstein and Sandra Blakeslee. *Second Chances: Men, Women, and Children, a Decade After Divorce: Who

Wins, Who Loses—and Why. New York: Ticknor & Fields, 1989, p. 82.

14. Judith G. Smetana, Jenny Yau, Angela Restrepo, and Judith L. Braeges. "Adolescent-Parent Conflict in Married and Divorced Families." In *Developmental Psychology* 27(6):1008, 1991.

15. E. Mavis Hetherinton and W. Glenn Clingempeel. "Coping with Marital Transitions." In *Monograph of the Society for Research in Child Development*, vol. 57, 1992.

16. James H. Bray. "Adolescents in Stepfamilies." In *The Family Psychologist*, Summer 1992. Bray is reviewing the research of Abelson reported in *Family Process*, vol. 31, 1992.

5. "My Mother Would Kill Me"

1. Diana Baumrind. "The Influence of Parenting Style on Adolescent Competence and Substance Abuse." In *The Journal of Early Adolescence* 11(1), 1991. Baumrind provides an excellent review of theories of adolescent development.

2. Laurence Steinberg, Nina S. Mounts, Susie D. Lamborn, and Sanford M. Dornbusch. "Authoritative Parenting and Adolescent Adjustment Across Varied Ecological Niches." In *Journal of Research on Adolescence* 1(1):19.

3. The term "authoritative parenting" was coined by Diana Baumrind of the University of California at Berkeley, who followed families for a period of ten years. Laurence Steinberg and others have extended her research. Many adolescent parenting studies rely on Earl Schaefer's brilliant research first published in 1959, "A Circumplex Model for Maternal Behavior," in *The Journal of Abnormal and Social Psychology*, vol. 59, and his 1965 work, "Children's Report of Parental Behavior," in *Child Development*, vol. 36.

4. Throughout the discussion of "authoritative parenting," I will be referring to Baumrind's research, including: "Parenting

Styles and Adolescent Development" in *Encyclopedia of Adolescence*, ed. R. M. Lerner, A. C. Peterson, and Jeanne Brooks-Gunn. New York: Garland, 1992; "The Influence of Parenting Style on Adolescent Competence and Problem Behavior," an address given at the American Psychological Association's annual meeting, New Orleans, August 1989; "Sex-Differentiated Socialization Effects in Childhood and Adolescence in Divorced and Intact Families," an address presented at the Society for Research in Child Development, Kansas City, April 1989; and "Effective Parenting During the Early Adolescent Transition," an address at the Family Research Consortium, Santa Fe, June 1987.

5. My application of Baumrind's studies to family life is derived from my discussions with mothers of adolescents and my personal experience as a mother of six.

6. Reported by Felicia R. Lee in *The New York Times*, February 9, 1993, p. B2.

7. Betsy Speicher. "Adolescent Moral Judgment and Perceptions of Family Interactions." In *Journal of Family Psychology* 6(2), 1992.

8. Arnold J. Sameroff and Barbara H. Fiese. "Family Representations of Development." In *Parental Belief System: The Psychological Consequences for Children* (2nd ed.), ed. Irving E. Siegel, Ann V. McGillicuddy-DeLisi, and Jacqueline J. Goodnow. Hillsdale, N.J.: Lawrence Erlbaum Associates, 1992.

9. Grace M. Barnes and Michael P. Farrell. "Parental Support and Control as Predictors of Adolescent Drinking, Delinquency, and Related Problem Behaviors." In *Journal of Marriage and the Family*, November 1992, p. 763.

6. Mother-Talk, Son-Talk

1. John Gray. *Men Are from Mars, Women Are from Venus: A Practical Guide for Improving Communication and Getting What*

You Want in Your Relationships. New York: HarperCollins, 1992.

2. Deborah Tannen. *You Just Don't Understand: Women and Men in Conversation*. New York: William Morrow, 1990.

3. Phame M. Camarena, Pamela A. Sarigiani, and Anne C. Petersen. "Gender-Specific Pathways to Intimacy in Early Adolescence." In *Journal of Youth and Adolescence* 19(1), 1990.

4. Reported in the American Psychological Association's *Monitor*, October 1989. A study by Janice Stapley and Jeannetter Haviland of Rutgers University.

5. James Youniss and Jacqueline Smollar. *Adolescent Relations with Mothers, Fathers, and Friends*. Chicago: University of Chicago Press, 1985.

6. Richard Majors and Janet Billson. *Cool Pose: The Dilemmas of Black Manhood in America*. New York: Macmillan, 1992. Quote is from an interview with Majors in *The New York Times*, April 21, 1992, p. C7.

7. An excellent review of adolescent socialization is found in a special issue of *Journal of Youth and Adolescence* 18(6), 1989. Particularly useful is the summary of the issue, "The Life Space and Socialization of the Self: Sex Differences in the Young Adolescent," by Maryse H. Richards and Reed Larson. Quote is on p. 620.

8. Austen A. Ettinger. "Mum's the Word." In *The New York Times*, February 3, 1991, Section 6, p. 10.

9. Tannen *op. cit.*, p. 79.

10. Paul W. Swets. *How to Talk So Your Teenager Will Listen*. Waco, Tex.: Word Books, 1988.

7. "Why Do They Fight So Much?"

1. David D. Gilmore. *Manhood in the Making: Cultural Concepts of Masculinity*. New Haven, Conn.: Yale University Press, 1990, p. 75.

2. *Ibid.*, p. 77.

3. David G. Perry, Louise C. Perry, and Robert Weiss. "Sex Difference in the Consequences that Children Anticipate for Aggression." In *Developmental Psychology* 25(2), 1989.

4. Perry, Perry, and Weiss review the literature on self-esteem and aggression in the article mentioned above.

5. Myriam Miedzian. *Boys Will Be Boys: Breaking the Link Between Masculinity and Violence*. New York: Doubleday, 1991.

6. Reported by Philip J. Hilts in *The New York Times*, June 10, 1992.

7. Charles Callahan and Frederick Rivara. "Urban High School Youths and Handguns." In *The Journal of the American Medical Association*, June 10, 1992.

8. Reported by Michel Marriott in *The New York Times*, September 13, 1992.

9. Reported by Sabra Chartrand in *The New York Times*, June 11, 1992, p. B10.

10. Douglas S. Well and David Hemenway. *The Journal of the American Medical Association*. June 10, 1992.

11. Rand D. Conger, Katherine J. Conger, Glen H. Elder, Jr., Frederick O. Lorenz, Ronald L. Simons, and Les B. Whitbeck. "A Family Process Model of Economic Hardship and Adjustment of Early Adolescent Boys." In *Child Development*, vol. 63, 1992.

12. Elder and Conger research mentioned above and also written up in *Journal of Youth and Adolescence*, vol. 21, no. 3, 1992.

13. Judith Wallerstein and Sandra Blakeslee. *Second Chances: Men, Women, and Children, a Decade after Divorce: Who Wins, Who Loses—and Why*. New York: Ticknor & Fields, 1989.

14. Reported by N. R. Kleinfield in *The New York Times*, February 27, 1992.

15. Brandon S. Centerwall, M.D., in "Television and Violence: The Scale of the Problem and Where to Go from Here." In *The Journal of the American Medical Association*, June 10, 1992.

16. Study reported by Tori DeAngelis in the American Psychological Association's publication *Monitor*, May 1992, p. 11.

17. Leonard Eron is the chairman of the American Psychological Association's Commission on Violence and Youth. Quoted in the *Monitor*, May 1992.

18. Reported by Jonathan Rabinovitz in *The New York Times*, August 6, 1992, p. B7.

19. Reported by Felicity Barringer in *The New York Times*, September 20, 1992.

20. Denise B. Kandel, Victoria H. Raveis, and Mark Davies. "Suicidal Ideation in Adolescence: Depression, Substance Use, and Other Risk Factors." In *Journal of Youth and Adolescence* 20(2), 1991.

21. Reported by Clare Collins in *The New York Times*, May 3, 1992, Connecticut section.

22. Interview with Dr. David Brent from the University of Pittsburgh reported by Jane Brody in *The New York Times*, June 16, 1992.

23. Reported by Jane Brody in *The New York Times*, June 16, 1992.

24. Marjolein L. de Jong. "Attachment, Individuation, and Risk of Suicide in Late Adolescence." In *Journal of Youth and Adolescence* 21(3), 1992.

25. Thomas E. Blackburn. In a review of Myriam Miedzian's book *Boys Will Be Boys* in *The National Catholic Reporter*, April 3, 1992.

26. Bettie B. Youngs. *Helping Your Teenager Deal with Stress*. Los Angeles: Jeremy P. Tarcher, Inc., 1986.

27. Available from the Carnegie Council on Adolescent Development, 2400 N. Street, N.W., Washington, DC 20037–1153.

8. Living Up to His Potential

1. Theodora Ooms, Director of the Family Impact Seminar, moderator of panel discussion on "The Family-School Partnership: A Critical Component of School Reform," held on

February 21, 1991, Washington, DC. Copies of the discussion are available from Family Impact Seminar, 1100 17th Street, N.W., Suite 901, Washington, DC 20036.

2. "Turning Points: Preparing American Youth for the 21st Century" by the Carnegie Council on Adolescent Development, 2400 N. Street N.W., Washington, DC 20037–1153.

3. Gene H. Brody and Zolinda Stoneman. "Child Competence and Developmental Goals Among Rural Black Families." In *Parental Belief Systems: The Psychological Consequences for Children*, ed. Irving E. Siegel, Ann V. McGillicuddy-DeLisi, and Jacqueline J. Goodnow. Hillsdale, N.J.: Lawrence Erlbaum Associates, 1992.

4. Laurence Steinberg, Susie D. Lamborn, Sanford M. Dornbusch, and Nancy Darling. "Impact of Parenting Practices on Adolescent Achievement: Authoritative Parenting, School Involvement, and Encouragement to Succeed." In *Child Development*, no. 63, 1992.

5. Peter G. Christenson and Donald F. Roberts. *Popular Music in Early Adolescence*. A working paper of the Carnegie Council on Adolescent Development, 2400 N. Street, N.W., Washington, DC 20037–1153, 1990.

6. Jacquelynne S. Eccles and Carol Midgley. "Changes in Academic Motivation and Self-Perception During Early Adolescence." In *From Childhood to Adolescence: A Transitional Period?* ed. Raymond Montemayor, Gerald R. Adams, and Thomas P. Gullotta. Newbury, Calif.: Sage Publications, 1990.

7. Carol Goodenow. "Classroom Belonging Among Early Adolescent Students: Relationships to Motivation and Achievement." In *The Journal of Early Adolescence*, February 1993. Goodenow offers a good review of related studies.

8. James P. Garvin. *Learning How to Kiss a Frog: Advice for Those Who Work with Pre- and Early Adolescents*. Rowley, Mass.: New England League of Middle Schools, 1988. A wonderful monograph for educators and parents.

9. Steinberg, et al., *op. cit.* Another study found that parental monitoring in preadolescence positively affected school grades: "Parental Monitoring and Perceptions of Children's School Performance and Conduct in Dual- and Single-Earner Families," by Ann Crouter, Shelley MacDermid, Susan M. McHale, and Maureen Perry-Jenkins. In *Developmental Psychology* 26(4), 1991.
10. The National Center for Learning Disabilities is located at 99 Park Avenue, New York, NY 10016.
11. Sally B. Shaywitz. "Nice Quiet Girls Can Have Reading Problems Too." In *Their World*, publication of the Center for Learning Disabilities, 1991.
12. The American Psychiatric Association's Diagnostic and Statistical Manual of Mental Disorders, 3d Ed., revised.
13. Information about the Coalition of Essential Schools may be obtained from the Coalition of Essential Schools, Box 1969, Brown University, Providence, RI 02912.
14. More information about District 4 is available through the Manhattan Institute for Policy Research, 52 Vanderbilt Ave., New York, NY 10017. Attention: Colman Genn, Senior Fellow, Center for Educational Innovation. Sy Fliegel has written about the innovations in District 4 in his book, *Miracle in East Harlem*. New York: Times Books, 1993.

9. "Get Them into Something"

1. For a good review of the merits of organized programs, refer to "Constraints to Activity Participation in Early Adolescence" by Wendy Z. Hultzman in *The Journal of Early Adolescence*, August 1992.
2. An excellent review of studies about latchkey children and after-school activities can be found in a working paper of the Wellesley College Center for Research on Women. Fern Marx, "After-School Programs for Low-Income Young Adolescents: Overview and Program Profiles."

3. Hultzman, *op. cit.*
4. George Leonard. *The Ultimate Athlete.* Berkeley, Calif.: North Atlantic Books, 1990. A good review of newer phys ed programs.
5. *Ibid.*, pp. 3 and 19.
6. Andrew H. Malcolm. *Huddle: Fathers, Sons, and Football.* New York: Simon and Schuster, 1992, p. 79.
7. *Ibid.*, p. 99.
8. Ronald E. Smith and Frank L. Smoll. "Self-Esteem and Children's Reactions to Youth Sport Coaching Behaviors: A Field Study of Self-Enhancement Processes." In *Developmental Psychology* 26(6), 1990.
9. Myriam Miedzian. *Boys Will Be Boys: Breaking the Link Between Masculinity and Violence.* New York: Doubleday, 1991.
10. *Ibid.*, p. 205.
11. "Steroid Users." In *Chemical People*, newsletter funded by the Metropolitan Life Foundation, September/October 1992, p. 9. Quote by Neil J. Carolan, vice president of BryLin Hospitals in Buffalo, NY. This newsletter is the source of steroid information in this chapter.
12. "The Male Athlete and Sexual Assault." Reported by Gerald Eskenazi in *The New York Times*, p.1, Section 8, June 3, 1990.
13. Douglas H. Heath. *Fulfilling Lives: Paths to Maturity and Success.* San Francisco: Jossey-Bass Publishers, 1991, p. 297.
14. Marian Salzman and Teresa Reisgies. *150 Ways Teens Can Make a Difference: A Handbook for Action.* Princeton, N.J.: Peterson's Guides, 1991. This guide is available through bookstores for $7.95.
15. This program was reported by Douglas Martin in *The New York Times*, May 2, 1992. ScoutReach is located in New York City.
16. Jeylan T. Mortimer, Michael Finch, Michael Shanahan, and Seongryeol Ryu. "Work Experience, Mental Health, and Behavioral Adjustment in Adolescence." In *Journal of Research*

on Adolescence 2(1), 1992. This article gives a good review of research on adolescents and work.

17. Laurence Steinberg and Sanford M. Dornbusch. "Negative Correlates of Part-Time Employment During Adolescence: Replication and Elaboration." In *Developmental Psychology* 27(2):307, 1991.

10. "I Only Have Sex with Virgins"

1. "Facts at a Glance, 1992," published by Child Trends, Inc., 2100 M. St., N.W., Washington, DC 20037. Child Trends publishes an annual report of adolescent sexual statistics.

2. Mireya Navarro. "AIDS Cases Rise Under New Federal Rules." In *The New York Times*, March 22, 1993, p. B1. The federal definition of AIDS cases has been expanded to include more illnesses caused by AIDS and to reflect a more accurate count of the AIDS cases in women and intravenous drug users.

3. Reported in *The Family Psychologist*, Winter 1992.

4. "Facts at a Glance, 1992."

5. "Facts at a Glance, 1993."

6. William Marsiglio. "Adolescent Males' Orientation Toward Paternity and Contraception." In *Family Planning Perspectives*, January 1993.

7. Jane Gross. "Where 'Boys Will Be Boys' and Adults Are Befuddled." In *The New York Times*, March 29, 1993, p. 1.

8. Emily Rosenbaum and Denise R. Kandel. "Early Onset of Adolescent Sexual Behavior and Drug Involvement." In *Journal of Family and Marriage*, August 1990.

9. Ellie W. Young, Larry C. Jensen, Joseph A. Olsen, and Bert P. Cundick. "The Effects of Family Structure on the Sexual Behavior of Adolescents." In *Adolescence*, Winter 1991.

10. Jon Pareles. "The Eternal Seductions of Prince." In *The New York Times*, March 26, 1993, p. C1.

11. Peter G. Christenson and Donald F. Roberts. "Popular Music in Early Adolescence." Carnegie Council on Adolescent Development. A Working Paper. January 1990.

12. John J. O'Connor. "On Teenage Virginity or Its Loss, on TV," *The New York Times*, September 25, 1991, p. C15.

13. Herant Katchadourian. "Sexuality." In *At the Threshold: The Developing Adolescent*, ed. S. Shirley Feldman and Glen R. Elliot. Cambridge, Mass.: Harvard University Press, 1990, p. 333.

14. Fred M. Hechinger. *Fateful Choices: Healthy Youth for the 21st Century*. Carnegie Corporation of New York, 1992.

15. Marion Howard and Judith Blamey McCabe. "Helping Teenagers Postpone Sexual Involvement." In *Family Planning Perspectives*, January 1990. More information about postponing sexual involvement may be obtained from Grady Teen Services Program, Grady Memorial Hospital, 80 Butler St., S.E., Atlanta, GA 30335.

16. Gerald Eskenazi. "The Male Athlete and Sexual Assault." In *The New York Times*, June 3, 1990, Section 8, p.1.

17. C. J. Jung. *Aspects of the Masculine*. Princeton, N.J.: Princeton University Press, 1989, p. 59. A series of lectures and essays about the masculine given by Jung during his lifetime.

18. Ellen Hopkins. "Sex Is for Adults." An op-ed column in *The New York Times*, December 26, 1992.

19. Marion Howard. *How to Help Your Teenager Postpone Sexual Involvement*. New York: Continuum Publishing Company, 1989.

20. Philip Kestelman and James Trussell. "Efficacy of the Simultaneous Use of Condoms and Spermicides." In *Family Planning Perspectives*, September/October 1991.

11. "Kids Do What They Want"

1. *Chronic Disease and Health Promotion: 1990 Youth Risk Behavior Surveillance System*. U.S. Department of Health and Human Services, Centers for Disease Control, 1992.

2. *Adolescent and Young Adult Fact Book*. Children's Defense Fund, 1991.

3. The National Summary of PRIDE Questionnaire Report, 1991–92. PRIDE, Inc., 50 Hurt Plaza, Suite 210, Atlanta, GA 30303. Comparison with previous years reported in *Chemical People* (Winter 1992/93), National Media Outreach Center, 4802 Fifth Ave., Pittsburgh, PA 15213. This finding of increased use of drugs by eighth graders was confirmed in the 1992 survey of fifty thousand eighth, tenth, and twelfth graders funded by the National Institute on Drug Abuse and conducted by University of Michigan psychologists Lloyd Johnston, Patrick O'Malley, and Jerald Bachman.

4. Personal communication (December 2, 1992) from Robert L. Walsh, National Institute on Drug Abuse, U.S. Department of Health and Human Services, Rockville, MD 20857, to Leigh Rudd, co-author of *The No-Nonsense Parents' Guide* by Sheila Fuller and Leigh Rudd, 1992. Parents' Pipeline, Inc., P.O. Box 11037, Greenwich, CT 06831.

5. Information on marijuana may be obtained from the Committees of Correspondence, 57 Conant St., Danvers, MA 01923. Information may also be obtained from the Centers for Disease Control or the Department of Health and Human Services' National Institute on Drug Abuse.

6. Summary of PRIDE Report, 1991–92.

7. *General Reports on Youth and Alcohol*, Report from the Office of Inspector General, November 1991.

8. Michael Schicks's comments were reported by Nick Coleman, a columnist for the *St. Paul Pioneer Press*, and published in *Greenwich Time*, September 17, 1992, p. A13.

9. Rev. Calvin O. Butts 3d of the Abyssinian Baptist Church, New York, quoted in *The New York Times*, April 16, 1993, p. B3.

10. Michael Windle and Carol Miller-Tutzauer. "Confirmatory Factor Analysis and Concurrent Validity of the Perceived Social Support-Family Measure Among Adolescents." In *Journal of Marriage and Family*, November 1992.

11. Brian K. Barbar. "Family, Personality, and Adolescent Problem Behaviors." In *Journal of Marriage and Family*, February 1992.

12. *Youth and Drugs: Society's Mixed Messages*. Hank Resnik, ed. Office for Substance Abuse Prevention. U.S. Department of Health and Human Services, Rockville, MD, 1990.

13. Norman G. Hoffmann and Richard A. Kaplan. *Cator Report: One-Year Outcome Results for Adolescents*, 1991. Cator/New Standards, Inc., 1080 Montreal Ave., St. Paul, MN 55116. Quote from p. 6.

14. Reported by Barry Bearak, Los Angeles Times Syndicate. "Brushfires of AIDS Stoked in Shooting Galleries." In *Greenwich Time*, January 26, 1993.

15. See Note 4. Statistics on smoking also are from *The Adolescent and Young Adult Fact Book*, published by the Children's Defense Fund, 1991.

16. Brett Queener. "The Grip of a Vice." In *Dartmouth Alumni Magazine*, Summer 1992.

17. Grace M. Barnes and Michael P. Farrell. "Parental Support and Control as Predictors of Adolescent Drinking, Delinquency, and Related Problem Behaviors." In *Journal of Marriage and Family*, November 1992. A good review of literature on parental support and control.

18. *Ibid.*, p. 768.

19. James Youniss, James P. DeSantis, and Sandra H. Henderson. "Parents' Approaches to Adolescents in Alcohol, Friendship, and School Situations." In *Parental Belief Systems: The Psychological Consequences for Children*, ed. Irving E. Siegel, Ann V. McGillicuddy-DeLisi, and Jacqueline J. Goodnow. Hillsdale, N.J.: Lawrence Erlbaum Associates, 1992.

20. Quoted in *The Chemical People*, National Media Outreach Center, Pittsburgh, March/April 1992, p. 8.

21. Rebecca A. Turner, Charles E. Irwin, Jr., and Susan G. Millstein. "Family Structure, Family Processes, and Experiment-

ing with Substances During Adolescence." In *Journal of Research on Adolescence* 1(1), 1991.

22. Owen Lewis. "Paternal Absence: Psychotherapeutic Considerations in Boys." Essay published by W.A.W. Institute, 20 W. 74th St., New York, NY 10023, and printed in *Mothers and Daughters: Fathers and Sons*, proceedings from symposium sponsored by Common Ground: The Center for Adolescents, Stamford Hospital, Stamford, CT. Quote is on p. 268.

23. Lee Shifts. "Relationship of Early Adolescent Substance Use to Extracurricular Activities, Peer Influence, and Personal Attitudes." In *Adolescence*, Fall 1991.

24. Tina Adler. "Temperament Tied to Drug Abuse Risk." Reported in the American Psychological Association's publication *Monitor*, February 1990. A review of current findings on temperament.

12. "Is My Son Gay?"

1. Richard Green. *The "Sissy Boy Syndrome" and the Development of Homosexuality*. New Haven, Conn.: Yale University Press, 1987, p. 2.

2. This view is described and reinterpreted by Richard A. Isay in *Being Homosexual: Gay Men and Their Development*. New York: Farrar, Straus, Giroux, 1989. Also, Kenneth Lewes presents a history of psychoanalytic theory in *The Psychoanalytic Theory of Male Homosexuality*. New York: Simon and Schuster, 1988. Older studies do suggest that mothers feel an unusual closeness and intimacy with their sons ("The Transsexual Experiment" in vol. 2 of *Sex and Gender*. Jason Aronson, 1976). Others find that some homosexual men feel hostility from their mothers ("On the Genesis of Male Homosexuality: An Attempt at Clarifying the Role of the Parents." In *The British Journal of Psychiatry* 111:803–13, 1965).

3. Richard Green, *op. cit.*

4. Alan P. Bell, Martin S. Weinberg, and Sue K. Hammersmith. *Sexual Preference: Its Development in Men and Women.* Bloomington: Indiana University Press, 1981.
5. *The New York Times*, August 4, 1992.
6. Bell et al., *op. cit.*
7. *Hometowns: Gay Men Write About Where They Belong.* John Preston, ed. New York: E. P. Dutton, 1991.
8. *Ibid.*, p. 71.
9. Reported in the American Psychological Association's *Monitor*, November 1991. Also featured in *Newsweek*, February 24, 1992, p. 48.
10. Laura S. Allen and Roger A. Gorski. In *The New York Times*, August 1, 1992. Natalie Angier reporting on the proceedings of the National Academy of Sciences.
11. Michael Bailey and Richard Pillard's research is reported in the American Psychological Association's *Monitor*, February 1992. Len Heston comments in the same issue.
12. David L. Wheeler. "Study Suggests X Chromosome Is Linked to Homosexuality." In *The Chronicle of Higher Education*, July 21, 1993.
13. Reported in *Newsweek*, February 24, 1992, p. 48, and confirmed in telephone conversation with John Money's senior researcher.
14. Michael Ruse. *Homosexuality.* New York: Basil Blackwell Inc., 1988. "Study after study designed to elicit homosexuals' recollections of themselves as children have found that (on average) there are striking differences between the memories of homosexuals of themselves as children and comparable memories of heteros. In particular more male homosexuals remember having been sissies as children, much happier playing with girls and doing girls' things (like dolls) rather than with boys, but a substantial number do not remember" (p. 13).
15. Bell et al., *op. cit.*, and Green, *op. cit.*
16. Green, *op. cit.*, p. 137.

17. These boys were "feminine" and should not be confused with "androgynous." Androgynous children may be interested equally in boys' and girls' activities.
18. Green, *op. cit.*, p. 176.
19. *Ibid.*, p. 177.
20. David Gilmore. *Manhood in the Making: Cultural Concepts of Masculinity*. New Haven, Conn.: Yale University Press, 1990.
21. Bell et al., p. 189.
22. Textbooks on adolescence that do *not* mention homosexuality: *From Childhood to Adolescence* (1990) and *Biology of Adolescent Behavior and Development* (1989), ed. Gerald R. Adams, Raymond Montemayor, and Thomas P. Gullotta. Newbury, Calif.: Sage Publications. *Biological-Psychosocial Interactions in Early Adolescence*, ed. Richard M. Lerner and Terryl T. Foch. Hillsdale, N.J., Lawrence Erlbaum Associates, 1987. *Experiencing Adolescents: A Sourcebook for Parents, Teachers, and Teens*, ed. Richard Lerner and Nancy Galambos. New York: Teachers College Press, 1984.
23. *At the Threshold: The Developing Adolescent*, commissioned by the Carnegie Foundation and edited by S. Shirley Feldman and Glen R. Elliott. Cambridge, Mass.: Harvard University Press, 1990.
24. *Ibid.*, p. 336.
25. Alfred C. Kinsey, W. B. Pomery, and C. E. Martin. *Sexual Behavior in the Human Male*. Philadelphia: W. B. Saunders, 1948.
26. The first survey (1 percent exclusively homosexual) was conducted by the Battelle Human Affairs Research Center in Seattle, with a grant from the National Institute of Child Health and Human Development, and was based on individual interviews with a sample of 3,321 men. The second survey, conducted by Louis Harris and Associates, polled 739 men (ages 16 to 50). Surveys on sexual issues can be skewed by the type of questions asked and the gender of the interviewer.

27. John Money and Patricia Tucker. *Sexual Signatures: On Being a Man or a Woman.* Boston: Little, Brown & Co., 1975.

28. In many essays by gays, particularly in Preston, *op. cit.*

29. Laurence Steinberg and Ann Levine. *You and Your Adolescent: A Parent's Guide for Ages 10 to 20.* New York: Harper and Row, 1990, p. 101.

30. Moses Laufer and M. Egle Laufer. *Adolescence and Developmental Breakdown: A Psychoanalytic View.* New Haven, Conn.: Yale University Press, 1984, pp. 164 and 170.

31. E. L. Pattullo. "Straight Talk About Gays." In *Commentary,* December 1992. Pattullo states his reasons for believing that there are boys who fall in the middle of a continuum between gay and straight and would respond to influences directing them toward a heterosexual orientation.

32. Ruth Westheimer and Louis Lieberman. *Sex and Morality: Who Is Teaching Our Sex Standards?* New York: Harcourt Brace Jovanovich, 1988, p. 177.

33. G. Remafedi. "Adolescent Sexuality: Psychological and Medical Implications." In *Pediatrics* 79(3):326–30, 1987.

34. Paul Monette. *Becoming a Man: Half a Life Story.* New York: Harcourt Brace Jovanovich, 1992.

35. *Ibid.,* p. 10.

36. Jeffrey Schmalz. Reporting in *The New York Times,* February 4, 1993, p. C10.

13. "Soon You'll Be Wanting Us to Wear Bras"

1. Ronald F. Levant. "Toward a Reconstruction of Masculinity." In *Journal of Family Psychology,* March/June 1992.

2. *Ibid.,* p. 385.

3. *Ibid.,* p. 389.

Index

Abstinence, 220, 223, 225, 226
ACE Model, 126
Acne, 23, 25, 29, 35–36
Acting-out behavior, 152
Activities:
conversation combined with, 116–17
see also After-school activities
Adolescence:
entry into, 18–19
fears or self-doubt in, 2–3
puberty and, 19, 21–38
Adult life, preparing for, 91–92
After-school activities, 183–205
athletics, 186, 187–97
benefits of, 184–85
dropping out of, 185–86
jobs, 201–3
outside school, 59, 200–201
school clubs, 198–200
Aggression, 25, 107, 136
in sports, 190, 193, 194, 195
steroids and, 196
television and, 149–50
AIDS, 208, 210, 211, 227, 238, 263, 274, 276

Alcohol, 93, 144, 185, 202, 239–43
detecting use of, 247, 251
drinking age and, 239–40
drinking parties and, 232–33
extent of use of, 234–35
friends and, 248–50
parental responses to, 100, 101, 102, 240, 241, 242–43, 245–48, 250–51
personality factors and, 250–51
reading and contacts on, 252–53
risk factors for abuse of, 245–51
sex and, 213
Alcoholism, 233, 241, 248
Allen, Laura S., 263
Androgens, 24
Anger, 114
turning fear into, 144–46
Arguing, 154
Assertiveness, encouraging of, 106–7
Athletics, 186, 187–97, 269
avoidance of, 187–88
coaches in, 191, 193–94, 195, 196–97, 221
downside of, 195–97
drugs and, 196–97

Athletics (*cont'd*)
  as outlet for stress, 155
  physical education classes, 187–89
  sexual conquests and, 197, 220–21
  team sports, 189–96
  timing of puberty and, 23, 25
Attention-deficit disorder, 177–78
Attentiveness, sons' appreciation of, 90–91
At the Threshold, 269–70
Authoritative parenting, 92–94, 131
  schools and, 174
  setting clear standards in, 98
  see also Highly demanding mothers

Bailey, Michael, 263
Baker, Russell, 63
Baseball, 190, 194
Baumrind, Diana, 93, 94, 101, 103
Bedrooms, 105, 132, 169
Behavior:
  monitoring of, 99–100, 242, 246
  substance abuse and, 99, 178, 247, 251
  suicidal tendencies and, 152–53
Bell, Alan P., 260, 261, 265, 267
Bicycling, 190
Birth of son, 8–11
Blackburn, Thomas, 153
Bly, Robert, 1, 28, 46–47
Board games, organizational skills and, 177
Body hair, 25, 26, 27–28
Boundaries, maintaining of, 72–74, 84
Boyhood, 17–18
Boy Scouts, 200, 201
Boys Will Be Boys, 141, 195–96
Braun, Jenifer, 69–70
Breasts, enlargement of, 26
Brevity, in requests for son's help, 128
Brooks-Gunn, Jeanne, 28–29

"Calvin and Hobbes," 55
Career choices, 49–51
Carnegie Council on Adolescent Development, 23, 156, 162, 170, 173, 215–17, 269
Cartoons, violence in, 149, 150
Child abuse, 261–62
Children's Defense Fund, 235
Chlamydia, 210
Chodorow, Nancy, 65–66, 76
Churches, 201, 273–74
Cigarettes, 243, 244–45
Circumcision, 32
Classroom participation, 115
Coaches, 191, 193–94, 195, 221
  drug use and, 196–97
Coalition of Essential Schools, 179
Cocaine, 236, 243
Cognitive skills, 161
College, 166
  ability to pay for, 147
  applications for, 106
  preparing to leave for, 52–53
Coming Out Within, 274
Communication, 78–80, 111–34
  of adolescent boys, 116–18
  confiding and, 119, 125
  conversing vs. interrogating and, 129–30
  direct and explicit, 112–13
  distancing from mother and, 43
  excessive, 71–72
  about feelings, 114, 116, 117, 119, 122–23, 124, 133, 282, 285
  gender-typical differences in, 113–15, 132–33
  lack of, 95–96
  listening vs. hearing in, 125–27
  modifying patterns in, 124–32
  about moral issues, 96–97
  mothers' coded messages and, 78–79, 80
  with mothers vs. fathers, 118

negotiating vs. controlling and, 130–32
with preschool children, 11–13
requesting vs. nagging and, 127–29
between school and home, 173–75, 180–81
about sex, 209, 213, 214, 217, 223–28
sons who won't talk and, 121–24
verbal, need for, 96
about wide variety of topics, 167
Community activities, 59, 200, 201
Competence, 164
Condoms, 208, 211, 213, 223, 224, 225–26, 227–28
Confiding, 119, 125
Conflict, 285
avoidance of, 152
Conflict resolution programs, 156–57
Contraception, 225–26, 227–28. *See also* condoms
Control, 31, 44–45, 283
sons' desire for, 130–32
Controlling, negotiating vs., 130–32
Conversing, interrogating vs., 129–30
"Cool pose," 120
Corneau, Guy, 48–49
Covering up for son, 102
Crack cocaine, 243
"Cross-gender" behavior, 256
Crying, 148–49
Curfews, 98, 131
Custody, 154

Daley, Richard, 232
Date rape, 208
Dating:
girlfriends and, 218–20
by single parents, 81, 214
Daughters:
desirability of sons vs., 8–9, 10–11
raising sons vs., 3–4

Death:
of father, 81
witnessing of, 57–58
Delinquency, 93, 202
Demanding mothers. *See* Highly demanding mothers
Dependence, mature, 76–78
Depression, 151–52, 272
Dinner, as family ritual, 97
Directness, in requests for son's help, 112, 128
Disagreement, toleration of, 103, 104
Disciplinary actions, 93–94. *See also* Punishment
Distancing, from mother, 41–43, 66–67
Divorce, 56, 81–84, 104, 286–87
anger after, 144–45
economic effects of, 82–83, 147
Dobson, James C., 29
Drama, as after-school activity, 199, 200
Drinking age, 239–40
Driving accidents, 101
Drugs, 88, 93, 102–3, 131, 144, 185, 202, 233–39, 241, 243–44
athletics and, 196–97
behavioral changes and, 99, 178
detecting use of, 99, 247, 251
extent of use of, 234–35
friends and, 248–50
parental actions and, 245–48, 250–52
parents' attitudes about, 237–39
personality factors and, 250–51
reading and contacts on, 252–53
risk factors for abuse of, 245–51
sex and, 213
suicide and, 151, 152
Drunk driving, 112, 239

Eating habits, 36
Economic factors, 82–83, 147–49, 178

Ejaculation, 28–30
Elliott, Glen R., 269
Emotions. *See* Feelings
Energy level, 160–61, 185, 186
Erections, 30–31
Erikson, Erik H., 50, 73
Eron, Leonard, 150
Ettinger, Austen, 122

Failure, self-respect and, 164
Family, making sons integral part of, 94–96
Family dinners, 97
Family values, imparting of, 96–97
Fathering children, 102, 209
Fathers, 1
    absence of, related to homosex-
        uality, 260–61
    boys' communication with, 118
    caretaking role of, 13
    divorce and, 82, 83
    finding oneself through, 45–49
    gender identity and, 266, 267
    idolization of, 47–48
    lack of attention from, 48–49
    sexual matters and, 30, 209, 213,
        224
    as silent role models, 121
    sons' desire for closeness with, 286–
        87
    sons' lack of knowledge about, 129
    sons' longing for, 46–47
    sons' relationships with mothers vs.,
        42, 43–45, 51
    stepfathers and, 84
    substitutes for, 49
    touching between sons and, 75–76
    of urban boys, 89–90
    violence and, 153–54
Fear:
    acceptance of, 154
    turned into anger, 144–46

Feelings:
    of boys vs. girls, 18, 117
    concealing of, 152
    getting in touch with, 285–87
    hidden by "cool pose," 120
    men's inability to speak about, 65–
        66
    of others, learning respect for, 130
    sensitivity and, 281–87
    sex without, 220–22
    talking about, 114, 116, 117, 119,
        122–23, 124, 133, 282, 285
Feldman, S. Shirley, 269
Fighting, 136, 152, 154, 156–57
    discouraging of, 13
    gender-typical characteristics and,
        12–13, 17–18, 136
    hitting back and, 138–41
    among preschoolers, 12–13
    with real weapons, 142–44
    with toy weapons, 141–42
Fingers, Rollie, 101
Fliegel, Sy, 179
Football, 190–91
Freud, Sigmund, 42, 259
Friends, 164
    of preschool children, 15–17
    sexual activity and, 217
    substance abuse and, 248–50
Friendship:
    gender-typical differences in, 115
    mother-son, 72–73

Gaddis, Alan, 28–29
Gang rape, 221
Gangs, 56, 58
Garvin, James, 172
Gay-bashing, 274–75
Gaylin, Willard, 45, 55–56
Gender behavior, signals about, 266–
    67
Gender intensification, 34–35

Gender-typical characteristics:
  communication and, 113–15, 132–33
  emotional displays and, 18
  fighting and, 12–13, 17–18, 136
  fostering of, 12
  play and, 15–17
  toys and, 13–15
Genital warts, 210, 227
Genn, Colman, 179
Get-tough strategy, 249
Gilligan, Carol, 50
Gilmore, David, 33–34, 138
Girlfriends, 218–20
Goals, searching for, 49–51
Gorski, Roger A., 263
Henry W. Grady Memorial Hospital, 217
Gray, John, 113, 123, 127–29
Green, Richard, 256, 260, 265–66
Grounding, 101, 102
Guns, 142–44
  in home, 143–44
  suicide and, 144, 151, 152, 162
Guntrip, Harry, 77
Gynecomastia, 26

Hallucinogens, 244
Hammer, Dean H., 264
Handy, Richard, 30
Harter, Susan, 53
Hearing, listening vs., 125–27
Heath, Douglas, 31
Height, 26, 32–34
Helping Your Teenager Deal with Stress, 156
Heroin, 244
Herpes simplex, 210, 238
Heston, Len, 263
Highly demanding mothers, 94–103, 242
  behavior monitored by, 99–100
  clear standards set by, 98

family values imparted by, 96–97
  sons made integral part of family by, 94–96
  as supportive vs. punitive, 101–3
Highly responsive mothers, 103–8, 242
  assertiveness encouraged by, 106–7
  commitment of, 107–8
  individuality fostered by, 103
  self-regulation fostered by, 104–6
HIV virus, 210, 244
Hockey, 190, 191–92
Homework, 105–6, 165–70, 174, 175, 184, 185
  monitoring of, 165–67
  study skills and, 168–70
  working environment for, 169–70
Homosexuality, 255–80
  behavior in childhood and, 264–68
  being a "sissy" and, 256–57, 264–67
  being different and, 267–69
  biological factors in, 262–65
  causes of, 257–65
  changing of, 271–72
  and confusion about sexual orientation, 271
  father's absence and, 260–61
  memoirs about, 275–76
  mother-bashing theory of, 259
  parents' understanding and acceptance of, 276–78
  reading about, 278–79
  religion and, 273–74
  same-sex experiments and, 270–71
  seduction by older man and, 261–62
  statistics on, 270
  teaching tolerance of, 274–75
Hopkins, Ellen, 223
Hormones:
  homosexuality and, 262
  puberty and, 23, 24–25, 26, 37
Household chores, 104–5, 131–32

Howard, Marion, 226
How to Help Your Teenager Postpone Sexual Involvement, 226
Hyperactivity, 151–52, 177

Identity, 39–60
    distancing from mother and, 41–43
    "father hunger" and, 46–47
    finding oneself through father and, 45–49
    and liberation from identification with mother, 45–46, 47
    relationships' effects on, 51–53
    risk-taking and, 53–54, 58
    search for goals and, 49–51
    self-assuredness and, 58–59
Importance of Being Earnest, The, 80
Impulsivity, 25, 177, 250
Independence, 40, 54, 59, 91–92, 283
    extremes of, 76–77
Individuality, fostering of, 103–4
Inhalants, 243–44
Initiation rituals, 55–56, 138
Insulting comments, 117–18
Interdependence, 45, 47, 59, 76–78, 94, 283
Interrogating, conversing vs., 129–30
Intramural sports programs, 190

Jokes, 117–18
Jung, C. G., 23, 222

Katchadourian, Herant, 216
Keillor, Garrison, 22
Kiepenheuer, Kasper, 11
Klein, Carol, 68
Kornfield, Jack, 74
Kozol, Jonathan, 178

Laufer, Moses and M. Egle, 272
Learning disabilities, 175–77
Leonard, George, 189
Lesbianism, 256
Levant, Ronald, 284–86

LeVay, Simon, 262–63
Libraries, 168, 170
Listening:
    gender-typical differences in, 114–15
    hearing vs., 125–27
Little League baseball, 194
Love:
    sex separated from, 221–22
    "unconditonal," 74–75
    voicing expressions of, 85

Maccoby, Eleanor, 15–16
Macho attitudes, 154, 283
Majors, Richard, 120
Malcolm, Andrew, 47–48, 79, 80, 190–91, 193
Male Ego, The, 45, 55–56
Malt liquor, 241–42
Manhood, proving of, 53–57
Marijuana, 233, 235, 236–39, 240, 241, 243, 244
    parents' attitudes about, 237–39
Marital conflict, financial strain and, 147
Masculinity, 4, 17, 28, 138
    attaining of, 1–2
    Bly's theories on, 46–47
    gender intensification and, 34–35
    positive attributes of, 284–85
Masturbation, 29–30, 31
Math teachers, 171–72
Men Are from Mars, Women Are from Venus, 113, 127–29
Men's movement, 1–2, 28
Men's Silences, 66
Menstruation, 28–29, 37
Miedzian, Myriam, 141, 195–96
Milken, Michael, 102
Monette, Paul, 275–76
Money, John, 264
Montessori schools, 163–64
Moral development, 96–97

"MotherDaughterSon," 69–70
Mothers:
    attentive, sons' pride in, 90–91
    distancing from, 41–43, 66–67
    friendship between son and, 72–73
    highly demanding, 94–103, 242
    highly responsive, 103–8, 242
    idealization of, 68
    overinvolved in sons' lives, 71–72
    positive traits demonstrated by, 80
    reluctance to talk negatively about, 66–68
    single, 81–84, 147, 214, 247
    sons' bodies admired by, 64
    sons' curiosity about body of, 63–64
    of sons' girlfriends, 218–19
    sons idealized by, 69–71
    sons overprotective of, 81
    sons' relationship with fathers vs., 42, 43–45, 51
    stepmothers and, 84–85
    strong, 87–109
Movies, 149, 150–51, 226
Moving, "proving oneself" after, 145
MTV, 214–15
Murders, 143, 144, 148, 151
Music:
    as after-school activity, 199
    rock, 199, 214–15, 226
Music videos, 214–16, 226
Mustaches, 27–28

Nagging:
    about homework, 167
    requesting vs., 127–29
Negotiating, controlling vs., 130–32
News, talking about, 96, 167
Nondemanding attitude, 128
Note-taking skills, 168–69
Novello, Antonia, 247

O'Connor, John J., 216
Olivier, Christiane, 10

O'Neal, Shaquille, 94
150 Ways Teens Can Make a Difference, 200
O'Neill, Craig, 274
Ooms, Theodora, 160
Organizational skills, 168–69
    deficits in, 176, 177
Outdoor activities, 200–201

Pareles, Jon, 215
Parents and Friends of Lesbians and Gays (Parents-FLAG), 278, 280
Parents Resource Institute on Drug Education (PRIDE), 235, 253
Part-time employment, 201–3
Penis, 25, 27
    circumcision of, 32
    erections and, 30–31
    size of, 31–32
Personality, 11–12
    substance abuse and, 250–51
Petersen, Anne, 34
Physical affection, father-son, 75–76
Physical attractiveness, 35–36
Physical education classes, 187–89
Pillard, Richard, 263
Pituitary glands, 24–25
Play:
    homosexuality and, 256–57, 264–67
    of preschool children, 15–17
    roughhousing in, 136–37
Police, 101–2
Possessions, violent conflicts over, 145, 148
Poverty, violence and, 147–48
Pregnancy, 227
    holding boys responsible for, 102, 209
Preschool children, 11–17
    communicating with, 11–13
    fighting among, 12–13
    friends and play of, 15–17

Preschool children (*cont'd*)
toys for, 13–15
Prince, 215
Privacy, 64
Problem solving, 126, 154, 157
four-step process for, 156
thinking things through in, 123
Puberty, 19, 21–38, 130, 171
becoming "manly" in, 26, 34–35
food and sleep needed in, 36–37
heightism and, 32–34
hormones and, 23, 24–25, 26, 37
mother-son attachment and, 41
mustaches and, 27
penis size as concern in, 31–32
physical attractiveness and, 35–36
providing information about, 22–24
sperm development and ejaculation in, 28–30
spontaneous erections in, 30–31
timing of changes in, 25
voice changes in, 27
Pubic hair, 25, 26, 27
Punishment, 93–94, 101–3
for drug or alcohol use, 252
physical, 103
tied to deed, 101

Rape, 208, 221
Rebelliousness, 53, 105
Religion, homosexuality and, 273–74
Remarriage, 84–85
Requesting, nagging vs., 127–29
Research skills, 168–69
Respect, 105, 154–55
adolescents' need for, 163–64
for girls and women, 209, 221
for parents, 102
Responsibility, 250, 284
learning of, 104–6
Responsive mothers. *See* Highly responsive mothers

Restrictions, 89–90, 92
Retaliation mentality, 138–41
Risk-taking, 53–58, 98, 250
deaths resulting from, 57–58
as substitute for initiation rituals, 55–56
Rites of passage into manhood, 55–56, 138
Ritter, Kathleen, 274
Rituals, in family life, 97
Robocop, 151
Rock music, 199, 214–15, 226
Roughhousing, 136–37
Rugby, 190, 192
Rules:
setting of, 98, 103, 131, 246
about television watching, 150
Runaways, 95
Running, 190
Russell, Bertrand, 29
Rutherford, Jonathan, 65–66, 68

"Safer sex," 211
Sarcasm, 118
Savage Inequalities, 178
Schick, Michael, 240–41
School, 159–82
activity clubs at, 198–200
asking questions about, 129
attention-deficit disorder and, 177–78
boys' energy level and, 160–61
choosing, 179
classroom participation in, 115
cognitive skills and, 161
demanding attendance in, 164–65
dropping out of, 171, 172
elementary, transition to junior high from, 171–72
expectations and, 164–65, 173
impersonality of, 161–62, 171
influence of, 171–73
learning disabilities and, 175–77

mini-school configurations and, 180
mother's beliefs and, 163–65
parents' cooperation with, 173–75,
  180–81
part-time jobs and, 201–3
study skills and, 168–70
"underachieving" in, 160
in wealthy vs. poor neighborhoods,
  178
see also After-school activities;
  Homework
ScoutReach, 200
Scrotum, 25, 26, 27
Second Chances, 82
Self-assuredness, 58–59
Self-confidence, 283
Self-esteem, 139, 194, 272, 283
Self-regulation, 104–6
Self-respect, 164
Sensitivity, 114, 257
  combining strength and, 281–87
Separation, from parents, 91–92
"Serial monogamy," 212
Sex, 22, 24, 81, 185, 207–29
  abstinence or postponement of,
    220, 223, 225, 226
  athletics and, 197, 220–21
  and double standard for boys and
    girls, 208
  without feelings, 220–22
  with girlfriends, 218–20
  interest in women's bodies and, 63–
    64, 65
  multiple partners and, 211–12, 227
  music videos and, 214–16, 226
  parents' messages about, 226–27
  societal pressures and, 212–17, 225,
    226
  talking about, 209, 213, 214, 217,
    223–28
  in television programs, 216–17
Sex education, 209, 212, 223
Sexual assault cases, 197, 221

Sexually transmitted diseases (STDs),
  208, 210–11, 212, 227, 238
Sexual orientation, 255–80
  changing of, 271–72
  confusion about, 272–73
  see also Homosexuality
Siblings, 52–53
Silence, of men, 121–22, 123–24
Single mothers, 81–84, 211
  remarriage of, 83–84
Single-parent homes:
  economic tension in, 147
  sexual activity and, 214
  substance abuse and, 247
"Sissies," 256–57, 264–67
Size:
  heightism and, 32–34
  of mothers vs. adolescent sons, 93–
    94
Sizer, Theodore, 179
Skepticism, 58–59
Sleeping habits, 36–37
Smetana, Judith, 83
Smokeless tobacco, 245
Soccer, 189
Solitude, boys' need for, 121–22
Sons:
  adolescence entered by, 18–19
  birth of, 8–11
  in boyhood, 17–18
  desirability of daughters vs., 8–9,
    10–11
  as preschoolers, 11–17
  raising daughters vs., 3–4
  see also specific topics
Special-education classes, 175–76
Sperm, development of, 28
Sports. *See* Athletics
Springer, Jerry, 32, 33
Squirt guns, 141
Standards, setting of, 98
Steinberg, Laurence, 41, 271–72
Stepfathers, 84

Stepmothers, 84–85
Steroids, 196–97
Strength, combining sensitivity and, 281–87
Stress:
  financial strain and, 147, 148–49
  outlets for, 145, 146, 149, 153–55
  school-related, 172
Strictness, 89–90, 92, 103, 161, 223
"Study of High School, A," 179
Study skills, 168–70, 174
Substance abuse, 231–54
  suicide and, 151, 152
  see also Alcohol; Drugs
Suicide, 151–53
  factors contributing to, 151–52
  guns and, 144, 151, 152, 162
  homosexuality and, 269, 272, 273
Summer jobs, 203–4
Swets, Paul, 126
Synagogues, 201

Talking tough, 102–3
Tannen, Deborah, 113–14, 122, 123
Teachers:
  homosexual, 261
  influence of, 171–73
  mothers' communication with, 173–74
Team sports, 189–96
  coaches in, 191, 193–94, 195, 196–97
Television, 169
  American family as portrayed on, 92
  monitoring watching of, 150
  sexual activity on, 216–17
  time spent on homework vs., 170
  values reflected on, 97
  violence glorified on, 149–50
  watching, 95
Testicles, 25, 26, 27, 28
Testosterone, 25

Thompson, Mark, 262
Timing, of requests for son's help, 127–28
Tobacco, 243, 244–45
"Tough guy" role, 154
Toys, 13–15, 257
  weapons, 141–42
Trust, 283
  academic performance and, 167, 170
  vigilant, 100
  violation of, 100, 101–3
TV Guide, 216–17

Ultimate Athlete, The, 189
"Unconditional love," 74–75
Unspoken messages, 112, 113, 127

Values, 217
  family, imparting of, 96–97
  sexual, 223, 225, 228, 273
Video games, 172
Vigilant trust, 100
Violence, 135–58, 214
  economic factors and, 147–49
  glorified by media, 149–51
  roughhousing and, 136–37
  in team sports, 190–92, 193, 194, 195
  turned on oneself, 151–53
  turning fear into anger and, 144–46
  see also Fighting
Voice, changes in, 27
Volunteer work, 59, 200, 201, 204

Walker, Father Lee, 257, 258, 273–74, 278
Wallerstein, Judith, 82, 147
War games, 56
Waterson, Bill, 55
Weapons:
  real, fighting with, 142–44

toy, 141–42
Weekly planning sessions, 95
Westheimer, Ruth, 273
"Wet dreams," 28, 29
White, Nathaniel, 151
Wilde, Oscar, 80
Women's bodies, boys' interest in, 63–64, 65
Wording, of requests for son's help, 128–29

Working:
  during school year, 201–3
  during summer, 203–4
Work-study programs, 203

X chromosome, 264

You Just Don't Understand, 113–14
Youngs, Bettie, 156